DISILLUSI
DECAD

Ireland
1966-87

TIM PAT COOGAN

GILL AND MACMILLAN

First published 1987
Gill and Macmillan Ltd
Goldenbridge
Dublin 8
with associated companies in
Auckland, Dallas, Delhi, Hong Kong,
Johannesburg, Lagos, London, Manzini,
Melbourne, Nairobi, New York, Singapore,
Tokyo, Washington
© Tim Pat Coogan 1987
0 7171 1430 9
Print origination in Ireland by
The Caseroom Ltd, Dublin
Printed in Great Britain by
Richard Clay Ltd (The Chaucer Press)
Bungay, Suffolk

British Library Cataloguing in Publication Data

Coogan, Tim Pat
Disillusioned decades: Ireland 1966-87
1. Ireland — History — 1922-
I. Title
941.4082'3   DA963

ISBN 0-7171-1430-9

Contents

Acknowledgements

A book of this sort is a highly personal work inasmuch as the great majority of the facts and opinions contained herein were either observed by or formed within myself. Any printed source material is (or should be!) acknowledged in the text.

My main obligations therefore are to those friends with whom I either discussed the project while I was writing, or sought advice on completed chapters when the book was almost finished.

Accordingly, I should like to acknowledge my indebtedness to the following for their help, advice and encouragement:

Ruaidhri Roberts, Sean Healy, Con Healy, Joe Carroll, Austin Flannery, Damien Kiberd, Barbara Hayley, Brian Farrell, Philip Flynn, Andrew Boyd, Paul McGuinness, T.K. Whitaker, Mairead Dunlevy, Sister Stanislaus Kennedy, Gerry Adams, Padraig O hAnnrachain, Hugh O'Flaherty. That kindly human computer, Donal Nevin, was a font of statistical lore and James Sharkey, now Ambassador to Australia, was most helpful in supplying information about the Department of Foreign Affairs. I owe a particular debt of gratitude to my publisher, Michael Gill, for his forbearance and support during the frequently difficult period of his brainchild's gestation.

All opinions and value judgements are, of course, solely my own.

Tim Pat Coogan

Preface

MY book *Ireland Since the Rising*, published in 1966, was the first attempt to chart the progress of the country during its first turbulent fifty years of statehood. I concluded with the following:

'It is already clear that Ireland's future involves a closer relationship with Britain and with Europe. In the past, Ireland's greatest problem was that she lay too close to England for comfort or independence, yet was too far away for England completely to assimilate her. Today, however, she is near enough for friendship.

'Fifty years after the Rising, mindful of what the men of 1916 died for, Ireland is striving to make herself a country which the men of today and their children will be proud to live in: a land, not of revolution, but of evolution. Bail o Dhia ar an obair — God bless the work!'

Today, with Ireland a world trouble spot and her identity picked out in the subconscious of television viewers and newspaper readers by such words as 'hunger strikes', 'IRA', 'Paisley', 'murder', those words of mine would appear to many to be quaintly inappropriate. Yet my vision was not entirely flawed. A good deal of what I foresaw did come true, but overall much else went sadly wrong.

Firstly, of course, on the world scale was that villain beloved of economists, 'the oil shock', and its terrible spouse 'recession'. These worked their evil alchemy in Ireland as elsewhere. But in Ireland they intertwined with specifically Irish phenomena which exacerbated the situation beyond anyone's anticipation. To give but one example, at the time of writing, there are more people unemployed (240,000) than work in manufacturing industry or as farmers. Forty per cent of the Irish population depends to some extent on social welfare.

The truth is that contemporary Irish society is an outcrop of two forms of colonialism. One, which can be seen quite obviously working its bloody way through Northern Ireland, is British colonialism. At the time of writing the death toll of over 2,400 is the equivalent in American population terms of 350,000 dead, a colossal impact on a small country. The other, less obvious but all-pervasive nevertheless, is the colonialism of religion: to a degree that of the Protestant churches, especially in the North, but more potently that of the Roman Catholic Church.

These influences had an impact on all that has happened in Ireland since I laid down my pen in the closing weeks of 1965. Now, as I resume in 1987, let us examine how native and international forces combined to produce the Ireland of today.

TPC
Dublin, 31 July 1987

1

The Past Twenty Years

IN the mid-1960s nobody in Ireland looked much beneath the surface. Sean Lemass retired in 1966, having succeeded the aging Eamon de Valera in 1959 as Taoiseach and leader of Fianna Fail. His time as head of government had covered seven of the most productive years in Irish political history. He introduced new men, fresh ideas — and hope. A belief took hold, however briefly, that things could get better, not worse.

The brash young 'men in the mohair suits', as I christened them at the time, caught the mood of the country exactly. The single element most lacking in Ireland throughout the fifties had been confidence. The new men of Fianna Fail had an oversupply of this commodity. Nobody questioned their corner-cutting and wheeler-dealing too much because, along with the changes which they were effecting — or seemed to be effecting — in the political sphere, vast external changes were coming to bear in Ireland. The Second Vatican Council was in many people's eyes literally a God-send, and the charismatic personality of Pope John XXIII had a great influence in Ireland. Along with Pope John came the liberalising effect of television, the paperback revolution and the amelioration of the disgraceful censorship which had banned every decent living writer, particularly Irish writers, so that prior to the mid-sixties the lists of banned books were in fact an excellent guide to contemporary literature.

The country began to look more prosperous as hire purchase sent TVs, washing machines, electric cookers and new additions of all sorts winging their way into many Irish homes. The educational system was radically overhauled so that 'free' education (barring payment for books, uniforms, etc.) was brought within the reach of all. As a consequence opportunities multiplied also, including political opportunities.

In the sixties and early seventies, upward, outward and onward seemed to be the direction in which the wagon was rolling. This impression was greatly heightened by the impact of two notable print journalists, Douglas Gageby and John Healy, and one outstanding broadcaster, Gay Byrne.

Byrne's contribution to Irish society is nearly immeasurable. His long-running weekly TV programme, the 'Late, Late Show', has, since the early sixties, enabled widespread discussion to take place on topics which, without his courage and professionalism, would otherwise have been swept under the carpet. He continues the process with a daily hour and three-quarters radio programme, a routine that would kill a lesser man.

Douglas Gageby, Editor of *The Irish Times,* opened the columns of that once rather staid and unionist-oriented journal to all the new influences playing about the country at the time, with the result that readership soared and one writer in particular came into his own. This was John Healy who, under the pseudonym of 'Backbencher', established a new genre of Irish political journalism. His mixture of gossip and purple prose, interspersed with his own authentic vision and leaks from some of the new men of Fianna Fail who realised how useful he could be, meant that his column became an opinion forum. It could not be ignored by the decision-taking 'New Irelanders' springing up in the wake of Lemass's initiative.

Inside the party the old faithful, including sometimes Lemass himself, might rage at 'government by leak' but outside the influence of Healy and his sources increased. Lemass concentrated more and more on trying to build up industry and on doing the groundwork for EEC entry which in the sixties, prior to General de Gaulle's 'Non', seemed an imminent possibility. Even after the EEC door was temporarily closed the main thrust of Irish governmental policy was to prepare the country for eventual entry, which occurred in January 1973. This left various ministers to build up habits of independence which ultimately nearly wrecked Fianna Fail. Ministerial autonomy began to be emulated further down the line by powerful bureaucrats in the civil service and state company network, with sometimes disastrous results. Easy-going attitudes, combined with lax political over-seeing in areas where state supervision was supposed to ensure that semi-autonomous schemes and enterprises funded by the taxpayer would work for the public good, resulted in some awful waste (See Chapter 7).

The principal financial architects of contemporary Ireland were two former civil servants in the Department of Finance, Patrick Lynch and T. K. Whitaker, whose joint influence on Irish budgetary and governmental strategy for almost two decades, starting in the 1950s, was enormous. Whitaker, with Lynch's help, took the country into an expansionary turn with the *First Programme for Economic Development,* which was formally adopted as government policy in 1958. In his public and private life Whitaker personifies the more attractive side of the Irish Catholic ethos. A keen golfer and family man, this scholarship boy, educated by the Christian Brothers, obtained a Masters' Degree in Economics from London University for which he had to study in his spare time. He speaks several languages and has served as secretary of the Department of Finance, governor of the Central Bank, chancellor of the National University and chairman or director of several boards and conferences.

When Whitaker speaks out against financial policy he therefore carries, or should carry, something of the weight of the Pope criticising the state of Roman Catholicism. And speak out he has done very trenchantly, both in his role as a senator and elsewhere. The pith of his criticism is contained in a collection of his writings, *Interests,* published by the Institute of Public Administration in 1983.

Whitaker comments: 'The tendency for "getting and spending" by government to bulk ever larger in national activity has been common to many western countries over this sixty-year span but nowhere, I believe, to a more marked degree than in Ireland'. He cites the statistics on p.4 to prove his point. This table tells a horrific story of drift and fecklessness. It illustrates how the defects in Irish political philosophy mounted up in national terms — the bottom line of vote-buying, Irish style.

The 1972 budget set a trend that was to be maintained throughout the decade. Although output costs were a prime source of both unemployment and weak export performance, the Fianna Fail government flinched from restraint and went instead for a growth-based solution relying on a rising tide that would allegedly lift all boats. Taxation was not increased but social welfare payments were. Events were to prove that the only flow

Government Expenditure and Borrowing

Year	Current Expenditure		Capital Expenditure		Total Expenditure		Borrowing	
	£m	% GNP	£m	% GNP	£m	% GNP	£m	% GNP
1922	30	20	1	—	31	20	3	2
1950	77	19	25	6	102	26	23	6
1958	126	22	38	7	164	29	21	4
1972	665	29	251	11	916	40	151	7
1977	1,944	36	695	13	2,639	49	545	10
1982	5,897	50	2,000	17	7,897	67	1,945	16

that would ensue was that from the opening of the flood gates of inflation. The 1970 national pay agreement had conceded a rise of 17.9 per cent for an average male worker; the 1972 agreement gave 21 per cent over eighteen months, with 29.4 per cent following in 1974 and 16.5 per cent in 1975. This, combined with the effect of the rise in agricultural prices which followed EEC entry, and the oil shock, had the annual rate of inflation at 21 per cent by 1975.

A coalition government of Labour and Fine Gael, which had come to power in 1973, were slow to recognise danger. Indeed they initially exacerbated it with a period of inactivity which government insiders say was largely due to preoccupation with the Sunningdale negotiations and their sequel. (See Chapter 2). Then, faced with a yawning deficit in the current account, the policy of drift was replaced by one of borrowing as the government again flinched from either cutting expenditure or raising taxes. In 1974 people simply were neither disposed nor conditioned to believe that the huge energy cost increases signified a permanent change in expectations and, with the taste of recently acquired prosperity in the mouth, the nation embarked on a 'spend now, pay later' policy. Though the next two years saw more moderate pay settlements and industrial production went up by 10 per cent in 1976, the nation fell with whoops of joy on a positively immoral give-away election manifesto from Fianna Fail in 1977.

Once in power again, Fianna Fail introduced tax cuts and public expenditure rose — although, as the figures for industrial production indicate, the country was pulling away so strongly from the oil shock that it did not require any budgetary stimulation. Public borrowing went up to 13 per cent of GNP and both the politicians and the people allowed feet to float so far from the ground that in June 1978 a White Paper was issued, and accepted without arousing either noticeable scepticism or derision, which envisaged full, repeat *full,* employment (100 per cent) in the eighties. In fact, the eighties were to see 18 per cent unemployment — which would be over 30 per cent were it not for forced emigration — and a climate of opinion well illustrated by one managing director who said to me, as I was researching this book: 'You know, with the taxes, the unions, the economy, everything, I've gone through a complete change. I used to be proud that I employed four hundred, five hundred men and looked forward to the day when I'd employ seven hundred, a thousand maybe. Now my whole idea is how many can I get rid of. Redundancy's the name of the game'.

That is a typical Irish manager's attitude today. The idea of employment creation in the public sector is as dead as Sean Lemass himself.

Why did no one shout stop? The fact is that the general appearance of the country gave every indication that government policy was correct, and that the new decision-takers knew what they were doing. Between the years 1962 and 1982 Irish industrial growth was, on average, the best in the European Community. The IDA (Industrial Development Authority), which had been set up as far back as 1955 with a view to attracting foreign investment to Ireland, was highly successful in achieving this aim in the euphoric sixties. There was a general move away from protectionism, and the dismantling of barriers to free trade. But appearances were deceptive.

The international business consultancy firm, Telesis, was commissioned by the government in 1982 to examine Irish industrial promotion. The team which visited Ireland appeared to have absorbed the Irish spirit of blarney, the art of managing to convey bad news as though it were good. Telesis praised the IDA as 'the most dynamic, most active, most efficient and most effective organisation of its kind in the world', but went on to lambast wide areas of IDA policy. The report found that too much was being offered to attract foreign firms, and not enough to boost native exporters. Allowing for business vicissitudes such as job losses and closures, the report found that of jobs approved in government-sanctioned projects during 1972–8, only 20 per cent were actually in place at the end of the period. One would have thought that the country's political watchdogs would have monitored this state of affairs but, as Telesis rightly pointed out, governmental controls on such matters existed in name only.

The 'job approvals' routine, for instance, says something about the largely cosmetic nature of much Irish governmental activity. It is common for a minister to attend a sod-cutting ceremony at which much publicity is generated by talk of 'jobs approved now' and 'it is hoped that the project will ultimately provide' so many jobs. Telesis drily commented that while Irish industrial policy 'aimed to create jobs', 'it expends too much energy on creating job *approvals*'. In a thunderous burst of stating the obvious, Telesis pointed out: 'The two are not synonymous'. No indeed. But in the increasingly PR-led world of Irish public life, where image was all and the symbol of progress was the glossy Annual Report (dominated by pictures of the Chairman, the whole produced in glorious technicolour by an ad agency, and usually unwrapped at a liquid press lunch designed to entertain rather than to inform) it was very often made to appear that jobs and approvals were one and the same.

Another rarely discussed but more serious criticism of the IDA's activities, or rather of the political watchdogs' failure to regulate them properly, is that so much of what the IDA has achieved falls as a direct burden on the taxpayer, whose pockets are lightened to provide the wherewithal to create Brigadoon-like 'job approvals' but who reaps little benefit from the profits. These are repatriated to whatever country or flag of convenience the parent companies operate under. One billion pounds Irish left the country in 1984 this way. This, of course, is also a question mark over the much vaunted 'growth in exports'. Should the expatriation of the fruits of so much Irish initiative, work, resources and services out of the country be considered as 'exports' or as 'haemorrhage'? The 'Black Hole' has now grown so deep, partly as a result of mounting taxation, that almost £1½ billion, not only in profits but also in smuggled savings and purchases in Northern Ireland, flowed outward in 1986. And it was January 1987 before the IDA announced that it was tightening up its grant package so as to relate payment to performance.

In the sixties, scarcely a day passed without the news of yet another American factory coming to Ireland, and by the time the seventies drew to a close it was not unusual to hear people referring to the Irish 'silicon valley', so much were we all led to believe that we were exporting high technology. There was to be a rude awakening. In fact, under the surface gloss, employment did not rise at all between 1972 and 1982. Instead, the crash of bankruptcies grew ever louder in the land. A new class of gombeen-man arose. Belonging to the best clubs and holidaying abroad at least twice a year, these new plunderers included bankers, accountants and stockbrokers who performed prodigies of liquidation, accumulating paper profits as one old family company after another went to the wall.

Hostility grew between management and labour, accentuated by the growth of the class who talked managerial newspeak to each other — 'function', 'added value', 'take on the unions' — corresponding to the other side's, 'if those bastards want to fight, we'll give it to them', 'ah sure 'twill do,' 'the job'll last longer than the money'. Smokestack industries crumbled, agribusiness lay unexploited. As recession spread, many of the multi-nationals clipped off the toenails of their worldwide enterprises, their Irish subsidiaries. The clipping could, and often did, account for hundreds of jobs on the ground in Ireland.

Because of Roman Catholic teaching on birth control, the numbers of young people grew well beyond the European average as a proportion of the whole population. Demographers say that it will level off sometime after the year 2,000 but concede that the numbers in the 15–29 age-group will continue to grow at least to the mid-1990s. These young people face a clash of cultures: 'Dallas' on the television, father on the dole. Jobs are hard to come by and some people question whether the school and third level training systems do anything more than fit the youngsters for a world of employment which does not exist.

As the so-called 'good' businessman in these years was very evidently the one who could get the most from all concerned, from worker, customer, government, whomsoever, and give the least in return so as to maximise the profits, the 'good' trade unionist in turn became the one who could give the least and get the most in return for his services. The more favoured device for this was the grossly misnamed 'productivity agreements', whereby incentive schemes — again a laughable misnomer — were introduced widely throughout Irish industry in the seventies. The object was to increase the output in return for more money. The result in fact was to make the average job slower and dearer. In the public service, even the most dedicated trade unionist would admit privately that manning levels were some 30 per cent over what was required, and industrialists would claim that the figure could be over 50 per cent.

By 1986 the total National Debt was estimated at £21,000m. or 120 per cent of GNP. Of this debt, 47 per cent was in foreign borrowings (*Sunday Press* 17.8.86).

Extraordinary changes occurred in Irish population and employment trends between 1966 and the time of writing. The population went up steadily by almost 25 per cent to 3,535,000; the numbers employed in agriculture fell by half, whereas those employed in the public sector increased by nearly 100 per cent. Overall unemployment went up nearly five hundred per cent and emigration reared its ugly head again, probably as many as 100,000 leaving the country in 1986. So many left as tourists, particularly for the USA, that it is hard to put an exact figure on this recurring scourge. Readers with a taste for statistics can peruse the tables from which these figures were extracted later. (See p. 244). I simply wish to underline the special problems posed for a well-intentioned, kindly but rather disorganised, small, agriculturally-based society faced with high transportation costs, the need to import raw materials and at the same time trying to cope with the effects of the micro-chip on numbers employed on the factory floor, and of Catholic teaching on birth control on numbers created in the bedrooms. Furthermore, one should bear in mind Noises Off: the threat posed by the Northern situation, falling agricultural prospects and rising oil prices. All combined to force people into cities, heightening the problems of both unemployment and urbanisation (Dublin has a heroin problem equivalent to New York's in percentage terms) while worsening both the ratio of producers to dependants, and the lot of the tax-payer.

2

Politics, 1969–79

Clientelism; Southern Parties; Northern Parties;
North and South; The Arms Trial;
The IRA; Fianna Fail Revives

THE distinguishing characteristics of Irish political life are better examined in rural Ireland, particularly west of the Shannon, that great river that bisects Ireland between east and west.

Clientelism

West of the Shannon the land is generally poor. In places like Connemara, Donegal, Leitrim or Roscommon, against a historical backdrop of rack-renting poverty, a TD (*Teachta Dala,* a deputy or member of parliament) is expected to provide his constituents with a variety of services which have no place in classical political theory.

'Blue Cards' which ensure free medical treatment (often for people well above the income level entitling them to such benefit), the dole, home improvement grants and farm subsidies of all sorts (even if they are not remotely merited) feature strongly in the concerns of a rural member of the Irish parliament.

Apart from such rarified matters as securing a contract for the more wealthy constituents, services such as having summonses quashed for after-hours drinking, or putting subsidised 'red diesel' tractor fuel in private cars, or poaching or trespass or assault or tax evasion, are considered the proper duties of a country TD.

This attitude permeates all sections of the administration, from the most junior garda (policeman), who each week watches

Sean or Pat 'sign on' at the police station to qualify for unemployment benefit in the full knowledge that both Sean and Pat are in fact working, to the most senior minister in Dublin. In fact, a minister is expected not to show higher standards in such matters, but rather, because of his greater power, a higher return in 'perks' for those who have voted for him.

Another side effect of the political culture is the undue politicisation surrounding some police force appointments. One of the scandals which helped to discredit the Haughey administration of 1979–81 surrounded an attempt to transfer Garda Sergeant Tully in County Roscommon. It was widely believed that the transfer of this efficient and conscientious policeman stemmed from precisely those causes — he had frequently proved himself honourably immune to the blandishments of 'red diesel culture'.

Fianna Fail in particular has had a two-fold reason for keeping rural culture flourishing. As the party most committed — under de Valera, at all events — to keeping the Irish language and culture alive, the west of Ireland, the poorest and most Gaelic part of the country, was a logical philosophical target for assistance, being the perceived reservoir of traditional Irish and Catholic culture. Also, to stay in power Fianna Fail required the rural vote generally, and the western vote in particular. Actually, today the main thrust of language revival is to be found in the cities; concerned parents have come together to found Gael Scoileanna schools wherein children are taught through Irish. These schools have an excellent reputation and their numbers are growing each year, but the number of people who actually use Irish as a first language in day-to-day communication is diminishing. Only about 30,000 to 50,000 people throughout the Gaeltacht areas now use Irish as their principal means of communication.

The classic exponent of rural clientelist culture is the ex-policeman and former Minister for Justice, Sean Doherty, who resigned from Fianna Fail for his role in the illegal bugging of journalists' telephones in February 1983, was re-admitted in December the following year and proved himself in successive general elections to be the most popular politician in his west of the Shannon Roscommon constituency.[1] Interviewed on the RTE programme 'This Week' on suggestions that he had inter-

1. R. Smith, *The Quest for Power,* Aherlow Press, Dublin 1986.

fered with the work of gardai, Mr Doherty gave the following widely quoted replies:

'I have not at any time stated that I would deny making representations on behalf of my constituents to the gardai or, indeed, to any public service body. It is my duty as a Dail deputy to communicate the views of my constituents to any particular area that I am requested to do so. I have done that in the past and I will do it in the future and I make no apologies for doing it.

'The fact that I became Minister for Justice or Minister of State as I was in the past, doesn't necessarily mean that I have to be silent when it comes to my constituents. If that were the situation they would have themselves with a Minister for Justice and lose themselves a TD. I am primarily a TD where my constituents are concerned — at a greater level I am Minister for Justice in the context of the national interest'.

He agreed that he had made phone calls to individual gardai at garda stations: 'I have communicated to the gardai as I have to many other public service bodies on many occasions insofar as the views of my constituents need to be expressed to them. I make no apology for having done that and I will do it again'.

'When I represent my constituents it's at the bottom and that's in my constituency and I represent them as Sean Doherty, Dail deputy.'

However, the rural vote is the one most susceptible to corrosion by emigration. Hence, as an American political scientist[2] has observed: 'Fianna Fail's response was to lengthen and retard the demise of this traditional political sector. The expansion of Ireland's social welfare programme under Fianna Fail has included a number of direct and indirect subsidies to the poorer countrymen, aimed at keeping them on the land'.

This inculcates a cavalier attitude to spending the taxpayers' money, and it tends to make the party responsive to the wishes of the conservative rural periphery on moral questions like divorce and contraception. In an era of universal education policy problems can easily arise for the party, since an attitude that goes down well in Connemara can cost votes in suburbia, and vice versa. During the abortion referendum Roscommon, the constituency of the redoubtable Sean Doherty, voted 83.79 per cent for the pro-life amendment of the constitution, 16.21 per cent

2. Paul Sacks, *The Donegal Mafia*, Yale University Press, New Haven and London, 1976.

against. In the urban east, Dun Laoghaire went 57.97 per cent against to only 42.03 per cent for — half the Roscommon poll.

An experienced deputy who has succeeded in getting tax-payers' money spent on building tarmacadamed drive-ways around constituents' houses to curry favour at election time,[3] and who has also succeeded in getting the county council to build a house for an unmarried mother, is far more likely to be criticised for 'encouraging them' over the latter initiative than over the former, which is perceived as nothing more than an ingenious exercise by patronage at government expense. The farming community by and large does not pay income tax and the black economy flourishes amid Ireland's 'forty shades of green'. Hence the fierce loyalty to Fianna Fail one encounters in places like Connemara, where it so often made survival possible by meeting unorthodox expectations.

Southern Parties

A distinguishing factor of Irish political parties is the fact that most in some way originated as a form of reaction to the British presence on the island. They either came out of the physical force tradition or had to make contact with that tradition as part of their normal function.

In the Republic both Fianna Fail, the largest party in the country, and Fine Gael are the outcome of the bitter family row that was the Irish civil war. This sprang up within the original Sinn Fein party over the Treaty terms that ended the Anglo-Irish war and established the independent Irish state.

The Labour Party stands partially free from, partially enmeshed in, the physical force tradition because James Connolly, who co-founded the party with James Larkin, was subsequently executed for the part he and his Citizen Army (formed from the ranks of Labour) played in the 1916 Rising. Throughout most of the century the conditions for socialism were unfavourable. As a result of the flood tide of nationalism which Connolly helped to unleash, the Labour Party did not contest the 1918 election in which Sinn Fein rose to power; neither did it figure in the war which followed. Subsequent Labour leaders in the Larkinite tradi-

3. *Irish Press*, February 1986.

tion were never able to bring Labour to power except as the junior partner in coalition, given the infrastructures and power bases set up by the revolution which Connolly helped to put in train.

Ironically, as firstly increasing urbanisation and stronger trade unionism and then increasing alienation brought on by recession and unemployment produced conditions more favourable to the left, it was the party which had most recently put down the gun and departed the physical force tradition that appeared poised to take over from Labour. The Workers' Party was an off-shoot of that wing of the IRA which, since the ending of the 1956–62 border campaign, had been edging towards constitutional socialism — although some members have shown no overwhelming doctrinal attitude against the occasional funding by bank robbery, particularly in Northern Ireland. The IRA, both left and right, hold strongly to that not insubstantial body of Irish opinion which believes in a theory of banking based on withdrawals rather than deposits.

Initially known as Sinn Fein, the Workers' Party, this party had its origins in the IRA split of January 1970. The section that wished to pursue the left-wing course espoused by Roy Johnston and his supporters within the movement, such as Tomas MacGiolla, Cathal Goulding and Sean Garland, regarded itself as the Official IRA. Its political wing was accordingly considered to be Official Sinn Fein.

Johnston was an unusual figure to find in IRA circles. A computer scientist at Trinity College, Dublin, who was also a Marxist, he had gained such an ascendancy over the then IRA leadership that he was appointed as a kind of educational commissar with the title of 'Education Officer'. Under his tutelage the movement had become involved in strikes, sit-ins and demonstrations over riparian rights and had been virtually demilitarised. When Protestant mobs invaded the traditional IRA strongholds of Belfast, there were no IRA 'defenders' to withstand them and the letters IRA appeared on gable walls in the Falls district in the form 'Irish Ran Away'. But even after this reverse the Johnstonites voted a few months later, in December 1969, to contest elections and enter parliament if elected, thereby ending the traditional policy of abstention. This decision gave a final impetus to the recreation of a full, traditional, physical force republican movement. The Provisional Caretaker Executive of Sinn Fein was the title adopted by those who left the Sinn Fein Ard Fheis in the Intercontinental Hotel at Ballsbridge in protest against the policy of the 'Officials'. They went instead to the Kevin Barry Memorial Hall (called after an executed hero of the Anglo-Irish War) to enroll in the new movement.

The Officials' teething period was not confined to Provisionals-versus-Officials dissension. It also had to contend with considerable public apathy at the 1973 general election; ten candidates offered themselves, none was elected and only one saved his deposit. However, the Officials must have preferred apathy to what happened next. Following a further split within the Official wing, the Irish Republican Socialist Party was set up in December 1974, having attracted Bernadette Devlin, now Bernadette McAliskey, to its banner. Following some bloody encounters between former Officials and an unsuccessful attempt on his life, the IRSP leader, Seamus Costello, was shot dead in October 1977 and the IRSP went into decline. Bernadette McAliskey was among those who left the party.

In January 1977 the Officials added the 'Workers' Party' description to their title, although in the election that year the voters showed little interest. Lost deposits were again the order of the day. In 1981, however, Joe Sherlock of Cork East was elected and was joined in the Dail in February 1982 by two more Workers' Party TDs, Patrick Gallagher and Proinsias de Rossa. The party in fact held the balance of power between the coalition and Fianna Fail, for whom it voted, thus bringing down the coalition. It was repaid in votes, though not seats, in the November 1982 elections, where it lost Sherlock but returned the party's President Tomas MacGiolla, along with de Rossa, gaining an almost 50 per cent increase in its Dublin vote.

At the time of writing, the Workers' Party is the Irish version of Eurocommunism. The most powerful figure in the party is the General Secretary, not its parliamentarians whose Dail salaries go to the party. The party in turn pays them an allowance based on the going rate for an industrial worker. The party's newspaper has a circulation of some forty thousand copies. It runs social clubs and a printing press and its publishing company Repsol owns the franchise for the distribution of Soviet Union publications in Ireland. At a Soviet Embassy social function I noticed that the Workers' Party guests were the most fêted by embassy staff.

The party is much more tightly controlled than its main rival on the left, the Labour Party, and its Central Executive Council holds sway over the organisation both north and south of the border (prior to the Ard Fheis of 1982 the Workers' Party in the North was known as The Workers' Party Republican Clubs). Members are thoroughly screened before being admitted and have to have attended new member classes, understand party policy and give a 'commitment to work for it' before joining. Anyone with a good income is expected to contribute to the party. The CEC runs advice centres and maintains a very high profile for such a relatively small party both in the constituencies and in the Dail. Its deputies, particularly de Rossa, have been amongst the most active in Leinster House.

The party does not like to be reminded of its IRA days.

Northern Parties

In Northern Ireland itself both major unionist groupings, the Official Unionist Party and the Democratic Unionist Party led by the Reverend Ian Paisley, owe their existence to their commitment in varying degrees of stridency to maintaining the British link, by force if necessary. Privately both parties express their disgust at Britain's lack of resolution in maintaining her side of the alliance, i.e. getting on top of the IRA.

The moderate Alliance Party, caught not alone in the vortex of unionism but of republicanism also, finds that the only meeting at the middle of the road which exists in Northern Ireland between the forces of nationalism and unionism is that which occurs when members of either side cross over to avoid sniper fire of the political or other sort.

The moderate Social Democratic and Labour Party was founded to work for reform within the system, not principally for a United Ireland. It grew out of the civil rights movement which sprang up in the late sixties to counteract the injustices towards Catholics which the unionists had been allowed to get away with by Britain ever since the state came into existence in the early twenties. Currently, even though it has benefited from the Hillsborough Agreement, it finds itself as much under threat from Sinn Fein as Labour comes under threat in the Republic from the

Workers' Party. This is because British governments consistently
bow to unionist pressure not to concede nationalist demands, and
support a system of 'justice' that sees nothing wrong in relying on
'Supergrasses'. Increasingly, after the hunger strike of 1981,
much nationalist opinion hardened to the belief that Britain
responds only to force. Despite Hillsborough, the same belief
exists in moderate political circles in the Republic also: not a
cheerful prospect but one which, borne in mind, will help
illuminate the more detailed examination of the Irish political
parties.

North and South

The years 1966 to 1970 marked the end of the period since the
foundation of the two states, north and south of the border, in
which the politics of the one could be generally considered independently of the other. During the Jubilee of the 1916 Rising in
1966 nobody paid much attention to the fact that a young Catholic
barman had been murdered in Belfast and that an organisation
called the Ulster Volunteer Force was apparently responsible for
the killing. But the death of John Scullion would be remembered
afterwards as the starting point in a recrudescence of the Ulster
Protestant opposition to Catholic nationalism.

In the south, the leitmotif of 1966 was of ageing 1916 warriors
— Eamon de Valera, Sean MacEntee and others — being
repeatedly photographed outside the GPO in Dublin where the
rebellion had begun. This set the tone for a veritable orgy of
commemorative tableaux all over the Republic and among
nationalists in Northern Ireland. At the end of that fairly
prosperous year, when Lemass retired, Fianna Fail chose Jack
Lynch to succeed him as a compromise between the main rivals
for the leadership, George Colley and Charles Haughey, Lemass'
son-in-law. No one at the time had the slightest inkling of the
forces which this rivalry would unleash long afterwards.

People talked about the rising tide of farmer protests or, in the
typically Irish preoccupation with international affairs, avidly
discussed the Vietnam War and the conflict between liberals and
conservatives which had broken out in the Roman Catholic
Church as a result of Pope John's Vatican Council. One was either
exhilarated or bored witless by the incessant discussions

encountered throughout the country, and particularly in the 'intellectual' circles of Dublin, amongst people who had excitedly discovered Vatican II via authors like 'Xavier Rynne', Michael Novak and Malachi Martin, or who had read theologians such as Rahner or Schillebeeckx. People mentioned 'John Charles', the ultramontane Archbishop McQuaid of Dublin, as frequently as Washingtonians would refer to President Reagan in our day. He was seen in those far-off days of ecumenical innocence as a far greater obstacle to progress than any other figure then existing north or south of the border.

Less than two years after Lemass left office an event of profound significance occurred, which showed the virulence of the Northern issue on Irish television screens for the first time and should have alerted the country to what was to come. This was the batoning of civil rights protesters on the streets of Derry by the Royal Ulster Constabulary on 5 October 1968. While this event enormously heightened an awareness of Northern Ireland in the south, attention was being more concentrated on the new men whom Lemass had brought forward and on the changes they were making. Lemass urged his top civil servants and state company heads to take on extra staff — viewing their operations as a means to increase employment. What was one era's 'job-creation' would be another's 'over-manning'.

The new ideas gripping the country found expression not alone in the established political power base of Fianna Fail, and to a lesser degree in its main rival Fine Gael, but also on the left, where a post-war generation of university-educated socialists began to dream of moving the country in their own direction via the Labour Party. Labour attracted a number of TV personalities whom the new medium propelled from the living rooms to the hustings, and these drew with them personalities from journalism and universities who would not normally have trodden a leftward path.

As this broadly familiar west European development was taking place, in Northern Ireland the colonial past suddenly placed its grisly fingers around the throat of Kathleen Ni Houlihan and squeezed hard. Serious violence erupted in 1969. The civil rights movement, led by young educated Catholics who had benefited from the British wartime Education Acts, had been so much publicised by the media that after the 1968 batonings many wishful thinkers in Dublin thought that the movement on its own would be able to bring about major change in Northern Ireland. In the event Protestant extremists — of whom the principal public figure was, and still is, the Reverend Ian Paisley — demonstrated against the Civil Rights Association (CRA) marchers, using the utterly misleading slogan 'CRA = IRA'. The result was that by August 1969 a position of such intensity was reached that British troops were forced on to the streets to quell rioting in Derry and Belfast.

The 'new men' of Fianna Fail constituted a major problem for Jack Lynch when he took over leadership of the party and the country in 1966. These colourful, corner-cutting characters may have 'pulled strokes', to use their own terminology (Donogh O'Malley said openly of political patronage, 'Of *course* we look after our own'), but they did change things for the better. O'Malley transformed the Irish educational system. Charles Haughey was one of the most effective and innovative ministers in the history of the Irish state in portfolios as challenging and diverse as Justice, Agriculture and Finance.

Neil Blaney, a bruiser at home in a smoke-filled backroom, looked after his own in his native Donegal where even today, as an independent, his machine is still a byword for effectiveness. Nationally he was a superb party organiser. Brian Lenihan, roly-poly and flippant in a way that belied his ability, also got things done, revolutionising the censorship laws, for instance, and bringing some badly needed improvements to the fishing industry. The doctor from Clare, Patrick Hillery, was quieter and less freewheeling, but he set in train the educational reforms which O'Malley saw through. George Colley, a former schoolmate of Haughey's, represented the style of the older wing of Fianna Fail. He was Haughey's principal rival when Lemass stepped down and was to speak openly about changes in Fianna Fail which brought about 'low standards in high places'. Though clearly his heart was in the right place, his tongue sometimes was not. When the tide of feminism first began lapping around Ireland's political shores he dismissed the claims of the Women's Movement as being nothing more than the preoccupation of 'well-heeled, articulate women', creating an uproar.

Lynch took over a party in which the new Fianna Fail and the old-style party were moulded together like one of those Chinese dishes in which pieces of duck and prawn are covered in glaze. When the Northern Ireland troubles finally erupted uncontrollably less than three years after he assumed the leadership, the glaze of expediency melted in the fires of burning nationalist homes in Belfast, combined with a high degree of personal rivalry and ambition in the party, and fish and flesh began to come apart.

On the one hand, the Republic joined the EEC. Cattle prices rose. Trade union activity fattened pay packets, businessmen prospered and the sixties' euphoria persisted. The major controversy of those years centred around the disclosure that the O'Malley philosophy of mutual support had been institutionalised into a body known as Taca (Gift), made up of a group of businessmen committed to giving money to Fianna Fail. Much criticism burst around Jack Lynch's head as a result, but it was as the gentle rain from heaven compared to what occurred when Fianna Fail republicanism began to sizzle in the Northern heat.

The Pavlovian reaction of the extremist Protestants of Northern Ireland to the civil rights marches and the perceived 'gains' of the nationalists was such that rioting and pogroms which broke out in Belfast and Derry seemed to be of a scale and intensity which made civil war throughout the whole island inevitable. In the nation generally there was a whiff of grapeshot in the air. Refugees were pouring south. Television and the newspapers were filled with graphic accounts of burnings and shootings.

Under pressure from the hawks in the Cabinet, notably Blaney and Kevin Boland, on 13 August 1969, Lynch went on radio and TV to make a ringing declaration that: 'the Irish government can no longer stand by and see innocent people injured'. During the broadcast he asked for a UN peace keeping force to be sent in, called on the British to stop the 'police attacks on the people of Derry' and announced that units of the Irish Army were being moved to the border to provide 'field hospitals' for people who did not wish to be treated in Northern Ireland institutions.

However, the doves ultimately won out and Lynch was able to pull back (relievedly) from his TV position. The hawks flew on. In the north the 'field hospitals' were regarded as the harbingers of an invasion and the tension rose even higher. Two days later the British Minister of State at the Foreign Office told Dr Hillery that the UN request was not on and Hillery unsuccessfully appealed in person to the UN on 19 August. Because of the Lynch/Hillery initiative (largely cosmetic, given the fact that Britain, which claimed that the matter was a domestic affair, has a right of veto in the Security Council) or because of the actual rioting, or the spectacle of Bernadette Devlin on TV breaking up bricks to throw at the Derry police, the British Army was sent into Belfast and Derry and the troubles temporarily subsided.

The Arms Trial

August 1969 was indeed a wicked month in Ireland, particularly in the North, where amongst Catholics in the traditional ghetto districts the political reality was the fear of assassination. Because of these fears messages went out north, south, east and west seeking weapons for defence. Very respectable people from all walks in Northern Ireland, particularly in Belfast, banded themselves together in defence committees and came south looking for weapons from the government of the day. As one of these emissaries, John Kelly, said later[4], these were not courtesy calls: 'I want to be very emphatic here, that we were coming from all parts of the Six Counties not to indulge in tea parties, not to be entertained, but to elicit in so far as we could what was the opinion of the government in relation to the Six Counties . . . We did not ask for blankets or feeding bottles. We asked for guns and no one from Taoiseach Lynch down refused that request or told us that this was contrary to government policy . . .'

The point about that statement is that he made it in the dock, after a number of prominent figures, including Charles Haughey had been charged (ultimately unsuccessfully, as it proved) with gun-running. Kelly afterwards got six months in the Special Criminal Court for IRA membership.

Kelly, of course, was a novice in the Republic's political ways and in the distinctions made between public-house republicanism ('Guinness Republicanism') and putting militant utterances into practice. On every hand's turn, he and others like him had been met with promises of aid from the southerners for their fellow nationalist tribesmen in the Fourth Lost Green Field. I heard

4. *Orders for the Captain*, published by Captain James Kelly, 1971, Dublin p.171.

from one key figure of the period that 'everyone we met promised us guns — except Paddy Hillery'. Hillery's caution was certainly a minority attitude in the fervid atmosphere of the time in which it seemed that the minority were all to be slaughtered immediately and groups gathered in the streets of Dublin chanting 'give us the guns' (after closing time, usually).

Fianna Fail sources established contact with the IRA through a priest in London. After various clandestine meetings in London, Dublin, Northern Ireland and elsewhere, involving Fianna Fail at ministerial level, plans were laid for the importation of arms to Northern Ireland. Official funds were placed in bank accounts in border areas in the names of prominent people in the nationalist community. An Irish Army officer, Captain James Kelly, made contacts in nationalist circles — and tongues began to wag. Certainly I heard rumours of what was happening in republican circles (I was concluding research on my book on the IRA at the time) throughout the late autumn and the early winter of 1969. Apparently, so did the garda Special Branch. So did British intelligence. How Jack Lynch managed not to hear of it remains a mystery to this day. An unsuccessful attempt was made to break the story by circulating Dublin newspapers with a brief, anonymous gestetnered tip-off. Then Garda Special Branch sources took action. Liam Cosgrave, leader of Fine Gael, was given some information and went to see Jack Lynch. Uproar ensued.

A quantity of arms was seized at Dublin Airport en route from Vienna and subsequently the government made unsuccessful attempts to recover money from a Hamburg arms dealer, who it was believed had been paid from public funds. In May 1970, a titanic upheaval took place within the Fianna Fail government: Jack Lynch sacked Ministers Charles Haughey and Neil Blaney, alleging that they did not fully subscribe to government policy on the North. Other government figures resigned in protest, but somehow the government held together.

All this of course caused tremendous public outcry, both in the Dail and outside it — far greater in fact than the original disturbances in Northern Ireland. Inside Fianna Fail it struck to the very core of the party's philosophy.

An anecdote told to me by a former *Irish Press* political correspondent, Brendan Malin, precisely illustrates why. He described an election meeting in O'Connell Street at which de Valera spoke. Unemployment and poverty were rife, but de Valera did not address himself to these minor matters. Instead he went into a long onslaught against those (unnamed) who said Fianna Fail was retreating: 'We are *not* retreating. We shall *never* retreat'. 'He kept on saying things like that all through, and the crowd loved it', recalled Malin. 'They roared and cheered, even though no one had said anything about retreating beforehand. Dev never made it clear where he was supposed to be retreating, or who from. That was Dev!'

That was Fianna Fail too. No one had to explain the retreat which had to be avoided. Going back to the formation of the party, when constitutionalism was still an itchy garment, many a member of a Fianna Fail cumann (branch) by day was an IRA man drilling by night. There was only one issue, one reason, for the party (or for that matter, the drilling). Partition. Standing up to Britain and the Orangemen over Ireland's inalienable right to be one and undivided was the party's main reason for existence; in 1987 Gerry Adams remarked to me of Sinn Fein's support, 'we draw from the same pot as Fianna Fail'. At the time of the sackings, this policy seemed to be in retreat to a significant number of the party's supporters and deputies. This sense of retreat, of betraying Fianna Fail's 'moral community', led to the formation of a new party, Aontacht Eireann, by the former Minister for Social Welfare, Kevin Boland, who had resigned from Fianna Fail. But it did not lead to the demise of Fianna Fail itself, as had seemed inevitable in the early period of the sackings

I remember on the night of Boland's resignation Vivion de Valera, Editor-in-Chief of the *Irish Press* and eldest son of the paper's founder Eamon de Valera, came into the office. He was obviously consumed with anxiety to read my leader. He considered that, given Boland's stated reason for departure, it was the most important leader I had ever written. It was the most fraught, certainly, for the balancing act between the reality and the fear of 'retreat' was particularly difficult to maintain at that time and in that atmosphere. But reality won out. Those who had joined the party for reasons related to jobs, houses, professional advancement, contracts or the quashing of the summons for the illicit use of red diesel proved themselves a majority at the ensuing Fianna Fail Ard Fheis in February 1971. A noisy and sometimes bitter gathering agreed overwhelmingly with the attitude expressed in a ringing phrase by Patrick Hillery who told his surging audience, 'You can have Boland, but you won't have Fianna Fail'.

The IRA

If Fianna Fail held together, the North did not. Appalling sectarian violence continued in the course of which hundreds of lives were to be lost. The IRA emerged from the shadows of Irish history, initially, at least, to protect the Catholic areas of Belfast and Derry from Protestant assassination squads.

The year 1972 was one of particular violence in Northern Ireland, witnessing amongst other events the Bloody Sunday shootings and the fall of Stormont. As the troubles mounted and their effects came to be felt more and more in the Republic, the Fianna Fail government on 28 November circulated a bill amending the Offences Against the State Act 1939, proposing changes in the law of evidence so that it would be possible for a Garda Chief Superintendent to secure a conviction by swearing in court that he believed the accused person to be a member of the IRA. Fines or imprisonment for twelve months were to be imposed on persons refusing to give an account of their movements.

The proposed bill, which also limited RTE's freedom to report IRA affairs, was greeted with vehement opposition in many quarters. Dr Conor Cruise O'Brien, for instance, then a Labour Party TD, said that he was 'astonished' at how far the bill went and that his party was not prepared to give the government a blank cheque for the take-over of RTE and the giving of such powers to the police.

However the government, spearheaded by the Minister for Justice, Des O'Malley, pressed ahead with its proposals, even though elements within Fianna Fail were known to be unhappy about it. Fine Gael was completely divided on the issue; Liam Cosgrave and prominent front-benchers such as Paddy Donegan, later to become involved in controversies over emergency powers legislation himself, stood against other sections of the party, in which Paddy Cooney was prominent, who felt that the legislation was too Draconian.

It appeared inevitable that the bill would fall, but as the debate reached its final stages on 1 December, there were two bomb blasts in Dublin, the perpetrators of which are still unknown; two people were killed. The bill passed through the Dail at 4 am on 2 December, by 69 votes to 22.

Had the bombs not gone off Lynch would have called a snap election and Cosgrave would almost certainly have been promptly dethroned as leader of Fine Gael, so great was the antipathy to the measure not alone in his own party but throughout the country. At one stage in the debate the Dail was in a virtual state of siege, and as the stage was debated thousands of troops and gardai ringed the Dail to keep back the huge crowds of demonstrators.

The United Kingdom government suppressed the parliament of Northern Ireland in 1972. In February 1973, Fianna Fail went out of office in the Republic, having presided over Ireland's accession to the EEC. Right-wing Fine Gael and left-wing Labour managed to put aside their differences, offered themselves to the voters as a 'National Coalition' and emerged from the general election victorious, under the leadership of Fine Gael's Liam Cosgrave and Labour's Brendan Corish, ending sixteen years of Fianna Fail rule. The coalition's period in office (1973 to 1977) was to be characterised by a very heavy-handed but ultimately unsuccessful approach to security.

The major effort of the coalition towards negotiating with the unionists and the British over this period was also unsuccessful. This was the Sunningdale Agreement, called after the Sunningdale Teachers' College in Berkshire where it was concluded between representatives of the British and Irish governments, the Official Unionists (though not the Paisleyites), and the Social Democratic and Labour Party. The Agreement attempted to set up a Council of Ireland comprised of members drawn equally from the Dail, and from the Assembly which had been elected in place of the abolished parliament in Northern Ireland. The council would have had a ministry consisting of members of the Irish government and of the power-sharing Executive of unionists and nationalists already constituted in the North. The council of Ireland would have formally linked Belfast and Dublin. The Agreement incorporated declarations that the status of Northern Ireland as part of the United Kingdom could be changed only by consent of the Northern majority. It was to be registered at the United Nations.

However, even thus limited, the Council provoked the loyalists into a strike which destroyed the Executive without trace in 1974. Direct Rule, provided by Britain, was introduced, and despite various experiments no new parliament arose in Northern Ireland. In the Republic, preoccupation with the security aspect of the Agreement resulted in the formation of the 'heavy gang', a specially-picked squad of tough detectives whose treatment of republican suspects earned considerable unpopularity for the government which set it up.

One of the factors which heightened Fine Gael's strong inclination towards taking a firm 'law and order' approach over the North, and security generally, was the fact that the coalition faced two particularly emotional challenges during its term in office. Both took that very Irish form of protest, the hunger-strike, although both the men involved — Michael Gaughan and Frank Stagg — died in British, not Irish, prisons. Michael Gaughan, who died at the age of twenty-four in Parkhurst Jail on the Isle of Wight on 3 June 1974, was the first hunger-striker to die in an English jail since Terence MacSwiney, Lord Mayor of Cork, more than fifty years earlier. Gaughan had been jailed for his role in robbing a North London bank of £530 in 1971 as part of an Official IRA fund-raising exercise. He had been on hunger-strike since 31 March in a demand for political status with a group which included Frank Stagg of County Mayo, who had been sentenced in 1973 on conspiracy charges. Stagg was ordered off his strike by the Provisional IRA after Gaughan's death.

Gaughan's funeral was a huge affair. From the time he was brought back to Ireland until he was buried in Mayo, the cortege was accompanied by a large banner inscribed 'Support the IRA' and by other more tangible forms of protest, such as petitions by doctors to the Home Office urging the transfer of such prisoners to the North on medical and humanitarian grounds. What perturbed the hardliners in the coalition government, and in particular the Taoiseach himself, Liam Cosgrave, was the gigantic publicity bonanza reaped by the IRA from the huge funeral and accompanying police escort that followed Michael Gaughan to his last resting place.

Two years later, when Frank Stagg died after another hunger

strike in Wakefield Prison, Cosgrave took an extraordinary decision. The plane bringing Stagg's remains back to Ireland was
diverted in mid-air by government order away from Dublin
Airport, where a reception party of prominent Provisionals
awaited it, and landed at Shannon. Here the coffin was removed
under Special Branch escort to County Mayo and buried in a
concrete-encased grave in Leigue Cemetery, Ballina.

When the subsequent controversy had simmered down, the
IRA, working at night, dug up Stagg's remains and re-interred
him in the nearby Republican plot as he had wished, to the
accompaniment of prayers from a sympathetic priest.

There was further security legislation controversy as a result of
the Sunningdale Agreement. The government moved on 2
January 1974, by publishing an order under which people accused
of murder in the North could be arrested and tried for the alleged
crime within the jurisdiction of the Republic. In practice this
didn't mean a great deal in terms of convictions, as the Northern
authorities continued to prefer to seek extradition from the
Republic rather than to avail of the Sunningdale provision.

Three other events which occurred during this administration's lifetime had a bearing on the government's attitude to
security. These were the murder of a Fine Gael senator, simul-
taneous bombings in Dublin and Monaghan which ultimately
killed thirty people, and the murder of the British Ambassador.

On 11 March 1974, Senator Billy Fox inadvertently arrived on
the scene of an arms raid in County Monaghan and was shot dead
by one of the raiding party. During the raid, the house, belonging
to Mr. Richard Coulson, and a mobile home belonging to his son
George were burned down. The raiding party, members of the
Official IRA, were apparently acting on the mistaken belief that
there were arms in the Coulson house.

The following June, five men from the Clones area were
sentenced to penal servitude for life for murder. The attitude of
all administrations in the state to this, the first killing of a
member of the Oireachtas since the death of Kevin O'Higgins in
1927, may be gauged by the fact that one of the raiding party,
Michael Kinsella, is still being held in custody, despite the fact
that there have been many appeals for his release on well-
documented medical grounds.

The Republic's 'Bloody Friday', as it instantly became known, occurred on 17 May 1974 when loyalist bombers struck at Dublin and Monaghan. Twenty people died when 'no warning' car bombs went off at the height of the rush hour in Dublin city. Scores more were injured and maimed in the worst bombing incident to befall the Republic since Hitler bombed Dublin during World War II. I vividly remember the destruction and shock I witnessed as I walked through the city shortly after the explosions. Yet there was no hatred expressed. Dubliners' most pronounced reaction was to queue in their thousands to give blood.

The bombs are believed to have been connected with the loyalist protest against Sunningdale, and unsubstantiated allegations have been made ever since that the loyalists may have been aided by some undercover British 'dirty tricks' unit anxious to step up its anti-IRA campaign.

Irish parliamentarians probably came under more pressure as a result of the blowing up on 21 July 1976 of the British Ambassador, Christopher Ewart-Biggs, near his official residence at Sandyford, County Dublin, than they had done over the Fox death. In a carefully-planned assassination, a bomb was placed in a small drain running across a quiet by-road and was detonated electrically from a field about 200 yards away. No one was ever successfully prosecuted for the Ewart-Biggs slaying, although police subsequently issued a photograph of a much sought-after Provisional IRA bombing expert known as Michael O'Rourke, who had escaped from the Central Criminal Court in Dublin two years earlier after a bomb blasted a hole in a wall adjoining his cell.

It was understood that the gardai also wanted to question O'Rourke in connection with another explosives death, that of Garda Michael Clarkin, who was killed by a booby trap set in a cottage near Mountmellick, County Laois, in October 1976.

At the time of the explosion Portlaoise Jail, not far from Mountmellick, was the centre of a controversy arising from riots and hunger strikes, all aimed at securing the same aim for which Gaughan and Stagg died, that of political status. Portlaoise continued in an unsettled and dangerous condition until after the 1977 general election which ousted the coalition. The Fianna Fail administration unofficially came to an agreement with the republican prisoners whereby de facto, if not de jure, political status was conceded. To this day the prisoners' command structure is recognised. They negotiate with the prison authorities only through their elected leadership, and have secured the sort of concessions with regard to visiting rights, the wearing of their own clothes, and freedom of association for which the hunger strikers in the H-Blocks outside Belfast were later to launch their campaign.

Fianna Fail Revives

I unwittingly played a part in the Fianna Fail resurgence which began *circa* 3 September 1976, when Bud Nossiter of the *Washington Post* interviewed the Minister for Posts and Telegraphs, Dr Conor Cruise O'Brien, on the anti-IRA legislation which had been proposed in the aftermath of the murder of the British ambassador.

Nossiter asked O'Brien, who had told him that he was intent on 'cleansing the culture' of the infection of nationalism, how he intended to operate the Act towards this end and O'Brien replied by pulling open a desk drawer to display a pile of cuttings of Letters to the Editor of the *Irish Press*, all either hostile to the government or expressing a strongly republican viewpoint. Aghast, Nossiter asked did he intend to pursue people who wrote letters to the papers? O'Brien replied that it was not the writers who would be bitten but the editor. This wasn't quite the way they saw things at the *Washington Post*, so Nossiter interviewed me also, warning me *inter alia* that I had better look out for myself.

I did! I declared editorial war on O'Brien and on the general proposition that the state should extend the sort of control it exercised over the national airwaves into the newspapers. Many people thought like me. A controversy over the issue itself, and over freedom of the press generally, escalated. Fianna Fail mounted a fine parliamentary performance — to the accompaniment of some enthusiastic support from the *Irish Press*, needless to say — and forced a change in the projected legislation which excluded the newspapers from its purview.

It was the first reverse suffered by the coalition and was as beneficial to the opposition as it was wounding to the government, which suddenly appeared unexpectedly vulnerable. It stayed that way until the general election the following year in which the main protagonists of the offending legislation, O'Brien and the Minister for Justice, Patrick Cooney, lost their seats. The idea of the intrusion of the executive into what people might write or read in public had raised a spectre of Big Brotherism that the fundamentally democratic Irish electorate found repellent.

By 1977 the government's unpopularity was overshadowed by a public outcry at the unpleasantness of living in southern Ireland in the aftermath of the 'Oil Shock'. Not even the everloving embrace of the Common Agricultural Policy could extend Brussels' aid and comfort to the tax-paying section of the community. A good deal of ill-advised economic and political experimentation was undertaken in an effort to redress the situation, and the general election was held in June.

Fianna Fail produced a 'shopping bag' manifesto which proposed increased government spending in order to promote industrial expansion: political code wording for 'borrow now and pay later'. It undertook to abolish car tax and housing rates. Politically and economically this manifesto, the brain-child of Martin O'Donoghue, an economist from Trinity College, Dublin, was unnecessary as the economy was in fact improving, and Haughey consistently opposed it. Beguiled by the prospect of electoral success, however, Fianna Fail embraced O'Donoghue's philosophy of spending its way out of a boom.

The gadarene rush to the polls in response to these proposals returned Jack Lynch and Fianna Fail to power with the largest majority in Irish parliamentary history, twenty seats. Liam Cosgrave resigned as leader of Fine Gael and was succeeded by Dr. Garret FitzGerald. Even in opposition Jack Lynch had commonly been referred to by the more fervent Fianna Fail supporters as the 'real Taoiseach'. Now he seemed to be the Taoiseach with such overwhelming reality that his reign was assured in perpetuity. However, the storm clouds were to blow him out of office after only two years in power. Rarely anywhere had such a majority achieved so little and lasted for so short a time.

A youthful 'Think Tank' was set up by Frank Dunlop, Esmonde Smith and Seamus Brennan. Brennan had succeeded the veteran Tommy Mullins as the party's General Secretary. These men were of a technocratic outlook that sat uncomfortably with both the deeper emotions aroused by the Northern conflict within Fianna Fail and the essentially conservative bias of the majority of the party on moral issues.

Dunlop, after a highly successful spell as Press Secretary to the party and then as head of the Government Information Services, later drifted out of active politics and became first a civil servant and then a PR consultant. Esmonde Smith, too, left active politics, returning to the law. Brennan, after re-organising the party and in particular introducing a youth section, Ogra Fianna Fail, would one day find himself siding as a TD with the dissidents who attempted unsuccessfully to overthrow Charles Haughey. He eventually made his peace with Haughey in time for the 1987 General Election, after which he became a junior minister.

Urged on by Martin O'Donoghue, who had become Minister for Economic Planning and Development, Fianna Fail also broke the 150-year-old link with sterling. Ireland joined the European Monetary Fund, with her currency now allied to the deutschemark and other continental currencies in the 'snake'. However, Ireland continued to do some 45 per cent of its trade with Great Britain, the sterling area, and the wage discipline which was implicit in joining the EMS did not materialise.

Lack of progress on the economic front was paralleled by lack of progress on Northern Ireland. This combined with animosities dating from the Arms Trial period, crystallised within Fianna Fail after Lord Mountbatten was murdered by the IRA in County Sligo in August, 1979. Lynch was first criticised for not getting back from his holidays in Portugal quickly enough (in fact there was no flight available when the news broke) and secondly, and more importantly, for giving too much away to Britain on the security front when he met Mrs Thatcher; he was visibly deflated by the psychological effects of the Westminster Abbey memorial service for Mountbatten in the presence of world leaders earlier in the day.

One of the most unusual problems to confront Jack Lynch in the closing stages of his reign was a speech by the youngest member of his party — nineteen year old Sile de Valera, granddaughter of Fianna Fail's founder. Speaking at the commemoration ceremony in Fermoy of the Civil War hero, Liam Lynch, she made a strongly republican oration, which was widely interpreted as a veiled attack on Jack Lynch's alleged departure from republican orthodoxy.

Miss de Valera was also in the news under Mr Haughey's

regime, but this time her remarks, a broadside attack against Mrs Thatcher's handling of the hunger strike issue, did not have the effect which her Fermoy remarks had had on Jack Lynch's already weakening grip on power. She had been speaking during a pre-election campaign in County Donegal and, following her remarks, she either left or was asked to leave the campaign and no more was heard of the incident after Fianna Fail's candidate, Clem Coughlan, won his seat. In any event, the difference in the two controversies lay in the fact that her remarks in County Donegal were obviously aimed at Mrs Thatcher, whereas, in Cork, Lynch's critics interpreted them as being directed against him.

Political and economic fall-out combined in what became known as 'overflights issue' in December of 1979 and Lynch, who had just seen two by-elections lost in his native Cork, resigned.

3

Politics, 1979–87

Fianna Fail in Turmoil; Charles Haughey;
Haughey in Power; The 'Heaves'; The Presidency

Fianna Fail in Turmoil

There were a number of reasons why the party rounded on a leader who had served it so well. One was the increasingly gloomy world economic scene, complicated in Ireland by the fact not alone that costs had not been kept in check — a *sine qua non* if the 1977 manifesto were to work — but a wage explosion had taken place rather than wage restraint. Secondly, the 1977 defeat of the coalition had produced a new and charismatic leader for Fine Gael, Dr Garret FitzGerald. Thirdly, Haughey and his cohorts were flexing their muscles within the party; fourthly, Fianna Fail's Northern philosophy actually switched from retreat to attack.

The cause of Lynch's final fall from office was significant in as much as it was here that the 'Hidden Ireland' of Irish politics became visible. What I might term the genuine patriotic, or nationalistic, feeling of the average Fianna Fail member, and in particular the elected member, councillor or TD, began to predominate over the public-house republicanism typical of many loud-voiced people earlier in Lynch's tenure of office.

Lynch, diffident in manner, born in Cork, where he grew up to become a GAA hero, lived his early life about as far away from Belfast as one can get in Ireland without actually stepping into the Atlantic. He had combined law studies with a background of steady progress up the lower rungs of the civil service before Fianna Fail tapped him as an ideal candidate. Ideologically he could just as easily have gone into politics for Fine Gael. To him the difference between the two parties lay in the mind and personality of Eamon de Valera. At a time when politics in Ireland were for or against the slogan, he was 'Up Dev'.

On his entry into politics he very definitely saw his future arena of activity as the twenty-six counties. He did not come out personally in favour of Irish unity until November 1975, when a similar call made a little earlier by the not unduly nationalistic Michael O'Kennedy prompted him to do so also.

When he speculated out loud in Chicago in November of 1979 that part of a forthcoming pact with Britain might include a security system whereby there would be 'overflights' into the Republic's territory by British aircraft, the pot boiled over. Fianna Fail had just lost two by-elections in Lynch's own citadel of Cork on economic issues and the overflight question served to bring together the discontent of the Haugheyites, economic pressures and the Northern crisis.

Fianna Fail headquarters was deluged with irate phone calls, the tenor of which may be gauged from the following small, but revealing, first-hand experience.

I had been asked to give a talk to a group of American students who were visiting my father's birthplace, Castlecomer, County Kilkenny. The venue was the local school. By the time the hour for giving the talk arrived the school was jam-packed. The students, who were to have constituted the bulk of the audience, were completely outnumbered. After my talk speaker after speaker stood up to ask 'questions' which were in fact comments, tirades not on what I had said but on the overflights issue.

To a man, the speakers were Fianna Failers, the chairman of this cumann, the secretary of that, and their collective message was summed up by one man who wanted me to 'go back up to Dublin and tell Jack Lynch that if he's given away our sovereignty and allowed the British to fly over our territory, he'll get the greatest dressing any man ever got. We fought long and hard for any bit of sovereignty we've got and I'm damned if we're going to have any overflights with this thing going on in the North'.

A few days after my lecture a more diplomatic version of the same message was delivered to Lynch himself by senior party figures, who warned him that if he did not step down open warfare would break out. He duly stepped down on 5 December, being succeeded by the man he had once sacked.

Charles Haughey

Charles J. Haughey was born in County Mayo, the son of a prominent IRA officer from Swatragh, County Derry, who had joined the Free State Army for training in order to return to the North to continue the struggle. He continued in the army when the civil war proved the futility of his intentions. Haughey's father died when he was a boy and he was reared in the North Dublin suburb of Donnycarney by his widowed mother, a remarkable woman who presided over the education of her four sons and three daughters. Haughey studied law and accountancy at University College, Dublin, married Sean Lemass's daughter and from his earliest days in politics gave evidence of those qualities that were to both buoy him up and bedevil him throughout his career: courage, hard work, intelligence, loyalty to his friends, an intolerance of criticism near to paranoia where the media was concerned, a tendency to allow the vision of a statesman to be overlaid by the expediency of the smoke-filled back room. In many ways, particularly in the characters of those with whom he sometimes surrounded himself, he appeared more of an old-style Irish-American political 'Boss' than a contemporary Irish political leader.

Because of his flamboyant wealth, his racehorses, his collection of paintings, his island off the Kerry coast and his palatial home at Kinsealy in north County Dublin, Haughey was credited during the prosperous sixties and early seventies with being behind every property deal in the country. But he is too complex to be simply described as a wealthy politician. From his interests there stemmed two of the strongest stimuli the arts have received in contemporary Ireland, the provision in the 1969 Finance Act whereby artists and writers are tax exempt, and the Aosdana Scheme which allows a small annual income to whole-time artists.

His interest in the family led to the Succession Act which protected the rights of widows and children. His interest in the sea and in islands prompted his proposal for a Department of the Marine in 1985 — an out-of-office initiative which suggested how the scandalous under-utilisation of Ireland's fisheries might be rectified. Above all, his Derry origins have given him a deep commitment to Irish unity, albeit tinged, especially since the hunger strikes, with anti-British feelings.

One factor, though, more than any of his defects has prevented him from achieving greatness — the quality which Napoleon sought in his generals, luck. Somebody, somewhere in Haughey's background appears to have offended the gods. As far back as 1966, he appeared to be the logical successor to Lemass at a time when he was an energetic, forceful Minister for Agriculture. But because of a dispute over milk prices, for which he was not primarily responsible since the refusal to grant a price rise was a cabinet decision, not his own, the farmers picketed the Dail. Haughey refused to meet them and referred to their protest as a 'circus'. The farmers retaliated by camping on the steps of Government Buildings and sending up shock waves in the party which cost Haughey vital support when Lemass stood down.

The saga of Charles Haughey's survival is one of the most incredible stories in west European politics. He was literally down and out when Lynch sacked him, lying in a hospital bed after falling off a horse. Haughey recovered from the sacking, recovered from his subsequent prosecution, recovered even from the ignominy of having to vote confidence in James Gibbons, the Minister for Defence at the time of the incidents which led to Haughey's prosecution. Gibbons's evidence and Haughey's had been so diametrically opposed on key issues during the trial that that vote must have been a bitter pill for Haughey to swallow. But swallow it he did and commenced the quiet, diligent circuit of the country that rebuilt his political fortunes. He hardly spoke in the Dail at all for three years, but was likely to turn up at everything from the Kilruddery Game Fair to the opening of an art exhibition.

He thus accumulated a large store of grass-root support and when the 1977 election swing restored Fianna Fail to power, Haughey too was restored to office as Minister for Health and Social Welfare. He performed with his normal efficiency and when the tide of popularity began to turn against Lynch there was no doubt within the party as to who the two main rivals for succession would be, himself, and his former schoolmate, George Colley. Haughey beat Colley, but it was an ominous victory.

Haughey had the support of the grass-roots and the parliamentary backbenchers who, ironically in view of his later espousal of the 'presidential' style, or virtual one-man dictatorship of the party, gave him their votes largely because they felt alienated from the leadership. At the time there was a widespread sense of being shut out from decision-taking which evolved, at least partially, from the formation of the 'think tank' and its apparent commandeering of the corridors of power. Against Haughey were ranged the front bench with one exception — Michael O'Kennedy, from North Tipperary, whose speech in 1975 had impelled Lynch towards an espousal of Irish unity. His defection from cabinet ranks proved decisive for Haughey.

What was an unhealthy 'them' and 'us' divide from the outset was worsened within days of Haughey's victory by a statement from Colley to the effect that he was going to give only 'qualified loyalty' to the leadership because of the lack of loyalty which he felt had been shown to the earlier incumbent in office. It is generally believed that Lynch had meant to resign in January anyhow, but that the Haugheyites, fearful that the extra month might, with Lynch's assistance, tilt the balance towards Colley, staged a pre-emptive strike.

Later, Colley would have aligned with him such figures as Seamus Brennan, Charles McCreevy and in particular Desmond O'Malley, but even apart from these names there were enough arrows flying about to make Haughey's back *the* political pincushion of the period. As yet the general public was not aware how deep the divisions ran within the party. Fianna Fail, prior to the 'arms trial' era, was unused to public dissent or to doing anything other than following in the de Valera-established tradition of accepting the tablets handed down from the Chief, at least in public.

Haughey in Power

When, in the first major policy statement he made after his election, Haughey went on television on 9 January to tell the nation that it was living beyond its means and that an era of belt-tightening would have to come, it was expected that such a policy would soon be implemented. Not so. Either through insecurity because of his political position, or because it took him some time to adjust to the difference between being a cabinet member and a prime minister, Haughey proved curiously indecisive. The forthright doer became a ditherer, caving in to one interest group after another as pay claims mounted. As the

tables in Chapter One show, the public finances drifted
hopelessly. In one area, however, he did appear to be making
progress — ironically, in view of what was later to happen, that
of Anglo-Irish relations.

According to his own account, he got on famously with Mrs
Thatcher when the pair first met as prime minister to prime
minister at 10 Downing Street in May, 1980. Haughey made her a
gift of a Georgian silver teapot and at his subsequent televised
press conference remarked that the meeting had been the most
satisfactory he had had. He went on to talk about the benefits
which he claimed were going to flow from this meeting to such an
overblown extent that expectations were built up and inevitably
doomed to fail.

In Mrs Thatcher's creed the Irish, the coloureds, the unions,
the Communists and members of the EEC have to be equally
confronted, put down and kept in their proper place. Or, in more
practical terms, the last vestige of the Union, symbolised by the
Cross of St Patrick in the Union Jack, had to be maintained intact
within the United Kingdom of Great Britain *and* Northern
Ireland. Mrs Thatcher is an ideologically convinced unionist. Yet
Haughey went around for some considerable time after the
Downing Street meeting making statements which seemed to
indicate that the link between Britain and Northern Ireland
would soon cease to exist. This impression was certainly
heightened by the fact that Mrs Thatcher herself led one of the
most high-powered British delegations ever to come to Ireland in
the following December, to begin a reciprocal round of talks in
Dublin Castle.

The delegation included such political heavyweights as Sir
Geoffrey Howe and, in particular, Lord Carrington who provided
both a stabilising force on the British side and (from the Irish
point of view) a distinctly encouraging influence on progress. It
was Carrington who defended to Mrs Thatcher the insertion by
the Irish in the final communiqué of the famous phrase 'the
totality of relationships' in a paragraph which announced that a
top level study group would be set up between the two countries
to explore ways forward.

Though Mrs Thatcher assured the unionists that their
sovereignty was not impaired, they not unnaturally felt as deeply
suspicious as the Dubliners felt jubilant. The idea that the

'totality of relationships' between Ireland and Britain could be 'studied' without the strong likelihood that a change in those relationships would be recommended was hard to swallow.

The period around the two summit meetings was Haughey's honeymoon in office. The summits served to obscure the effects of a U-turn on the economic front, and he made such capital out of his meetings that it did appear something of substance was occurring in the historic mountain of misunderstanding that constituted Anglo-Irish relationships. People were led to believe that perhaps Irish unity *was* a real prospect at last. Knowledgeable Fleet Street journalists and TV reporters, however, shook their heads in puzzlement and said things like: 'Tim Pat, we can't find any resonance for Irish unity in Whitehall. The best that we can pick up is that Mrs Thatcher as a gesture of goodwill is letting your Mr Hockey make mileage out of the meetings, but she's telling her backbenchers and the unionists there's no question of any give on the constitutional guarantee'.

The chickens of the dichotomy between the Irish and the English interpretations of what had transpired at the summits came home to roost in a dramatic fashion very shortly. Hunger strikes broke out in 1980 in the H-Blocks of Long Kesh where IRA prisoners were seeking political status. A settlement in which Haughey played an energetic and helpful role — as I can testify from personal involvement at the time — seemed to defuse the situation with an announcement of cessation on 18 December. However, the strikes broke out again the following March because the terms of the agreement were not honoured by the authorities — chiefly in relation to the prisoners' right to wear their own clothes.

This strike, which will be examined in more detail in a later chapter, was led to the death by Bobby Sands, who before he died was elected to the Westminster parliament. Sands was to be followed to the grave by nine other hunger-strikers, one of whom, Kieran Doherty, was elected to the Dail. All died apparently without achieving their demands, but in terms of Northern Ireland politics their seemingly futile deaths had something of the same effect on the nationalist community as the executions of the 1916 leaders had on nationalist sentiment throughout the country. Where Haughey was concerned, these effects lay in the future.

Had Haughey done a Falklands over the hunger strike and gone for world opinion at the UN, the EEC and elsewhere, Sinn Fein and the IRA generally would have backed him as a nationalist leader and a highly popular truce could have been secured which might have led on to — who knows what? I was in touch with the Sinn Fein leadership of the period and I can attest that that was their policy — and hope — at the time.

However, to the republicans he appeared to dither on the issue and as the tide of sympathy swung inexorably towards the dying men in Long Kesh, H-Block fever swept the country and he lost crucial support in the June 1981 election as a result of which Fianna Fail lost power. Dr Garret FitzGerald became Taoiseach, with Michael O'Leary, leader of the Labour Party, as Tanaiste.

Haughey's 'special relationship' was clearly in tatters. Not alone had it not served to avert the hunger strike, it had actually proved of so little worth that Mrs Thatcher allowed matters to develop to the point where he lost altogether, which *inter alia* contributed substantially to his subsequent difficulties within the party. An out-of-office leader was more vulnerable to his critics within the party than one who was actually running the country.

The 'Lynch factor' was particularly strong in Munster where the party had lost considerable support. Public dissent from Haughey's leadership tended to concentrate around the personality of Charles McCreevy, a Kildare deputy, who argued that the tough budgetary measures that the coalition introduced were necessary and that Fianna Fail should have stuck to the policy first enunciated by Haughey on television rather than indulge in a splurge of foreign borrowing.

However, the threat posed by McCreevy was somewhat blunted when the coalition fell over the budget of January 1982 and Haughey returned to power with the aid of the independent deputy Neil Blaney, who had never rejoined the party after the Arms Crisis though he continued to vote for it in the Dail, and of a former republican Tony Gregory, who represented an inner Dublin constituency and succeeded in wresting considerable commitments from Haughey to revivify the inner city in return for his vote. It was a precarious position, made doubly so by a public attack on Haughey's leadership — this time by Desmond O'Malley, a supporter of George Colley.

The period 1966–86 was certainly the most volatile in Fianna

Fail's history since that party had first entered the Dail in 1927. There were two sets of forces at work within the party, one largely philosophical, the other a matter of personality.

The philosophical clash arose out of the traditional relationship with Fianna Fail between the nationalist and republican ideology of many of its members and the big business ethos of those who had joined it because, along with some commitment to its nationalist ideals, they perceived the party as the soundest where business was concerned. Haughey always appealed to the latter sort. Everything about his track record encouraged the belief that he was *the* brain of the cabinet. I would rate his political ability as the greatest of anyone to step on the Republic's political stage since 1966. He, and in the North, John Hume, Gerry Adams and Ian Paisley, all in their different ways, possess qualities of a different and higher order than those of their contemporaries.

However, some of Haughey's bloom wore off under the impact of the Arms Trial. While it helped to establish his nationalist credentials with some sections of the party, it gravely disquieted others. Within the party, Haughey was caught between personality and ideological forces. There was also what he himself was responsible for christening, albeit unwittingly, the 'GUBU factor', which we will come to shortly.

Irish debates on republicanism have a certain air of *déjà vu* about them. They all proceed by, with or from the border and the British heritage, that other colonialism, how to accommodate to it or alter it, and they tend to recur with a certain superficial newness in each generation.

Eamon de Valera, in an attempt to prove that his version of constitutional republicanism was not 'soft' on the border issue, on one famous occasion brought a pile of dictionaries into the Dail to help illustrate the various definitions of the term and was subsequently frequently taunted with attempting to create a 'dictionary Republic'. A decade later Sean MacBride helped to put de Valera out of office and gave the term new currency with the formation of a new political party, Clann na Poblachta, which also attempted to end the physical force tradition by ending partition. The government in which he became a minister did declare the twenty-six counties a Republic, but the border remained.

Now in the 1980s it was the turn of Haughey, Garret Fitz-Gerald and Desmond O'Malley to attempt to make their vision of the term 'republicanism' come true. None, as yet, has succeeded but the attempts gave rise to enormous controversies whose intensity gives an idea of the strength and complexity of the issues. There were, for instance, three open attempts against Haughey's leadership between February 1982 and February 1983.

The 'Heaves'

The first challenge, led by Desmond O'Malley, fizzled out on 25 February 1982 when O'Malley withdrew his opposition at the first meeting of the Fianna Fail parliamentary party, held after the general election of the previous week but before the Dail met on 9 March to elect a government. The idea of opposing Haughey's selection as leader of the Fianna Fail party, normally a foregone conclusion for the man who led the party in a general election, had first been publicly mooted by James Gibbons, the former Minister for Defence, as the results were still coming in after the election. These, though incomplete, indicated that Haughey was likely to be the next Taoiseach. Three days later O'Malley, Martin O'Donoghue and George Colley met in Dublin to decide whether or not a leadership challenge to Haughey could succeed. At that stage it appeared to both Colley and O'Donoghue that either might muster the necessary support. This view was not borne out in subsequent soundings and they decided to combine behind O'Malley.

Initially there was some debate between the three and their supporters as to how the Haughey challenge should be presented — by means of a vote of 'no confidence', an open vote between O'Malley and Haughey, or the garnering of sufficient signatures of dissident deputies to convince Haughey he should step down. The open vote formula was finally decided on because they reckoned that O'Malley could count on some votes, but in their efforts to copper-fasten those votes before the crucial parliamentary party meeting, the conspirators alerted the Haughey faction as to what was afoot.

Three of Haughey's closest supporters, Ray MacSharry, Albert Reynolds and Sean Doherty led the counter charge. O'Malley was to say after his first leadership tilt that he hadn't realised either

the deficiencies of the Irish telephone service or the extent to
which funerals took Irish TDs from their homes! But his opponents ploughed ruthlessly through these obstacles. Unlisted telephone numbers of TDs were obtained and hitherto unknown
flats and hotel rooms discovered in a campaign which lasted
night and day right up to the last moment before the meeting. By
then the O'Malleyites had become so disorganised that when
O'Donoghue spoke at the meeting he proposed that *no* vote be
taken, lest this be taken as divisive by the watching public.
O'Malley realised the battle was lost and didn't even let his name
go forward when MacSharry proposed Haughey as the party's
nominee for Taoiseach. The motion was carried unopposed.

But the war went on.

Haughey had in his favour the constituency organisations and
the traditionalist, grass-roots Fianna Fail supporters who
believed still in the goals for which the party had been founded, a
thirty-two county Republic. This Republic, by ballad at least if not
by bomb or bullet, favoured a 'Brits out' unitary state. This state,
once achieved, would be open and generous in its laws and
constitution towards the unionist tradition and, with the irritant
of the border removed, would live in permanent peace and unity
with Britain. Such thinking did not favour changing the laws and
constitution of Ireland in advance of a British departure so as to
make the southern state more acceptable to the North. A round
table Constitutional Conference embracing the unionists should
only be held when it was clear that a British departure was
inevitable.

An average male Haughey supporter, to be found in particularly large numbers in the west, north-west and along the border
counties, would be more inclined to be found at a Gaelic football
or hurling match than say a rugby or soccer match. Haughey also
appeals to women, partly because of his personality but also,
particularly where older women are concerned, for the improvements which he has brought to Irish society in areas as diverse as
safeguarding families' inheritance rights and providing free travel
for pensioners. And though somewhat tarnished by his U-turn
on the economy, Haughey also had considerable support amongst
the business community, particularly in that traditionally Fianna
Fail-favoured section of the economy, the building industry.

Above all there was the word 'loyalty'. Loyalty to the party, to its ideals and beyond all else, loyalty to its leader. As the major recipient of the not inconsiderable level of 'loyalty' left in the Fianna Fail reservoir since 'Dev's' day, Haughey was able to appeal for loyalty as a right and at the same time draw from his followers great supportive outrage at the sacrilegious behaviour of his opponents in denying it to him.

O'Malley drew his strength from different well-springs. He had come into politics via a by-election caused by the death of his famous uncle Donogh O'Malley, who had revolutionised the Irish educational system. As Minister for Justice at the age of thirty-one, Des O'Malley put through the Forcible Entry Bill, making squatting a crime, which made an unlikely legislative harbinger of the liberal positions he adopted a decade later. His views on Northern Ireland and republicanism were shaped by his own experiences and by those of his wife's family. A particularly tough Minister for Justice, the IRA was his natural foe. He once proposed banning the use of the letters 'IRA' in the media, preferring to use some such formula as 'an illegal organisation' and was chided by *The Irish Times,* which pointed out that he was on dangerous ground because while he was making the proposal (June 1970) the then Taoiseach, Jack Lynch, was helping to launch my book *The IRA* in Dublin's Gresham Hotel!

As the troubles wore on, to the memory of the IRA threats he incurred as Justice Minister there was added the impact of the Provisionals' burning down of a pub in Northern Ireland owned by his wife's family, the MacAleers of Omagh, County Tyrone. After witnessing the destruction of the Sunningdale Agreement by the loyalists' strike, he became further convinced that the traditional republican view on the North was wrong. Even if the British did withdraw from Northern Ireland, he felt the unionists would still have to be accommodated, unlike Haughey, who believed that Dublin and London could and should come to an agreement over Belfast's head.

Accordingly O'Malley openly and fundamentally differed from Haughey in proposing that the Republic first move to change the nature of the south's society and economy, as Lemass had advocated, so as to make the unionists eager to be associated with the Republic. In the first major interview he gave after the formation of the Progressive Democrats (*Magill*, January 1986) O'Malley made it clear that he was prepared to put the whole question of the North on the back burner.

He said: 'The very fact that it (Sunningdale) was destroyed, and the way it was destroyed, has given an encouragement to unionists to act in a way that I think they wouldn't have acted up to 1974. We have a much harsher reality to face in that respect. In a time of emotion such as the present, unfortunately, you've got to face the facts that the reality of the general unionist position is pretty entrenched and we just can't go on down here (in the Republic) making speeches about our ideals for the unattainable, because it *is* unattainable in the foreseeable future'.

O'Malley and his supporters also had more tangible reasons for supposing that a fresh political horizon beckoned. These were based on the findings of a secret political survey commissioned by elements in Fianna Fail after the failure of the first O'Malley 'heave'.

The survey showed that eastern Leinster, comprising all of Dublin and large tracts of the 'home counties' of Louth, Wicklow and Kildare, the traditional sphere of British influence, known as the 'Pale' area, had as one might have imagined a more urbanised ethos than rural Ireland. British TV programmes, BBC, ITN and channels such as UTV, Wales and increasingly Channel 4, vie with the home-produced programmes of RTE to the same extent as do British newspapers with their Irish counterparts. Some 34 per cent of all newspapers are British, chiefly popular tabloids such as the *Mirror* and *Sun*, but also a complement of *Guardian*, *Times*, *Daily Mail*, *Express* and so on. As any newsagent can tell you, a picture of Princess Diana on the cover of a woman's magazine will guarantee a sell-out in many areas.

The findings of the survey made it clear that whether one thought in terms of 'Anti-Haughey', 'Yuppie', 'Dublin' or 'Rural', changes were occurring in Irish political culture and that the dichotomy between rural and urban political attitudes offered possibilities for a new political initiative. A narrow majority of those polled showed a preference for O'Malley over Haughey, 39 per cent to 37 per cent.

The survey said that O'Malley was seen as the 'most apt at working for the political and economic stability of Ireland' and its findings indicated that he had the edge with younger urban voters who felt a new party would be 'beneficial'. The rural over-fifties preferred Haughey. And the survey found, perhaps most significantly, that some 60 per cent of the population were dissatisfied with the functioning of the political system. This finding could of course have been related more to the overall economic situation than to strife within Fianna Fail.

The survey confirmed the O'Malleyites in two beliefs, (1) that a new party could have a future and (2) that failing radical change within Fianna Fail, Fine Gael under the attractive 'new' leadership of Garret FitzGerald would benefit from the increasingly youthful electorate.

The second abortive 'heave' took place on 6 October 1982. Again it underestimated the 'loyalty' factor within Fianna Fail, Haughey's own fighting qualities, and the fact that he had his hands on the party's internal levers of power. Prior to the parliamentary party's vote on his leadership, for instance, he secured 76 out of a total of 78 votes from the party's national executive by a show of hands on a motion backing his leadership.

The second 'heave' was masterminded by Charles McCreevy, who had been expelled from the party the previous January for criticisms he made of Haughey in an interview with Geraldine Kennedy in the *Sunday Tribune*. He only regained admittance after the coalition's unexpected fall a month later. He had initially campaigned for Haughey against Colley after the Lynch departure, but began turning his allegiance towards O'Malley after Haughey failed to deliver.

McCreevy believed he had learned from the disorganisation of the abortive February 'heave' and kept the planning of the 'October Revolution' entirely to himself until five days beforehand when he arranged to have two copies of a 'no confidence' motion delivered simultaneously to the party's Chief Whip, Bertie Ahern, at Government Buildings and to Charles Haughey personally at his home in Kinsealy, County Dublin, on the afternoon of 1 October.

Central to McCreevy's strategy was that balloting on the 'no confidence' motion should be by secret vote. A secret ballot, given the climate existing in Fianna Fail at the time, seemed certain to go against Haughey. However on the prestigious 'This Week' programme, listened to by the largest radio news audience in the country each Sunday for an hour from one o'clock, Haughey countered by calling on all deputies to 'stand up and be counted', and demanded moreover the full support of his cabinet.

This last call precipitated O'Malley and O'Donoghue into sub-

mitting their resignations as ministers on the morning of the
vote. The refusal to hold a secret ballot resulted, after an unprecedented twelve hours of political soul-searching for Fianna Fail,
in Haughey winning on a show of hands by 58 to 22.

The twenty-two became known as the 'Club of 22' and some of
them were to join O'Malley when he ultimately did form his new
party, notably Mary Harney of Dublin, a compelling, lucid orator,
Bobby Molloy from Galway, one of the best vote-getters in Dail
Eireann, and Pearse Wyse, a Cork deputy second in popularity
only to Jack Lynch himself.

Their attack, and that of the rest of the 'Club of 22' centred on
the sort of people Haughey surrounded himself with, and a litany
of 'strokes' and 'deals' which he had engaged in to hold power.
Some of the 'deals' referred to were part of his inexplicable
U-turn on the economy. For instance, the decision to bail out the
ailing Dublin car assembly plant, the Talbot Motor Company,
though it saved (temporarily) some hundreds of jobs, had no
long-term economic justification. And his critics could concede
neither short nor long term justification to the decision to go
ahead with Knock Airport when there was already an international airport two counties away to the south at Shannon which
had the thriving city of Limerick close by. Knock had (and has) no
such catchment area of population nearby — a necessary prerequisite for such an airport — and, once built, its critics feared that
according to aviation experts the initial £10m outlay would soon
appear small compared to its upkeep costs. It appeared, so the
'Club' argued, that it was merely being built for vote-buying
purposes. The 'Gregory deal' which had ensured the vote of the
inner city Independent deputy Tony Gregory would, had it gone
through, have cost £100m to revamp Gregory's constituency, but
it fell with the government the month after the 'heave'.

The difference between a 'deal' and a 'stroke' may not immediately be apparent to readers not familiar with Irish political
nomenclature, but the 'Club' was quite clear what was meant by
the term — the Burke 'stroke', for instance, was widely condemned. Haughey had sought to lessen his dependence on
Gregory and other support such as that of the Workers' Party by
attempting to woo away from Fine Gael the party's Dublin West
deputy, Richard Burke, offering him the position of EEC Commissioner which had become vacant when Fianna Fail's Michael

O'Kennedy had returned home from Brussels to win a Dail seat. After much hesitation and controversy within Fine Gael, Burke accepted the post, but the controversy swung from within the ranks of Fine Gael to those of Fianna Fail when the Fianna Fail candidate and former deputy, Eileen Lemass, whom Haughey had banked on to win the seat, lost the by-election to Fine Gael's Liam Skelly.

Ironically, Skelly would later turn out to be a maverick, a constant thorn in the side of Fine Gael, who would lose his seat in the 1987 election, but for the moment he caused Haughey to be roasted for giving away a plum job to Fine Gael and then not reaping the benefit of a seat in return.

The plain speaking of the day had a long-term effect on the party; after the 1987 cliff-hanger general election Haughey pointedly refused to offer Gregory a 'deal' and only scraped into power as a minority government when Gregory abstained and the Chair gave its casting vote to Haughey. But in the short term all Haughey won was a breathing space and his opponents an assurance that rumours of a 'death list' of TDs hostile to Haughey, which Mary Harney insisted had been drawn up, would be investigated and its perpetrators suitably chastened. Outside the meeting McCreevy was amongst the anti-Haughey deputies to be jostled and cat-called as gardai cleared a way to his car.

There was such bad blood in Fianna Fail that it was inevitable that 'Heave' No. 3 would occur sometime. But it had been accelerated by the events of 1982, such as that in April, when Haughey's election agent and solicitor, Pat O'Connor, was accused of having applied for voting papers at two different polling booths at the February general election.

The so-called Dowra Affair took its name from the small town in Cavan where one night the brother-in-law of the Minister for Justice, Sean Doherty, became involved in a fracas, as a result of which he was charged with assault. When the case came to trial, a principal witness against him failed to turn up and the case was dismissed. It later emerged that the missing witness, a man of exemplary character, had been picked up in Northern Ireland by the RUC and detained, without charge, until the case was over. The Dowra affair's damaging effect on one of Haughey's closest supporters had been greatly heightened by the controversy over Sergeant Tully's transfer protest. This spread as far afield as a programme on RTE entitled 'The Roscommon File' and an article in the *Sunday Times*. Throughout the summer there was widespread rumour of improper interference with gardai in the performance of their duties.

In August the police raided a luxury flat complex at Bullock Harbour in County Dublin and arrested Malcolm MacArthur, who was subsequently convicted of having killed a nurse in the Phoenix Park. The arrest took place in the home of Patrick Connolly, the Attorney General.

Though Connolly had no knowledge of MacArthur's 'Mr Hyde' personality and had no connection with MacArthur's activities other than the fact that he was friendly with his 'Dr Jekyll' persona, the affair was enormously damaging for Haughey. It made headlines abroad, and sent out shock waves domestically which surely would have toppled the government had MacArthur been arrested when the Dail was sitting. Connolly resigned. Haughey gave a press conference at the height of the controversy during which he described the affair as 'grotesque, unbelievable, bizarre and unprecedented'. Conor Cruise O'Brien took the initials of these adjectives to coin a new word, 'GUBU', for the Irish political vocabulary.

There were serious rumours of phone-tapping. Bad and unsettling as these reports were, they remained unconfirmed despite a Fine Gael call for a judicial inquiry into the gardai, and were speedily forgotten in the wash of events as Fianna Fail suffered the added trauma of a second general election defeat inside eighteen months. One Fianna Fail deputy, Bill Loughnane, had died on 18 October and Jim Gibbons had suffered a heart attack. The Workers' Party withdrew its support from Haughey on a Fine Gael-sponsored motion of 'no confidence', and Fianna Fail were defeated. The party suffered a further defeat at the general election held three weeks later on 24 November 1982, dropping to only 75 seats.

The hawks prepared to fly at Haughey again. Their claws were sharpened when on 18 December a keen young journalist, Peter Murtagh, security correspondent of *The Irish Times,* revealed that the phones of Bruce Arnold of the *Irish Independent* and Geraldine Kennedy of the *Sunday Tribune* had been tapped by Fianna Fail. Murtagh's scoop was then confirmed in dramatic fashion by Doherty's successor as Minister for Justice, Michael

Noonan, who on 20 January 1983 revealed that Doherty had not alone caused Geraldine Kennedy's and Bruce Arnold's phones to be bugged, he had also been instrumental in having a sensitive garda recording device made available to Ray MacSharry so that MacSharry could 'bug' his colleague Martin O'Donoghue, and that as a result the careers of two top garda officers were now terminated: the Commissioner, Patrick MacLaughlin, and his deputy, Joseph Ainsworth, resigned. The reason for MacSharry's 'bugging' of O'Donoghue was because the conversation centred, as MacSharry expected it would, on the fact that if financial considerations were the problem, money could be procured to enable MacSharry to cease supporting Haughey.

This time it seemed certain that Haughey would fall. To lose an election in which the 'Haughey factor' was often stressed on the doorsteps as a reason for not supporting Fianna Fail was bad enough, but the bugging was the last straw. Even though Haughey protested strongly that he knew nothing about the phone-tapping, and Doherty corroborated his statements, both MacSharry and Doherty resigned from the front bench the day after Noonan's disclosure. An internal committee of inquiry was set up into the affair within Fianna Fail and another motion challenging the leadership, drafted with the aid of George Colley, was put down in the name of Ben Briscoe, the party's assistant Chief Whip, and seconded by Charles McCreevy. It read: 'The Fianna Fail members of Dail Eireann request the resignation of Mr Charles J. Haughey as party leader now'.

The National Executive, the body which had given him almost unanimous support at the time of the last 'heave', subjected him to a barrage of criticism on the bugging issue and the GUBU trail generally four days before Briscoe's motion was due to be voted on. One speaker said bluntly that Haughey was now a greater electoral liability than Dr Conor Cruise O'Brien had been to the coalition in his time. After the meeting Haughey was so depressed that he visited Gerry Collins in hospital and suggested that he should lead the party.

But this time Haughey's luck held — in tragic circumstances. A popular Fianna Fail deputy, Clem Coughlan of Donegal, who might have voted against Haughey, was killed in a road accident as he travelled to Dublin on the eve of the vital vote, the date of which was then transferred from 2 February 1983 to 7th, in circumstances of great controversy. Jim Tunney, the Chairman of the meeting, adjourned it after Haughey had opened it by paying a tribute to Coughlan and all present had recited a short prayer and stood in silence for a minute. Tunney announced the adjournment in Irish and had walked out of the room before the 'Club of 22' realised what had happened.

Tunney afterwards pointed to the fact that the parliamentary party had adjourned before for a week when a deputy died and that the use of Irish was appropriate as Coughlan represented a Gaeltacht constituency. He refused a petition signed by forty-one deputies, a clear majority of the party, urging him to reconvene the meeting before the weekend. The 'Club' guessed correctly that Haughey would use the respite to his advantage.

The night of Coughlan's death, thousands of pro-Haugheyites converged on Fianna Fail headquarters to sign a book approving of his leadership and a Nurembergesque rally was held in the street outside in which the 'media conspiracy' against Haughey was thunderously denounced. This theme was taken up stridently in the interval before the crucial vote. Hundreds of denunciatory phonecalls poured into newspaper offices and a similar blizzard of phonecalls hit the homes and offices of wavering TDs.

On the night Coughlan was buried Haughey went over the heads of the dissidents by issuing a statement to 'all members of the party to rally behind me' and gave a clear indication that the theatre of the war might be broadened by saying that 'the Ard Fheis will give a clear direction to the party'. In other words, he would if necessary use the power of the party's forthcoming annual conference to override that of the elected representatives. That had a decisive effect on some waverers.

Another factor which began to affect the issue was that along with O'Malley other candidates, Gerry Collins and Michael O'Kennedy, were presenting themselves for leadership. This had the effect of dividing the opposition to Haughey.

On the morning of the crucial vote itself, Haughey delivered his master stroke. The meeting began not by discussing his leadership, but by considering the report into the bugging! After it had been read Haughey proposed that at the next parliamentary meeting the whip be withdrawn from Doherty and from Martin O'Donoghue, Doherty for the bugging and O'Donoghue for suggesting that money could buy a change in leadership, and that Labour would support Fianna Fail if Haughey quit.

So one sacrificial lamb was offered from the Haughey camp and one from the dissidents, and the meeting spent the entire day discussing both the impropriety of bugging and that of 'big business attempting to control Fianna Fail', so that O'Donoghue came in for as much, or more, criticism as did Doherty.

By the time that the leadership issue arose, after 8 pm, the opposition was divided and exhausted and after only three hours of discussion Haughey carried the vote by 40 votes to 33. O'Malley and his camp knew finally that Haughey could not be dislodged from within Fianna Fail. Round 4 would have to be fought outside, and the lamp of the 'new party' idea flickered ever more brightly thereafter.

The appalling atmosphere which all this generated within the party may be gauged from the fact that Haughey's opponents were said to have been subjected to a campaign of intimidation and abuse. Certainly I have been given to understand that this was the case and this type of atmosphere was to continue.

It could be argued that Haughey was a hapless tool of fate. Things seemed to go against him at decisive moments. In 1981, for instance, it was generally believed that the Ard Fheis held in February was intended to be the occasion for a ringing declaration of a general election, which Fianna Fail seemed certain to win. On the very eve of the Ard Fheis an appalling fire broke out at the Stardust Ballroom in Haughey's constituency and forty-eight people were burned to death in an inferno from which they could not escape because some of the windows were barred and safety doors locked. The fire and subsequent controversy caused him to postpone the election announcement and week by week the postponement drifted until June, as unemployment mounted and the H-Block situation escalated with results already described.

All this and the GUBUs, too, would be a burden for any man's reputation. Understandably the Haughey factor is strong, particularly in Dublin and in urban areas.

The Presidency

Since the period under review contained a fair share of controversial legislation and threatened crisis, it is of interest to consider the role of the President in such situations.

The President is not an executive head of state in the same way as the President of America for instance, but neither is he a figurehead. No bill may become law without his signature. He can refer bills to the Supreme Court to be tested for constitutionality before signing them. He formally appoints the Taoiseach and members of the government and summons or dissolves the Dail on the advice of the Taoiseach. He can refuse a dissolution of the Dail where the Taoiseach has lost his parliamentary majority. He accepts the credentials of visiting Ambassadors. He is titular head of the armed forces, as Commander-in-Chief, and it is he who gives cadet officers their commissions.

Under Eamon de Valera, who retired having served the maximum of two seven-year terms in 1973, the office was stately and uncontroversial, taking its dignified tone from the personality of 'Dev' himself. He was succeeded by Erskine Childers of Fianna Fail, son of the author of *The Riddle of the Sands* who had been executed by the Free State side during the Civil War. Childers, who defeated Tom O'Higgins of Fine Gael in an election in which many people voted for him because he was a Protestant, raised the profile of the Presidency. He spoke out on many issues and travelled widely throughout the state to an extent which caused some of the Fianna Fail old guard to grumble privately that he was a little too visible and opinionated. He was widely popular, and there was countrywide regret when he died suddenly in November 1974, of a heart attack, while speaking on the problems of stress in modern life at the Royal College of Surgeons in Dublin.

He was succeeded without an election by Fianna Fail's nominee, Cearbhall O Dalaigh, an agreed candidate. O Dalaigh was a distinguished jurist and linguist. Before becoming President he had been a judge of the European Court, a member of the Irish Supreme Court and a former Chief Justice. He was a noted traveller who spoke several European languages, but his first love was Ireland, her culture and people, and especially her language. Though scrupulously correct in his duties as President, his Fianna Fail background and his fondness for Irish did not endear him to Fine Gael.

O Dalaigh, who had also been a former Irish Editor of the *Irish Press,* took a keen interest in the laws affecting the press and from time to time while he was in Europe, used to send me material concerning press freedoms, or legislation affecting newspapers. I was not surprised therefore when, particularly after controversy surrounding Dr O'Brien's interpretation of the uses to which the Emergency Powers Bill might be put, he decided to refer the Emergency Powers Bill to the Supreme Court on 24 September 1976 to test whether it was 'repugnant to the Constitution' before signing it into law.

Many members of the government were dismayed at O Dalaigh's action in that year of riots in Portlaoise prison, the murder of the British ambassador, and the security situation generally, but criticism was uttered privately — until on 18 October the Minister for Defence, Paddy Donegan, opened a new canteen at Columb Barracks, Mullingar. Speaking about the security situation in the context of the Emergency Powers legislation, Mr Donegan said that O Dalaigh was a 'thundering disgrace' for his 'amazing decision' to refer the Bill to the High Court.

Such a comment by a Minister for Defence in the presence of officers who had received their commissions from the President was of course unheard of, and a governmental apology on behalf of Donegan was issued almost as soon as the news broke. But Donegan neither resigned nor was transferred or sacked. Following the failure of a Fianna Fail motion aimed at forcing Cosgrave to sack Donegan, O Dalaigh resigned from the Presidency on 22 October to establish his own integrity and the unassailable nature of the office of the President.

There was bitter controversy, but political hackles ultimately subsided to the point whereby agreement was reached that O Dalaigh's successor would be Dr Patrick Hillery, Ireland's EEC Commissioner for Social Affairs. He was named the unopposed President-elect on 9 November, being sworn in on 3 December.

Hillery, who maintained a deliberately low profile after the O Dalaigh excitements, was sometimes criticised for becoming 'the prisoner of the Park'. He spoke to me once of his hope that he and his wife Maeve, like himself a doctor, would be able perhaps to put in some years in the Third World as volunteer medics. Once, in a distinctly unwelcome manner, his 'low profile' approach almost altered into his becoming a figure of major international controversy, on the eve of the Pope's visit in 1979.

Hordes of Fleet Street journalists began descending on Dublin on foot of a spate of rumours that Hillery and his wife were about to separate because of another woman. Such rumours concerning an Irish President at any time would have been, to coin a phrase, slavering stuff of the first water, but on the eve of the Pope's visit . . . I was one of the Irish national newspaper editors whom Hillery invited for lunch to his residence, Aras an Uachtarain, the week before the Pope was due to arrive. He emphasised that there was no truth whatever in the rumours, but that he understood that they were about to break in an Irish paper and he thought in at least one Fleet Street publication. What should he do? I suggested that he should give a limited press conference for Irish political correspondents and that he should prepare a statement so that whatever comment was made he could at least be sure of having this on the record in full. He accepted the suggestion and, later in the afternoon, met the correspondents from the Irish daily papers and RTE and gave a statement which was slightly more anodyne than the one I had drafted. Within a few days the gossip subsided. The Pope came and departed happily untouched by any scandal, having delivered a broadside against divorce during his last speech in Ireland. When his term ended in 1983, there was an all-party reluctance to fight yet another divisive and expensive election in that election-rife period and he yielded to an unprecedented all-party appeal to remain on as President.

He took a more active role thenceforward, attending public events and being photographed and written about as a result, but this second term in office has been marred by the death of his adopted daughter, from leukaemia. The tragedy occurred after a period during which the role of the Presidency was again under scrutiny; there had been widespread speculation following the February 1987 election that Haughey might not succeed in forming a government and that Hillery might have to intervene. In the event intervention was unnecessary, but the 1987 election result has served to underline the potential of the presidential role.

4

Partners in Coalition

Fine Gael; FitzGerald as Leader; The Labour Party;
Uneasy Partners; The Fate of the North

Fine Gael

When Garret FitzGerald succeeded Liam Cosgrave as leader in 1977, Fine Gael benefited, if that is indeed the correct term, for the first time from an infusion of Fianna Fail-style organisational muscle. A group popularly known as the National Handlers was set up (christened by John Healy, after the not overly scrupulous fraternity who handle the dogs at greyhound meets). These, studying the results of the 1977 campaign, decided that what Fianna Fail could do well, they could do better. They included Enda Marren, a prosperous Dublin-based solicitor; Bill O'Herlihy and Pat Heneghan, partners in a large Dublin PR and advertising agency; Derry Hussey, financial director of the Jones group of companies and husband of Gemma Hussey, later a forceful Minister for Education; Joe Jennings, a former *Irish Press* journalist and public relations officer with CIE, who was to become head of the Government Information Service; and above all Peter Prendergast, a marketing expert, not merely the government's Press Secretary but, it was often said, its brains and antennae as well.

Other figures within the ranks of Fine Gael supporters who made important contributions to this think-tank were Frank Flannery, who would become Chairman of the Rehabilitation Institute and a member of the Broadcasting Authority, and Ted Nealon, another former *Irish Press* journalist and broadcaster who became Minister for the Arts. This group was formally expanded and augmented as a new and powerful body within

Fine Gael, the Election Committee, during the Christmas week of 1980. It eventually evolved into a strategy committee to direct the conduct and policy of the party before, during and after the election campaigns of the eighties.

The strategy committee, presided over by a Fine Gael stalwart from Cork, Sean O'Leary, took aboard such political heavy-weights as Jim Dooge, who was to prove himself an able and effective Minister for Foreign Affairs, and Peter Sutherland, who became Attorney General. Another lawyer, John McMenamin, was put in charge of speechwriting, and two businessmen, Sean Murray and Vincent Ferguson, took over financial control and fundraising. The committee later added regional organisers throughout the country: Marren, Myles Staunton, Peter Curran and Peter Kelliher.

Initially at least, the impact of these groups on Fianna Fail, racked by internal divisions, was devastating. The effect of the new men and their policies was further heightened by the overall tactic of targeting Haughey as the chief enemy, not alone of Fine Gael but of the people at large. Encouraged by this approach, some of Haughey's other adversaries took the tactic into the realm of 'Dirty Tricks': for instance, circulating religious leaders and conservative-minded people with photostats of a scurrilous *Private Eye* article about the Fianna Fail leader's private life.

From the time Haughey was formally declared Taoiseach on 11 December 1979, FitzGerald chose to attack him, referring to his 'flawed pedigree' in a memorable Dail speech on the day Haughey was named Taoiseach. No one was quite certain whether he meant this to be taken as a reference to the Arms Trial or to the fact that Haughey's father had been a member of the Free State forces which had crushed the republicans during the civil war. The descendants of the republicans were now the very people whom Haughey had allegedly tried to assist in Northern Ireland, and FitzGerald was leading the party that had evolved from the major Free State grouping, Cumann na nGaedheal. At all events this speech, delivered in the presence of Haughey's family, including his mother, set the tone for a relationship between the two men of a bitterness which had not been seen in Irish politics since the civil war.

Although Fine Gael is seen as the most 'conservative' of the two Irish major political parties, it is ironic that since the twenties the party has not been able to hold power without the aid of the left. The result is almost invariably that supporters of both right and left feel betrayed at the end of the day — the day in question usually being polling day.

In the bright dawn of the sixties both main parties began making progressive noises. In Fine Gael these came mainly from Declan Costello, the son of the former Taoiseach John A. Costello, who had presided over the declaration of an Irish Republic in 1949 in order, as he said, to 'take the gun out of Irish politics'. The gun remained, and so did the conservatism of Fine Gael despite the fact that Declan Costello won support, after much argument within the party, for what was presented in the 1965 general election campaign as the 'Just Society' document. This laid heavy emphasis on planning, social welfare and education. However, on 21 April 1965 following the election the party's leader, James Dillon, retired and was succeeded by the conservative Liam Cosgrave, a son of the first leader of the Cumann na nGaedheal party.

Liam Cosgrave, low-sized in stature and deeply religious was, and is, a man very much in tune with the middle ground of Irish politics. He had been in the army during the war, qualified as a barrister and had twenty-one years of politics behind him before Dillon stepped down. By arrangement the conservative Gerald Sweetman, an archetypal figure of 'fiscal rectitude', nominated Cosgrave as soon as Dillon's resignation became known. This came as a surprise to the party at large but not to the inner circle, and the matter was over and done with before Costello's supporters could mount a challenge. Nevertheless the 'Just Society' document, which also advocated price control and a degree of intervention in the private sector, remained at the back of the minds of the more intellectual membership of the party, surfacing later during the leadership of Garret FitzGerald.

Cosgrave became leader at the time of the Vietnam War, and the FitzGeraldite wing's distaste for that war was at variance with Cosgrave's staunch pro-Americanism. So was its foreign-sounding notion, aired unsuccessfully at the 1968 Fine Gael Ard Fheis, to change the name of Fine Gael from 'Fine Gael, the United Ireland Party' to 'Fine Gael, the Social Democratic Party'. This suggestion was to become significant in the seventies when the party was in coalition with the Labour Party. Labour's spokesman on the North, Dr Conor Cruise O'Brien, expressed distaste for working towards a united Ireland.

Prior to the link with Labour, the old Sinn Fein radicalism that still lay dormant in some Fine Gael breasts showed itself in opposition to such a change. FitzGerald continued to advance within the party, particularly after he had been elected to the Dail in 1969, but Cosgrave, an enthusiastic horseman in private life, remained firmly in the saddle holding on to the reins of power. He received widespread publicity, much of it critical, when he used the terminology of the hunting field to refer to his party opponents at the May 1972 Ard Fheis as 'mongrel foxes'. These, he said, he would 'root out and chop'. He referred to his critics in the party and the media as 'blow-ins' to the country. This was taken to refer in particular to Bruce Arnold, a distinguished art critic and political commentator who, as we have seen, was also singled out under Mr Haughey's regime for special attention by having his phone tapped.

The year 1972, of course, saw the fall of Stormont, abortive British-IRA talks and appalling violence, some of which spilled over to the Republic in a highly suspicious manner. Cosgrave went on to scale his highest pinnacle of success in February of the next year when a general election was called and he successfully negotiated a coalition pact with Labour.

Weakened by the Arms Trial crisis, Fianna Fail fell to skilful use of the PR system by the coalition partners; each benefited from the other's transfers. Overall, though the party's first preference vote went up, it lost parliamentary ground, returning with only 69 seats as opposed to the 75 it had held in 1969. Cosgrave became Taoiseach, remaining both as Taoiseach and Leader of Fine Gael until he lost the 1977 general election and handed over to Garret FitzGerald — the most mongrel of foxes in Liam Cosgrave's eyes.

FitzGerald as Leader

Articulate, the fastest talker in what is probably the fastest-talking public life in western Europe, Garret FitzGerald has the reputation of being able to enter a room talking, talk his way through it and leave still talking. Affable and urbane, 'for a good part of his public life he travelled so fast that he left his mistakes buried behind him', as a former admirer of his in the Department of Foreign Affairs put it to me.

FitzGerald's stint as Minister for Foreign Affairs began in March 1973. Typically, he was so keen to take up his new post that the porter arriving to open up for the day found the newly-appointed minister waiting for him at the front door. Once inside FitzGerald blasted currents of fresh air through the place. Salaries, morale and prestige mushroomed within the department. He became particularly friendly with Sean Donlon, who at thirty-eight had been appointed by Jack Lynch as the youngest-ever Ambassador to America. FitzGerald's respect for Donlon was to have important consequences in the future, both when Haughey tried to shift Donlon and when FitzGerald himself was negotiating the Anglo-Irish Agreement unveiled at Hillsborough in November 1985.

FitzGerald is almost invariably well spoken of internationally. Unlike Haughey, he is at ease with and liked by journalists. His personality makes it almost impossible to dislike him — although Charles Haughey tries hard to do so and was ably assisted in this on a basis of reciprocity by FitzGerald himself. The two men became personally friendly after FitzGerald resigned the Fine Gael leadership in 1987, but in political opposition they clashed continually. The two men's antagonism was based on styles, culture, everything that one can think of politically. Cultured, middle-class Dublin is epitomised in FitzGerald, by contrast with the back-room image of nationalist-inclined Haughey, the boy from Donnycarney who made good and who maintains a millionaire's lifestyle while upholding traditional working class values.

It was on Northern Ireland that Garret FitzGerald set out most determinedly to break new ground. Here he fundamentally differed from Haughey who held the traditional thirty-two county view to be inviolable, sometimes to a point where he left himself open to justifiable criticism of being intolerant. I remember on one occasion being invited to an Ogra Fianna Fail meeting to share a platform with Seamus Brennan, the SDLP's Seamus Mallon and the Alliance Party's John Cushnahan. When I got there I found the young organisers reeling from their first dose of *real-politik*. They had had to convey to Cushnahan an hour earlier the fact that his invitation to speak at the meeting had been withdrawn on instructions from on high, because of some criticism of Fianna Fail policy which he had expressed.

FitzGerald on the other hand deliberately sought to open up debate on the North, particularly amongst the young Fine Gael group which he encouraged to a degree that he possibly regretted later; the young tigers went after his blood on issues which became tied up with Northern policy such as the abortion referendum.

One of his early passions in government was to reform the Irish Constitution, a document sacred to Fianna Fail since de Valera had drawn it up. He believed that the Constitution should be redrawn to reflect the 'pluralist' nature of modern Ireland instead of reinforcing Roman Catholic doctrines accepted by most, but not all, citizens of the state. FitzGerald once told a group of unionists that they would be 'bloody fools' to opt for a United Ireland under the existing Constitution. To Haughey in particular, this proposal came as would a suggestion to the successor of Moses that the Tablets should be revised. Where the unionists were concerned, the idea that the south should re-word its Constitution was interesting, but their priorities required the south to defeat the IRA and forget about Irish unity.

FitzGerald, an economist, a university lecturer by profession, a statistician and a journalist by inclination, is the son of a former Cumann na nGaedheal Minister of External Affairs. A former President of the EEC Council of Ministers, he is devoted to the idea that men of good will can meet at a centre, particularly if they are internationally minded, have a grasp of continental languages and a well-bred sense of humour.

But as the lovable koala bear of Australia can inflict a nasty wound from a concealed poisonous claw, so does the FitzGerald/Haughey antagonism bring out what divides Fine Gael and Fianna Fail ideologically against all logic, sixty years after the civil war. Each thought the other unsuited for public life or high office and said so vehemently at different times in his career. The relationship between Lynch and FitzGerald was far more cordial. FitzGerald once assured Lynch in the Dail that if he had any difficulty in forming an administration from his own ranks — a reference to the Lynch-Haughey rivalry — then he could count on support from the Fine Gael side of the House.

However, in recession-struck Ireland with the Northern pot

threatening to boil over, FitzGerald, while projecting an image of great integrity, frequently struck the public as the absent-minded professor who would be better off back in his university than trying to deal with the problems of ordinary people, with whom he plainly could not empathise anyway. In 1985 and 1986 his wife's health added to his problems. Earlier, the absent-minded air had been epitomised by a famous occasion on which he appeared in public wearing odd shoes — a fact noted by an alert photographer — because, struggling into his clothes in the dark, he had taken whatever shoes he could lay hands on rather than forage further and disturb his sleeping spouse.

Nevertheless, while the Dublin man's jibe was that the difference between Haughey and FitzGerald was that if Haughey found a bank note lying on the street, he would pocket it whereas FitzGerald would lose it, this kindly, confused, fundamentally decent image helped rather than hindered FitzGerald with the public as a whole. What lost him popularity was his inability to run his government efficiently. A cabinet reshuffle in February of 1986, intended to boost the government's image, went disastrously wrong when the Minister for Health, Barry Desmond of Labour — unpopular over health cuts — simply refused to be shifted. This heightened criticism both from Fianna Fail and within Fine Gael that the government was a prisoner of the left. Then Fianna Fail and the left swung over to the charge that the liberal FitzGerald was a prisoner of the right after the *Irish Press* revealed on 29 March 1986 that prominent members of his government, who were active in lobbying for a concession on oil exploration on behalf of companies drilling in the Irish Sea, were in fact share-holders in one of these companies, Atlantic Resources, themselves.

Few of the liberal crusades with which FitzGerald was associated — the implementation of the Just Society policy, the proposal to change the Constitution so as clearly to separate church and state, the proposal to give limited access to divorce —came to anything. His biggest success was the signing of the Anglo-Irish Accord, which did mark high water of sorts for Irish constitutional nationalism. However, the agreement had no effect on southern electoral attitudes in an era dominated by unemployment and the economy.

Probably FitzGerald's main contribution to Irish politics was

his ability to put a decent face on public life and to convince some
people, particularly amongst the young, that a man could be
articulate and straightforward in speech and still achieve some
success in politics. His weakness lay in his inability to become as
enthused by people, particularly working-class people, as by
ideas. He also allowed his distaste both for the constitutional
republican strain of Irish political life and the IRA version of it to
blind him to the force (and dedication) which the republicans
both represent and generate.

The Labour Party

In 1963 the Labour Party was joined by the stormy petrel of
Irish politics, Dr Noel Browne. Dr Browne had resigned (over a
clash with the bishops) from the inter-party coalition that put de
Valera out of office in 1948, had spent some time with Fianna Fail
and then had founded his own party, the National Progressive
Democrats. Two years after the NPD dissolved and Browne
joined Labour, Labour won sixteen Dail seats in Dublin at the
1965 general election making a total of 22, equal to its highest
ever obtained at the election of June 1927. This precipitated
something of a rush of blood to the head, and in 1966 it celebrated
the anniversary of the 1916 Rising by formally proclaiming itself
a socialist party, joining the Socialist International a year later
and proclaiming confidently at its annual conference that year
that 'The seventies will be socialist'.

Brendan Corish, the leader, was well placed to further these
developments from a trade union and socialist point of view. He
had been an active member of the ITGWU, but he was also
generally liked as a good family man from County Wexford
— fond of attending coursing meetings, a popular country
pastime. He succeeded his father at a by-election in 1945 and had
been elected to succeed William Norton as leader of the party in
1960, when he was a member of the rising progressive wing of
the movement. From the outset Corish had made it clear that he
wanted the party to be a political force in its own right, not
merely the trade union movement's parliamentary pressure
group. As the sixties wore on it appeared to some people at least
that the seventies could possibly be 'socialist'. Certainly Labour
began conducting itself like a party which intended to have a say
in government, even perhaps to form one.

I remember a Labour Party friend at the time who spoke about the changes which would be brought about by 'the Labour government'. These were to have included the nationalisation of building societies. When I suggested to David Thornley that this might be a mistake akin to cutting one's own throat, I was airily brushed aside. The euphoria of the period did not permit proposals to nationalise financial institutions to be seen as in any way incompatible with Irish political wisdom.

David, who died tragically young in 1978, I will always consider to have been one of the best brains of my time. A lecturer in Trinity College in Political Science, he was also a boxer, a writer and a national figure through his appearance on the top RTE current affairs programme, 'Seven Days'. Other television personalities to join the Labour Party at this time were Justin Keating and Dr Conor Cruise O'Brien, who had won an international reputation as a writer and controversialist from the days of the Congo/Katanga uprising.

Later the influx of these intellectuals to Labour would result in jibes about 'smoked salmon socialists'. But as the 1969 general election approached it appeared that Labour was set for a massive breakthrough. In fact it proved something of a breakdown because, though its vote went up (17 per cent overall), it lost four seats and the truth of the sort of thing I had warned David Thornley about was borne out. Jack Lynch spoke publicly but mildly of the party's 'alien ideologies'. Privately Fianna Fail canvassers spoke more fiercely about a 'red menace'; they capitalised particularly on Dr Conor Cruise O'Brien's remark that he would be more in favour of opening an embassy in Cuba than in some of the traditional Catholic countries.

Uneasy Partners

The question of coalition inevitably came to be discussed. Despite the determination of Corish and his supporters in the sixties that the party should not be an adjunct to anybody else but a force in its own right, it was obvious to realists that this was not to be. A special conference called in December 1970 voted nearly two-to-one in favour of considering coalition in the future. Even though Labour, unlike Fine Gael, was opposed to joining the EEC and had campaigned against entry (ironically, alongside Sinn

Fein) in the May 1972 referendum, it ultimately formulated a joint manifesto with Fine Gael on which the two parties successfully fought the 1973 election, promising to encourage worker participation in state enterprises, to cut prices and unemployment and to increase spending on housing.

However, the right-left dichotomy continued to disturb both parties throughout the four years of coalition. The increasingly deteriorating situation in Northern Ireland, together with an overspill of violence into the Republic, drove Fine Gael to introduce ever more Draconian anti-IRA legislation, as we have seen (Chapter 2). Dr Cruise O'Brien and those who thought like him in Labour favoured these steps, which alienated much of Labour's traditional republican support. At the same time some of Labour's left-wing policies, such as the introduction of a wealth tax and the introduction, in principle at least, of income tax for farmers, alienated Fine Gael supporters, though in practice the farmers managed to fight off the taxation threat. Meanwhile, of course, the oil shock, rising inflation and unemployment levels began to erode government support overall.

Left-wing Labour particularly had cause to question its continuation in coalition in July 1974, during the vote on a coalition-sponsored family planning measure to regulate the law; this followed a supreme court decision which recognised the right of married couples to buy contraceptives. On a free vote Liam Cosgrave and the Minister for Education, Richard Burke, were amongst those who crossed the floor to vote with Fianna Fail against this proposal. Cosgrave had not consulted any of the party before doing so and his action struck the progressive wing of Fine Gael, and all shades of Labour opinion, like a bolt from the blue.

Coalition as a philosophy suffered an even bigger blow when, having gone to the country in June 1977, the coalition commissioned a public opinion poll *after* the Dail had been dissolved only to discover that it was trailing massively behind Fianna Fail. The poll predictions were borne out in the election results. Fine Gael lost eleven seats and Labour one; not a great deal numerically for Labour perhaps, but a continuation of a slide which had gone on since the 1965 peak of twenty-two.

In the immediate aftermath Liam Cosgrave resigned and on July 1st was succeeded by FitzGerald as leader of Fine Gael. In Labour Justin Keating and Conor Cruise O'Brien were amongst the defeated and Corish, who like Cosgrave resigned on learning the election results, was succeeded as party leader by Frank Cluskey, a Dubliner and a former trade union officer in the Workers' Union of Ireland, who had been in charge of Social Welfare in the coalition government.

Shades of the gathering difficulties in Fianna Fail also helped Fine Gael in the local government elections, wherein the party's vote rose to a record total of 36.5 per cent. In Cork Fine Gael doubled its vote to overtake Fianna Fail, an ominous indication of things to come for Jack Lynch, whom everybody hitherto had regarded as Cork's unquestioned darling. The Fianna Fail dissensions and the overall economic situation, coupled with the H-Block crisis, presented another opportunity for coalition in 1981 which Fine Gael and Labour gladly availed themselves of.

There was tension between Fine Gael and Labour. Fine Gael was plainly unhappy about the wealth tax and was at the same time seeking to make far heavier cuts in expenditure to balance the budget than Labour wanted. The desire for fiscal rectitude from the right triumphed over the views of the left in the January 1982 budget brought in by Finance Minister John Bruton. The budget contained a proposal to tax children's shoes; this was relatively insignificant among many weightier measures, but it lost the coalition the support of an Independent Socialist deputy, Jim Kemmy, and the government fell.

As has been noted, the coalition partners were lucky enough to have a second chance of government that year when Fianna Fail was forced to call an election in November. Fine Gael appeared to be heading towards overall single party government in the foreseeable future as the party won seventy seats, coming only five seats behind Fianna Fail. But the financial climate soon began to erode those dreams. The European Parliament elections of June 1984 showed a substantial drop in support for the government parties combined. But it was Labour which found itself in a particularly precarious position, having won only 8.4 per cent of the poll and suffered the loss of all its seats in the European Parliament.

As a result of the 1981 election Frank Cluskey lost his seat and was replaced by Michael O'Leary, Cluskey's former rival for leadership, a former minister and a coalition enthusiast. He was too much of an enthusiast for the Cluskey wing of the party, which sponsored a motion at the annual conference of October 1982 committing Labour to fight the next election on its own two feet, leaving the question of coalition over until the results were in. However, this displeased O'Leary so much that a few days after the conference, on 28 October, he resigned from the party and the leadership. He was succeeded by the former Irish rugby international, Dick Spring.

At thirty-two, Spring was the party's youngest TD and had been returned from a peculiar Labour enclave in North Kerry, where his father had preceded him. Spring, who had studied law at Trinity, had a disastrous interlude as full back for Ireland, appearing at Lansdowne Road against England in a game where he was unlucky enough to miss a catch, resulting in a try for the opposition. On hearing of his cabinet appointment a former international colleague of his remarked, 'thank God they didn't put him in Defence'. Spring, however, performed well in the unfavourable Labour climate, having to confront a general election campaign only a few days after assuming leadership. Rejecting overtures from Charles Haughey, Labour decided to take office again with Fine Gael, this time with Spring as Tanaiste.

Rejuvenated Fine Gael proved itself insensitive to Labour's wishes. Capital taxation was not raised, unemployment went up and cuts in public spending continued, though at a lower rate than if Labour had not been in power. One year after the party took office Frank Cluskey, who had regained his seat and who was then Minister for Trade, Commerce and Tourism, resigned from office specifically over the way the government was handling the natural gas resource, but in general indicating a dissatisfaction within Labour at the manner in which Fine Gael was dominating it.

A thumb-nail sketch of the difficulties 'Finegabour' experienced in attempting to function as a unit may be given for two key areas, the elimination of the budget deficit and the introduction of a land tax. The first was a Fine Gael priority in the 1982–3 coalition, the second a Labour one.

The target budget deficit in 1982 was IR£1 billion. Fine Gael proposed to eliminate this in four years. Under pressure from Labour, FitzGerald extended the deadline to five years. But by half-way through the coalition term, faced with a series of revolts over various proposals to cut public sector spending, to eliminate subsidies on food, and to reduce grants for health and education, FitzGerald was forced to concede in September of 1983 that the deficit would not be eliminated by 1987. Thus the cardinal point of Fine Gael's strategy was abandoned.

That fateful September, Croke Park rang to the unprecedented sound of a Taoiseach being booed as he arrived to take his seat at the All-Ireland Football Final. Labour's proposal for a 1 per cent land tax had surfaced as government policy. The Irish Farmers' Association swung into operation, querying local Fine Gael TDs in the provincial media about their voting intentions on the land tax. It became obvious almost immediately that at least half the Fine Gael parliamentary party, the rural half, did not want the proposal, though a few urban TDs with working-class unemployed in their constituencies argued for it, just as the same elements provided the ideological links which kept the left-right coalition from drifting apart altogether.

However, such links proved ineffective against IFA pressure, which took some spectacular forms. In County Wexford they issued a statement opposing the tax in the name of a group of Fine Gael TDs which included one of the junior ministers for agriculture, Michael D'Arcy.

The government altered the land tax policy on 2 October, proposing instead a three-year national economic plan entitled 'Building on Reality'. This proposed instead a land tax on £10 per 'adjusted acre' up to holdings of 80 'adjusted acres'. However this strange concept works out, it can be said with certainty that the Labour land tax was adjusted by the IFA's pressure on Fine Gael.

Labour had ensured the inclusion of a National Development Corporation in the 1982 proposals for government. They envisaged that it would have £500m to spend initially on such varied objectives as the development of fishing and forestry as well as industry. The idea floundered from the word go in the coalition bargaining process, and instead of £500m cash a promise of £200m was made, to be provided 'over a period of years'. Even this scaled-down sum could have created valuable incentives had the NDC been pursued with the same concentration of time and energy that was committed to the referenda on divorce and abortion (see Chapter 6), or for that matter was taken up by the negotiations which preceded the Anglo-Irish Agreement.

The truth of a Labour-Fine Gael Coalition in Ireland is that

Fine Gael largely represents the voice of the bigger farmers, the professions, merchants, and Old Money. Never mind the fact that, as with the British Tories, there is inevitably a large element of working-class support and, since the days of Declan Costello, an important 'Social Democrat' segment, typified by Garret FitzGerald. Labour, though poorly supported by the unions, is nevertheless trade union orientated and largely influenced by trade union thinking, or by the presence of former trade union members. In other words, Fine Gael are commonly thought of as the employers and Labour as the employed — involving, in British terms, the tendencies of Thatcherism and Scargillism (if not the personalities) sitting at the same cabinet table.

Against this left-right dichotomy there is the unique position occupied by Fianna Fail in Irish politics, which has meant in practice that, as Labour spokesmen have frequently said to me, Labour interests are best served by a Fianna Fail government in power negotiating directly with the trade unions who can rely on the Labour Party in opposition to support their view publicly in the Dail. This the trade unions cannot expect when Labour is uneasily sharing power with Fine Gael.

The Fate of the North

Labour will continue to have difficulty in coalition with Fine Gael over Northern Ireland. With inevitable individual exceptions, Labour attitudes still reflect the fact that James Connolly marched the movement into the GPO in 1916; Labour remains imbued with thirty-two county republicanism.

The equally patriotic Fine Gael is nevertheless descended from Cumann na nGaedheal, which took the harsh decision to execute republicans and so conclude the civil war in 1922. And some members privately, generally in drink and late at night, will say, 'it was done in 1922 and it can be done again'.

However, Fianna Fail does not suffer from this obvious ideological divide. Indeed the late-night Fianna Fail drinker is quite likely to mutter approvingly about the 'boys' — and then go off without a qualm the next day to vote for some Fianna Fail measure to curb the IRA. Nevertheless the root and branch of the party is emotionally at least in favour of a more 'forward' policy on Northern Ireland. There is no doubt, for instance, that

Haughey, though under pressure during the various 'heaves', always had a fundamental strength on his side — the fact that the grassroots perceived him as 'the man to stand up to Maggie'.

A new Secretary of State for Northern Ireland, the energetic and forceful Mr James Prior, had attempted to deal with the situation created by the hunger strikes by setting up a new Assembly in June 1981. This was going to function by a process known as 'rolling devolution', going from a committee system to a full-blown ministerial one, within the existing framework of London-Belfast relationships. It did not work. Boycotted by the SDLP and by Sinn Fein, which after the hunger strike won something approaching 42 per cent of the nationalist vote, the Assembly was a non-starter and the North continued in an unstable and dangerous condition.

The Republic also made a number of major contributions towards solving the Northern problem, beginning with meetings between Haughey and Mrs Thatcher in London and Dublin during 1980. However, the hunger strikes generated further bitterness on the nationalist side, derailing the Haughey-Thatcher relationship. Mrs Thatcher's intransigence over the issue was a direct contributory factor to the June 1981 election which forced Haughey out of power.

Garret Fitzgerald, at the urging of the SDLP leader John Hume, attempted to pick up the pieces of the Anglo-Irish relationship with an unusual initiative, the New Ireland Forum. Beginning in May 1983, all the Republic's constitutional parties and the SDLP began what amounted to a public enquiry into the realities of Northern Ireland and how a peaceful solution to the problems might be found.

Although Sinn Fein were not invited and the unionists boycotted the proceedings the Forum continued its work for a full year, a remarkable example of all-party co-operation. It finally published a report which defined three possible options for a 'new' Ireland:

1. A united Ireland governed from Dublin;
2. A federation, or confederation, of the two parts of Ireland;
3. A system of Joint Authority, with Dublin and London together responsible for the North.

As the Irish had engaged in a major re-assessment of the problem there was a general expectation in Dublin that the British would do so too, despite the fact that Haughey stated at the news conference when the report was presented that the unitary option was the only one acceptable to Fianna Fail.

However, at her press conference on the report given in London in November 1984, after she and FitzGerald had had two days of talks on the document, Mrs Thatcher made Haughey's position appear positively mild and flexible. She was seen on Irish TV screens saying: 'I have made it quite clear, and so did Mr Prior, when he was Secretary of State, that a unified Ireland was one thing that was OUT. A second solution was a confederation system: that was OUT. A third solution was Joint Authority: that is OUT'.

The Republic was aghast at this rejection of its political deliberations and it became known that FitzGerald himself described her remarks at a cabinet meeting as being 'gratuitously offensive'. International opinion, particularly in America, was also critical. Such reactions appeared to change Mrs Thatcher's attitude. She was more conciliatory towards FitzGerald when they met in Milan in June 1985 at a European Community Conference, and accepted his view that, if something were not done soon, Sinn Fein and Gerry Adams would replace the SDLP and John Hume as spokesmen for the North's nationalists.

After much discussion between the two governments and their civil servants, including in each case the secretary to the cabinet, the Hillsborough Agreement was signed at Hillsborough Castle outside Belfast on 15 November 1985. This Agreement gave the Republic a say in the running of Belfast's affairs for the first time since the Northern state had been set up.

An on-going inter-governmental conference was set up wherein, as of right, Dublin could voice its opinions on matters such as security and the administration of justice in Northern Ireland. An Irish government minister (Peter Barry, Minister for Foreign Affairs) was to represent Dublin, again as of right, and the Conference, which was to meet in Dublin, London and Belfast, was to have a permanent secretariat composed of Irish and British civil servants.

Opinions differed as to the actual significance of the Conference. Haughey, for instance, promptly rejected the Agreement, but the unionists understood the symbolism. The Dublin accents were drawing nearer. The tricolour, formerly an *illegal* emblem under the Flags and Emblems Act, now flew (however temporarily) over Hillsborough Castle, the seat of the former Governors of Northern Ireland. To a man the unionists were appalled, their MPs withdrew from Westminster and a programme of protest, which included sectarian assassination and the burning of policemen's homes, was embarked upon. The protests, though diminished, continue at the time of writing.

The Republic, less dangerous but nearly as volatile in November of 1982 as Northern Ireland was and is, saw Fianna Fail lose its slim majority following the death of a TD, Deputy Bill Loughnane from County Clare, and be forced back to the country, losing to another coalition which fell in February 1987.

The end of the 24th Dail came during the Christmas recess; Labour announced that it could not support Fine Gael's hairshirt budget and formally withdrew from the government. A general election became inevitable and one was declared for Tuesday 17 February 1987. Normally general elections are held on Wednesdays, but that week there were two big football matches in Scotland, a soccer and a rugby international, and it was felt that if the election date clashed with travel plans the polls would suffer, economic crisis or no economic crisis!

In the event the main sufferer was Fine Gael. Their vote fell by 27 per cent, returning the party with only 51 seats, 17 fewer than when the 24th Dail concluded. The main beneficiaries in the election were Des O'Malley's newly-formed Progressive Democrats, who gained 14 seats from nothing. But while the party had campaigned with a new broom image to mark 'an end to civil war politics', a new policy of 'reconciliation towards the North', tax revision and privatisation of state companies, its most apparent characteristic was the continuing anti-Haughey one.

Apart from the Fianna Fail TDs who had left the party before the election to join O'Malley, two of the successful candidates were the daughter of George Colley and a son of Jim Gibbons, respectively. The journalist, Geraldine Kennedy, who had successfully sued the state over her phone being tapped on Sean Doherty's orders, won a seat in Dun Laoghaire, having been imposed on the constituency by O'Malley.

Another effect of the Progressive Democrats' appearance was to deny Haughey an overall majority for the fourth successive occasion. A combination of bad vote management in a number of key constituencies — Clare, Kerry North and ironically enough his own North Dublin Central — combined with the Progressive Democrats' emergence to give Fianna Fail only 81 seats.

When the Dail re-assembled on 10 March in an atmosphere of great tension it was not certain until the last moment that Haughey could form a government. After all that had gone before, the party set its face against 'strokes' or 'deals' and it was only when Tony Gregory announced he would be abstaining on the vote for Taoiseach that Haughey was able to scrape through with the aid of independents. The final party line-up for the 25th Dail was FF 81, FG 51, PDs 14, Labour 12, Workers' Party 4, others 4. Labour's total of seats achieved with only 6 per cent of the vote raised questions about PR, always a source of annoyance to Fianna Fail, but it does not appear that PR will be dropped by the Irish electorate in the foreseeable future.

Fine Gael had in effect campaigned on the budget which Labour failed to support. Garret FitzGerald, who resigned after the election result, was succeeded as leader by Alan Dukes, former Fine Gael Minister for Finance, who pledged that his party would support Fianna Fail if it took the harsh measures which Fine Gael had proposed to reduce the national debt and lighten the public finances. Similarly, O'Malley pledged the PDs' support and on Tuesday 27 March Haughey duly became converted to fiscal rectitude, introducing a deflationary budget which slashed house grants, cut social welfare, introduced hospital charges and above all promised a public service pay freeze in the hope that interest rates would fall and recovery begin. The shadow of Mrs Thatcher now sat at the Irish cabinet table.

The election was notable for the way in which it highlighted the cleavage between rural culture and the urban ethos of the cities, particularly of Dublin and Cork. The new party, the Progressive Democrats, was most notably supported by the professional middle class and what their opponents termed 'yuppie' elements, thereby decimating this traditional Fine Gael source of strength. The polarisation could well be exemplified by the success of Geraldine Kennedy in the east and by Sean Doherty in his customary role as poll-topper in Roscommon.

However, another sharp cleavage which became apparent was that between the loose de facto alliance that formed amongst the parties of the right and centre-right, Fianna Fail, Fine Gael and the Progressive Democrats, and those of the left, Labour, the Workers' Party, (which gained two seats in the election, adding Joe Sherlock and Pat McCartan to Proinsias de Rossa and Tomas MacGiolla), the left-wing independent Tony Gregory and the leader of the Democratic Socialist Party from Limerick, Jim Kemmy, who along with Sherlock, made a second appearance for the left in the Dail.

The left remained resolutely opposed to the harsh measures of the budget, which the right-wing parties of course pushed through, and at the time of writing there is widespread speculation that at long last Irish political parties will begin to divide on left-right lines.

5

The Church and the People

Holding the Line; Morality Plays; In the Classroom;
Third World Radicals; A Nun's Story; Modern Pastors

THE Pope's visit to Ireland in 1979 stopped the country in its
tracks. The crowds for his open-air appearances were the greatest
of the century — over a million people attended Mass in the
Phoenix Park, Dublin, on the morning of his arrival — and there
was virtually no crime and little drunkenness for the three days of
his visit. He did not cross into Northern Ireland; he had intended
to go there, but the Mountbatten and Warrenpoint killings
changed his travel arrangements, and he went no nearer the
border than Drogheda, less than thirty miles north of Dublin.
There he delivered a speech that cynics say was written by the
SDLP, so strongly did it, in effect, support the party's position (in
fact, Bishop Cathal Daly is credited with having a hand in its
drafting).

While the visit proved the strength of Ireland's attachment to
the Faith for anyone who might have doubted it, its effects soon
wore off. The IRA rejected his appeal to abandon their campaign.
Vocations, which some churchmen hoped would resume a
permanent upswing, reverted to their downward movement a
year or two after he departed, and the younger people in
particular showed that they made a distinction between the man
and his message where issues such as divorce or contraception
were concerned.

To the extent that one can fully rely on surveys of any sort, the
best and most up-to-date plain man's guide to the practice of
religion in Ireland today is contained in the surveys

commissioned by the Council for Research and Development in Maynooth. These set forth all that can be gleaned statistically concerning religious beliefs, their implementation and attitudes towards the church in 1974 and 1984. The purpose of the 1984 survey was to 'discover whether patterns of religious belief, practice, moral values and attitudes towards the church' had changed in the Republic since a similar survey in 1974.

In the four categories it found that among the 'less well-accepted teachings' were those on family planning and divorce. Familiar concepts such as hell or papal infallibility had shown the greatest loss of popularity. 'Practice' showed an increase in the numbers of those praying regularly and attending Mass, but a decline in those making Confession.

'Moral values' showed that old Irish absolutism had declined, with fewer people opting for the category 'always wrong' and more for 'it depends on circumstances'. It also found, interestingly enough, that such views tended to be equally shared between women and men, whereas ten years earlier women would have taken up a more conservative position than men. Taking what can be learned from the survey, along with my own observations, I feel the following general picture may be painted with some accuracy.

While young people increasingly go their own way, the position of the devout, church-going laity is fairly subordinate in the Irish church. The laity's most important role is as fund-raisers; a few appearances in public are allowed, such as reading the lessons and helping to distribute the Communion wafers at Mass. The hierarchy have not proved responsive to suggestions for incorporating the laity into the church's structures in the manner in which this has happened elsewhere in the world — in Brazil, for instance, or nearer home (and more relevant because of the strong Irish quotient) in the Archdiocese of Liverpool.

However, as the abortion and divorce referenda showed, these failures have been deplored more by the Catholic intellectuals to be met at Dublin discussion groups under the auspices of the Dominicans or the Jesuits than by the laity at large, who enthusiastically fall in with the hierarchy's wishes. Despite this self-evident fact, the Irish are making a distinction between supporting the church as lay men or women and actually becoming priests, nuns or brothers.

The total number of church personnel declined by roughly a quarter between 1970 and 1985, from 33,092 to 25,944, and there is no indication that this pattern of decline will be halted. Thus, though the presence of the church is all-pervasive there has been a diminution in the grip which it is able to maintain on an increasingly well-educated society. Increasing affluence (of a sort) and mobility mean that people can move in and out of the purview of the church without permitting it to have any great influence on their conduct (unless, of course, they want an abortion or a divorce).

In the North, while turmoil has had its effect in terms of falling vocations and priests leaving the ministry, the truth of the saying, 'there are no atheists in a foxhole' is well borne out. The Church of Consolation flourishes despite underlying secularist trends, notably the use of 'the pill', which poses a far greater long-term threat to IRA support than anything Paisley or the British Army can devise.

Given the grotesque brutality of some aspects of the Protestant/Catholic divide in Northern Ireland, and that Paisley and his forces actively oppose any ecumenical trends, the state of ecumenism in Ireland is not all that bad. Relations between the Catholic and Protestant churches are formal but generally friendly. The principal source of annoyance to Protestants in the Republic is the requirement made of the Catholic partner in a mixed marriage which, in effect, means that the children are more than likely to be brought up Catholic. Paisley frequently makes capital out of the effect which he claims this requirement has had on Protestant numbers in the Republic, and points to this decline as a principal reason why Ulster must remain hostile to the blandishments of Dublin.

Holding the Line

Along with what might be termed the 'liberalising' influence of youth, one must take note of the marked rightward swing in the Roman Catholic church as a whole, accentuated by the effects of the recession. The Rightist swing, symbolised and furthered by Pope John Paul's visit, manifests itself markedly through the selection of bishops. There the Papal Nuncio, Dr Alibrandi, plays a prominent part in seeing that the Pope's conservative policies are furthered. The short-reigning Archbishop of Dublin, Dr Kevin McNamara, who died in April 1987, was thrust into the office after he had distinguished himself by a strong articulation of the papal line during the referendum held in 1983 to insert a pro-life amendment in the Irish Constitution.

The previous Archbishop, Dr Dermot Ryan, had been elevated to the Curia but died unexpectedly in Rome in February 1985. He had lobbied successfully against the appointment of either of two of his auxiliary bishops, Donal Murray and Dermot O'Mahony, on the grounds that they had not been loyal during the referendum campaign — they had spoken openly of the faithful using conscience as an aid in the decision-making process! From his Roman curial position Dr Ryan, a man of great charm and intellect, was also instrumental in vetoing the appointment of Dr Brendan Comiskey. The appointment, offered to and refused by the able but elderly Dr Harty, Bishop of Killaloe, finally went to Dr McNamara, at the time Bishop of Kerry.

Dr McNamara, a former Maynooth theologian, was known to have a terminal illness when he came to Dublin. His appointment can be regarded as something of a stop-gap amidst the conflicting forces of the Irish church and the political system. In his public utterances and pastoral letters there was no mistaking his devotion to the traditional school and to the Pope's wishes. These wishes can also be seen in the choice of Dr Dermot Clifford, who in March 1986 was named to succeed another of the four Irish archbishops, Dr Tom Morris of Cashel. He too, in church terms, is a man of the right. The appointment of Dr John Magee to the diocese of Cloyne in 1987, directly from his position as Pope John Paul's secretary, was another clear indication of papal preferences.

The single dominant influence in the Irish church should be that of the Cardinal. For nearly a century the red hat has been conferred on the Archbishop of Armagh (subtle Vatican underlining of the fact that though Armagh lies north of the border the Irish church, like the island of Ireland, is one). The present Cardinal, Tomas O Fiaich, exerts considerable influence in his native Armagh area, where the nationalists regard him as a folk hero. But throughout the country, apart from the fact that each of the other twenty-five members of the hierarchy is a power in his own diocese, the Cardinal has to contend with the fact that the bishops are as divided over the Northern issue as are the laity. Even in the Northern Ireland context, for example, Cardinal O Fiaich, a former President of Maynooth, takes a much more actively nationalist viewpoint than have either the present Bishop of Down and Connor, Dr Cathal Daly, or his predecessor Dr William Philbin.

O Fiaich, while a strong and unequivocal opponent of violence who has repeatedly condemned the IRA, nevertheless managed to make a distinction between the sinner and the sin while the hunger strike was in progress. After a visit to the H-Blocks he made a statement which included the following: 'One would hardly allow an animal to remain in such conditions, let alone a human being. The nearest approach to it that I have seen was the spectacle of hundreds of homeless people living in sewer-pipes in the slums of Calcutta. The stench and filth in some of the cells, with the remains of rotten food and human excreta scattered around the walls, was almost unbearable'.

He also placed himself in the centre of controversy when, in an historic interview with me in the *Irish Press,* he came out in favour of Irish unity. His stature has grown since his appointment, which displeased some among the better-off Dublin middle-classes because of his well-known advocacy of the Irish language and Irish culture — atavistic pursuits in the eyes of such sophisticates.

No longer does the influence of a Cardinal, any Cardinal, automatically reach down into every home in the land or his portrait hang in many homes. Lenten Pastorals, for instance, are very little discussed by the laity. The newspapers no longer automatically allocate several pages each year to lengthy extracts from each bishop's annual animadversion on sin and penance (wanting more of the latter and less of the former). One might thus deduce that the society is becoming more secular, yet one finds that the young priests emerging from seminaries such as Maynooth are markedly conservative, and individual priests can, and do, command as much respect and authority as have any of their predecessors in the past.

To take a literally very concrete example of the church's influence, one cannot underestimate the physical existence of the much-criticised Knock Airport. As a result of the criticism Knock Airport, built through the drive and organising genius of the late

Monsignor James Horan, parish priest of Knock, did change its name to Connacht Regional Airport, but continued to expand its runways! There was some criticism of the project in Fianna Fail, but the urban left was enraged, in particular the leader of the Workers' Party, Tomas MacGiolla, and the Labour Minister for Social Welfare, Barry Desmond. The attacks were directed against the idea of building — and even more costly, maintaining — an airport with runways capable of accommodating passenger jets out in the remote fogs and bogs of Mayo. The £10m airport, of course, is an amenity for the western area, questions of clerical and political skullduggery in procuring the finance notwithstanding. With the recent proliferation of 'moving statues', to be seen according to some of the faithful in various parts of the country, its apologists argue that an Irish pilgrimage site rivalling that of Lourdes may be on the way to fulfilment!

At the time of writing all that can definitely be said regarding the airport's long term viability is that Ireland is the only country in western Europe wherein such an undertaking could be carried out by a parish priest.

Morality Plays

Where morality is discussed within the Irish church it means sexual morality. Although individual priests show their humanity in a manner that reminds one of the significance of the Irish name Mac Entagart (Mac an tSagairt, son of the priest) — in paternal concern rather than literal paternity, let it be said! — the Irish church official does give off a faintly eunuchoid, rather foetid atmosphere concerning sex because most of the would-be arbiters of sexuality are themselves, at least presumptively, celibate. It's rather like teaching swimming from a book without ever having got wet oneself.

Three recent events illustrate the reality of life in Catholic rural Ireland. In 1984, a teenager died in childbirth in Granard, County Longford, apparently in an effort to leave the child, which did not survive, on the steps of the parochial house. No action was taken by her classmates, her teachers or her parents in regard to her pregnancy which, it emerged after the deaths, had been widely spoken of. But the stigma of illegitimacy in rural Ireland was still strong enough to prevent the young mother being given, as of right, the care which her own inexperience denied her.

The second case concerned a teacher in a Catholic convent in County Wexford, Eileen Flynn, who lost her job and a resultant highly-publicised court case for living openly with a married man whose wife had left him. The court agreed with the religious order involved that this was not the sort of example to be given to the pupils of a convent school — and so did most of the public, including her fellow teachers.

Both these morality plays from what might be termed the Theatre of the Irish Conscience were overshadowed by the long-running saga of the Joanne Hayes affair, which in the end proved nothing save that Zola was alive and well and living in County Kerry. The end came in October of 1985 when Mr Justice Kevin Lynch delivered the verdict of a tribunal set up ostensibly to inquire why the gardai had charged Joanne Hayes with the murder of an unnamed infant found at Cahirciveen, County Kerry, the previous year. This baby did not belong to her and forensic evidence proved that it could not have been born to her. The gardai had refused to co-operate with an internal garda inquiry into this point, after a district court had thrown out the case against Hayes. As a result the public tribunal was set up, at vast expense to the taxpayer — it's an ill wind that blows the lawyers no good. The tribunal found that Miss Hayes did not kill the Cahirciveen baby but that she had disposed of the body of another baby discovered near her home at Abbeydorney, County Kerry. The report managed to be critical of both Ms Hayes and the gardai.

The tribunal's investigation into Ms Hayes's sex life (and that of Abbeydorney generally) and the frequent conflict of evidence provided Ireland with salacious gossip for most of the year, but left behind nothing more substantial than some black humour (Question: What is the definition of confusion? Answer: Father's Day in Abbeydorney) and a national feeling that for a time a veil had been lifted on a primitive and rather terrifying Ireland that was probably more widespread than the good churchgoers of the country like to imagine.

The three cases taken together certainly underlined the fact that the laws of Ireland, reflecting church teaching, make it a disturbing place in certain circumstances for someone who either does not want a baby, or would like to have a mate.

In the cities things are different. Dublin Corporation would have hundreds of empty houses on its hands because of emigration, were it not for the numbers of unmarried mothers receiving state benefits.

Interestingly, not long after the publication of the Hayes tribunal's findings, I addressed a gathering of the combined clergy of the Archdiocese of Cashel at a media seminar and found that the main preoccupation of the priests present (over one hundred) was with 'the coming war on divorce'. This was the year before the divorce referendum, but one would have thought that Northern Ireland, unemployment, emigration and crime would also have been burning issues. However, rural Ireland is that bit more untouched by such problems. Many of the priests I spoke to seemed genuinely to believe that were it not for the media many of the problems of the hour would be seen to be far less grievous than was imagined. One lovely old man, the archetypal kindly Irish priest, sighed as he asked me rhetorically, 'Where did we go wrong? Sure we had all those journalists in the classroom. How did we manage to turn them out like that?'

Though marriages are breaking up at such a rate that a divorce referendum was felt to be necessary in 1986, the majority of Irish couples still prefer to get married in church, rather than opt for a registrar's office ceremony. Baptism, First Holy Communion and Confirmation are important occasions for families, particularly the women, and even the poorest will go to great trouble and expense to ensure that their offspring are well turned out to receive the sacraments. In fact, not only Catholic welfare agencies such as the St Vincent de Paul Society but state-run health boards will give needy parents money to help to equip their children for these landmark events.

The women of Ireland in particular are buoyed up by what one might imagine would bear them down, the church of child-rearing and child-bearing. It is they who hitherto have most sustained the church, both by keeping up the Catholic ethos in the home, and very often by acquiring the vocation which their sons subsequently suffered. It was, and to a large degree still is, the women who fuss over the priest and it is the conservative influence of the women, paradoxically enough, which inhibits any meaningful movement toward giving women a greater say in the Irish church. For all the froth of feminist media activity, the majority of women simply are not interested in change.

In the Classroom

The vast majority of the Republic's schools are under the influence of the church. Even in the state-run primary schools the parish priest is usually the school manager, with a say in the appointment of teachers. One of the present major controversies involving the church is a dispute between the Irish National Teachers' Organisation and the hierarchy, which is seeking to have it made mandatory on school teachers in national schools that they sign a declaration that they are practising Catholics. So far, though lay teachers are increasing in numbers throughout the school system, the religious still appoint the principal in secondary schools under their care and the laity prefer clerical-run schools to the exclusively state-controlled vocational schools.

The decline in vocations, particularly for nuns, poses long-term challenges to the security of the twin props of the church in Ireland, the family and the school — each reinforcing the other. The fabric of Irish society would be very different should the educational prop disappear — and despite the criticism levelled at the idea of clerical control of education, not necessarily for the better. Apart from the increasingly obvious trade unionism of teachers, the contribution of the Irish church to education has, objectively speaking, been enormous.

The Christian Brothers, despite excesses of discipline which persisted long after such rigours were frowned upon by educationalists world-wide, did educate the children of the Irish working class and small farmers. The brothers have co-operated in an historic education breakthrough; a decision in 1984 to appoint lay principals was implemented in 1986. Falling numbers played a part in the Brothers' decision, of course; of the 480 Brothers in Ireland's southern province, 160 were retired at the time of writing and only thirty were in the initial stages of training. But the Brothers are still receiving seminarians and their tradition is respected in Ireland.

The wealthier classes could go to the exclusive schools run by, say, the Jesuits or the Loreto nuns but until as late as the middle sixties, without 'The Brothers' and their counterparts in the communities of teaching nuns like the Sisters of Mercy, there would have been very little of an Irish educational system to build on. It would have been a case of construction, rather than expansion and reform. Moreover, while in terms of overall church strategy the system was geared to promote church policy, it did so very often at the expense of a well-recognised sacrifice on the part of the individual nun or priest.

Some of these exceptional people had a lasting effect on their pupils. For instance the dedication of Fr Aidan Lehane, currently a notable headmaster of the Holy Ghost Fathers, combined with the tradition of the order's schools commands great respect amongst pupils, ex-pupils and their families. The similar reputation of Sister Regina of the Order of Mercy, in charge of Carysfort Teacher Training College, rebounded badly on the coalition government when it tried to close down Carysfort at the beginning of 1986 because fewer teachers would be needed in the future. The personality of Sister Regina and the tradition of the college, which had included such distinguished figures amongst its staff as Eamon de Valera and the poet Seamus Heaney, created a national uproar that forced a rethink. The Irish do not want the old style narrowness but they have made it clear, particularly in an era of declining parental authority, that they do want the dedication and discipline of the church's influence in education.

Third World Radicals

Radical thinking on social matters is another facet of the Irish church, partly because of the traditional Irish streak of radicalism present in the church as elsewhere in Irish life, but partly because of the Irish clerical diaspora. The Irish contribution to Roman Catholic missionary activity has been monumental, positively or negatively. Positively, it has done much to spread the church's influence throughout the world, particularly in Africa, Latin America and the United States, where much of Irish-American strength was devoted not to political activity concerning Ireland but to building up the church. Negatively, it is fair to ask what these innovative, energetic and intelligent men and women could have meant to Ireland had they stayed at home to work at other vocations.

The returned missionaries have been influential on attitudes to international affairs; President Reagan's visit in 1984 became the subject of controversy very largely through the interest of Irish nuns and priests who had worked in Central America. Nicky

Kelly, a political prisoner who was widely believed to have been framed by the Special Branch, was released a few weeks after Fr Niall O'Brien, a Columban father who had been released from a Philippine jail, returned to Ireland to a hero's welcome in 1984 and the authorities became alarmed that he might join the picket-lines in support of Kelly.

The astonishing response of the Irish to Bob Geldof's Live Aid rock spectacular — providing the highest per capita donation in the world at over £8m — owned as much to the influence of long-gone Columban, Holy Ghost and other missionaries as it did to folk memories of famine or to Geldof's charisma.

The tradition of putting a penny in a collecting box each week to save the soul of a black baby, so widespread (and patronising) throughout Irish schools, at the time I wrote *Ireland Since the Rising,* showed the popular base for the vast prosyletising effort mounted by the Irish church over generations. This can be seen today in the voluntary work done by thousands of young Irish men and women, trained in various disciplines, who give of their time and knowledge to work in the Third World for various Irish relief agencies such as the hierarchy-sponsored Trocaire (Mercy), or the lay organisation GOAL, largely financed by sportsmen through the energetic endeavours of my colleague on the *Evening Press* sporting staff, John O'Shea. At the time of writing orders with missionary antennae speak out at home, and even get arrested, as in the protests organised by the Sisters for Justice in support of travellers. A former Franciscan, Seamus Claffey, publishes the radical magazine *Resource.* The Jesuits are active in a number of areas, including their centre for Faith and Justice, the school of philosophy and theology in Milltown Park and the Irish School of Ecumenics — a third level institution for the study of ecumenism and peace, founded by Father Michael Hurley in the palmy days of Vatican II which survives with an international reputation in the somewhat harsher climate of Pope John Paul.

The Conference of Major Religious Superiors not alone represents the orders in an organised fashion but speaks out on matters of social concern in a positive way, its stance on justice being particularly admired.

By and large men and women returning to Ireland today from the mission fields come home to the church that formed them radically changed by the churches to which it sent them out.

When I was leaving school my contemporaries who opted for life on the missions with the Holy Ghost Fathers were expecting either to follow in the footsteps of their predecessors, bringing with them a certain particularist form of Irish Catholicism, papalist, authoritarian and brick-and-mortar orientated, or to fit into an existing colonial regime. For instance, at the Holy Ghost Fathers seminary at Kimmage Manor, Dublin, they learned how to conduct themselves if 'presented to the Governor and his Lady', when they got to Africa!

What nobody could foresee was how they should conduct themselves when the Biafran civil war occurred. Many of them either became estranged from the eventually victorious Lagos regime and were expelled from Nigeria or, in reaction to the forces unleashed both by the Biafran famine and by Vatican II, left the priesthood.

They had gone to Africa prepared for a situation which was permanent, welcoming, even grateful. After all, most schools and hospitals in say Africa or the Caribbean were built by missionaries, but the end of the colonial era and the increased educational facilities which the missionaries had helped to initiate created a new and challenging world. Today the challenges are not mainly physical as they were in the fifties — malaria, typhoid and other hazards — but psychological also. 'It may only take a few hours after leaving Ireland to land in the Third World, but it takes a lifetime to adjust', a former school friend of mine, now a Holy Ghost Missionary, told me. Instead of concentrating on infra-structures, today's missionaries specialise in development and teaching communication skills.

The more recent difficulties which Irish missionary societies have had to face include the influence of Roman resistance to liberation theology. Local hierarchies, of course, are responsive to the papacy and tend to attempt to curb the missionary society activists. The average Irish missionary is less anxious today to promote religion in a particular form than to change the structure of society. They do not like the 'split consciousness' approach — merely to build a well, as in a purely 'Third World development' approach, or on the other hand to attempt to evangelise local culture out of existence. They see a connection between the well and God and suffering *now,* a mutuality between themselves and the black and the brown. Reflecting the world-wide effect of a conservative papacy, there tends to be a certain tension between the Irish hierarchy and the great Irish missionary societies, the Jesuits, the Dominican sisters, the Holy Ghosts, the Kiltegan fathers, the Holy Rosary sisters, the Columban fathers, the SMA and the rest of them.

The hierarchy tend to favour Trocaire which, though it is non-evangelical, is Irish, Christian and directly controlled by them. It is also an excellent development agency by world standards even though the volunteer development workers are often in the field only for periods of two years. The missionaries of course serve far longer periods, and it is they who more frequently come to criticise the economic dependency that has followed the achievement of political independence in the Third World. This makes them anti-American and opponents of multinationals, to the dismay of some Irish bishops (and sometimes of the government, as was seen during Reagan's visit).

This tension can be expected to grow rather than diminish as more Irish bishops are appointed according to Pope John Paul's three major criteria of doctrinal soundness, commitment to social progress and the ability to communicate. A fourth consideration, that the applicant be 'known', i.e. that he be publicly seen to meet the other three criteria in the eyes of a local hierarchy or nuncio, is also of great importance.

A Nun's Story

No group reflects the changes in the Irish church more than nuns. In common with the rest of the world, vocations in Ireland are down; the number of girls accepted as entrants to religious orders in 1985 was only 123, whereas in the same year 266 nuns died and ninety-six left the religious life. One of the brightest of the bishops observed to me that he did not think, on present trends, that there would be such a thing as a nun in twenty years' time — a prophecy which, if borne out, would enormously alter the impact of the church in Irish society. Irish womanhood reared without the influence of 'the nuns' would raise children with a far different attitude to church teaching and towards the church's authority than is easily visualised even now. Ideas on the family or politics, for instance, would be vastly altered.

But the qualitative shifts which are occurring are interesting also. A vigorous alternative view is put by Sister Stanislaus, probably the best-known nun in Ireland through involvement with Bishop Peter Birch's many social reforms in County Kilkenny and through her membership of the Commission on Poverty. Her book, *One Million Poor*, was deemed important enough to be launched by the Taoiseach, Dr Garret FitzGerald, such is the esteem in which she is held in high places. *Some* high places, that is; Charles Haughey disbanded the Commission. A public controversy which she had with him mirrored the many conflicts which 'Stan', as she is generally known, has had within her own order from time to time.

In 1987 Stan is forty-six, slight, of middle height, with a vivid open face radiating energy and enthusiasm that takes her through a routine of 24-hour days against a constant background of pain stemming from operations on her spine. Her view of the nun's role in Irish society is that, like the grain of wheat, it must die to be born again.

As she sees it, nuns are no longer 'on campus'; they serve the people at large by living in housing estates as opposed to enclosed religious communities. She argues that Irish nuns have adopted the idea of 'responsible obedience', in which the nun can give expression to her own charisma in fields of her own choice. In practical terms this means a reduction, additional to that caused by falling vocations, in the number of religious in schools, with nuns now working for state organisations, not the Community.

When I interviewed Stan herself it was in a refuge which she runs in Dublin for homeless girls. We were interrupted at one stage by a group who came in 'in fits of laughter' having dressed themselves up as clowns. Stan believes that this atmosphere is essential to running such a home. Her fiery temperament means that discipline does not suffer as a result — the girls, who without her would either be sleeping rough or living in homes afflicted by alcoholism, violence or incest, know that with Stan there is a line which they cross at their peril. Stan argues that there *is* a place for the religious woman in society.

She claims that, although improved levels of education and opportunity are causing women to look elsewhere for a career, the nuns who come into the sisterhood and then leave benefit individually from better training opportunities. Meanwhile, those who stay on react faster to the changes of Vatican II than many religious, whether dealing with the poor in Ireland or in missionary activity.

Mercy nuns in Zambia, for instance, talk of 'their culture', meaning the African culture. Irish nuns are to the fore in questioning their role to bring 'our culture', meaning Irish culture, 'our big institutions', to the mission fields. These, says Stan, are seen 'not as priceless gifts but as a halter round our necks'.

'We're much freer. We see our role as one of service. We have opted to work for the poor, away from power.'

Stan strongly believes that a nun living a life of prayer, and unlike a married, or even single, lay person, can devote more time and provide more of a source of inspiration for lay workers and the deprived than can the deprived themselves. Just as nuns in America have proven themselves willing to stand up to the Pope, Stan is prepared to speak up to the Irish hierarchy, who of course do not universally share her views. The late Bishop Birch was an exception; he admired the work of Jean Vanier, the French Canadian Christian philosopher who founded many hostels for the homeless all over the world. A more typical Irish bishop would not have given Stan the chance to develop as she has. Stan sees a future for nuns working for the church 'away from the altar' although she acknowledges that this type of activity may not win her adherence 'amongst the two-car families in Dublin 4'. However, she is adamant that 'the church of Mass on Sunday is not the answer'.

Attempting to define a new role in a conservative society such as Ireland, albeit one which is in considerable flux, is not easy. Even though Stan's type of operation is run on the belief that 'small is beautiful', she is still faced with having to spend eighty per cent of her time on fund-raising, apart from the attrition of dealing with her superiors. Only time will tell whether her courage, initiative and charisma, or the type of structured authoritarian church furthered by Pope John Paul through his choice of bishops, will prove to be the hallmark of Irish Catholicism in the future.

Modern Pastors

The rightist swing has tended to enhance rather than diminish the reputation of outstanding individuals and institutions. For instance, while it would be true to say that many of the best theologians, notably James Mackey, have left the country (and in some cases the priesthood itself), some men of great calibre remain, attracting general esteem whatever hierarchical reservations they may arouse. One of these is the well-loved Fr Austin Flannery, a Dominican, who edits the journal *Doctrine and Life*. This journal maintains an international level of scholarship that has gained it a position of status and significance amongst intellectual Irish Catholics.

On his sixtieth birthday Fr Flannery, a Tipperary-born theologian who studied at Oxford and Rome, was accorded the rare distinction of a *festschrift* written in his honour. It was presented at a reception in the headquarters of the Bank of Ireland which the Taoiseach, Dr Garret FitzGerald, attended, with a guest list that amounted to a Who's Who of contemporary Dublin.

On the other side of the country, and at the other end of the clerical spectrum, is Padraig Standun, an Irish-speaking curate on Inismaan. Standun is an ardent campaigner for Civil Rights who went to jail in Holy Week 1986 rather than pay his motor tax, in order to highlight the condition of the roads in the Connemara Gaeltacht. He was released almost immediately because someone paid his fine anonymously. Standun, who has been active in several causes on behalf of Connemara, is best known for his novel *Suil le Breith (Expecting Life)*, written in Irish, which tells the story of a young and beautiful girl who gets pregnant and is then taken on as a housekeeper by a priest. It can be bought all over Ireland including, significantly enough, the bookshop in Maynooth. Standun is well thought of by most of his parishioners, especially by young people, though to some older people he is a controversial figure. More likely to be concerned with the problems of finding the rent for a poor family than with the scruples of the devout in the confessional, he is also a priest in good standing with his bishop. The Irish church can sometimes show itself capable of an unexpected 'pluralism'.

Fr Harry Bohan, in adjoining County Clare, has founded a housing co-op run on such business-like lines that it should be adopted nationally as a model for providing Ireland with cheap, well designed housing.

In the North, the troubles have produced special challenges for priests. I have been present when one priest received a message from an IRA unit urging him to visit a local widow to tell her that her son would be shot if he did not leave the area immediately. I was present also when another got word that he was wanted to explain to parents that their son *had* been shot. Another had to leave my company to go on a tour of hospitals to see if a woman's husband, who had been shot by the army at a demonstration a little while earlier, was still alive.

In the North these would rate only as trivial incidents, droplets in the vast tide of human misery swelling in an area where prison building is the only growth industry and the innocent and the beautiful have more enemies than time. In this harsh milieu priests have tended to be somewhat overwhelmed by the scale of the thing, but an exceptional handful have caught the public eye. I know many who deliberately choose to keep out of it — Redemptorists such as Alex Reid or Brendan Meagher, for instance, who could if they wished shed a light on contemporary history that would make headlines, but who prefer to make their contribution away from the limelight. Their tales of the extra-ordinary interface between prisoners, their families, the authorities (sometimes the authorities at the highest level) north and south of the border, must await another day's telling. 'Contact', 'pastoral work', 'negotiation' even, carry nuances which could, if explained with reference to specific incidents, speak volumes for 'the role of the priest in Irish society'.

Others, however, have willy-nilly become national figures, notably Denis Faul, Raymond Murray, Brian Brady and Desmond Wilson, all diocesan clergy.

The first three names will occur and recur in the history of the Troubles for their work in compiling factual dossiers on the treatment meted out to nationalists (inevitably Catholics) by the security forces. They helped to prick the consciences which later set up the tribunals (Amnesty International, the Bennett report etc.) which confirmed the pattern of behaviour to which they first drew attention and had a marked effect on Irish-American opinion in particular.

Faul, through his visits to the prisoners at Long Kesh, and Murray visiting those in the women's prison in Armagh, gained enormous insight into, and influence over, the situation through-

Two decades, four leaders: Jack Lynch, Liam Cosgrave, Charles Haughey and Garret FitzGerald have each held office as Taoiseach since 1966.

G. A. Duncan

R.T.E.

The power of the pen: writers such as Brian Friel, Seamus Heaney, Jennifer Johnston and John McGahern enhanced their own reputations and those of Irish literature.

R.T.E.

R.T.E.

The power of the sword: on Bloody Friday, 17 May 1974, three car bombs in Dublin and one in Monaghan killed 31 people and injured 150. Two years later on 21 July 1976 the British Ambassador, Christopher Ewart-Biggs, was assassinated when his car was bombed. The perpetrators of these outrages have never been found.

Turbulent priests. Denis Faul and Desmond Wilson were stern critics of political and ecclesiastical establishments in Northern Ireland, while Niall O'Brien was jailed, amid international controversy, by the Marcos regime in the Philippines.

out the seventies. Faul became nationally known through his radio and TV appearances and his letters and articles in the press. Many people in Northern Ireland who had a son, father or husband assailed by the security forces, the IRA or loyalist paramilitaries thought of contacting 'Dinny' Faul, a teacher at St Patrick's Academy, Dungannon, before ever considering any other form of succour. He clashed with Cardinal Conway in 1969 for his criticism of the northern judiciary, but as the struggle wore on he came to be highly respected by church authorities. Deeply conservative, and as a churchman fundamentally opposed to violence, he helped to set up an underground escape route, largely paid for by himself, to help lads who wanted to quit paramilitary life to leave the country.

He lost some of his ascendancy over the nationalist community in the cauldron of passion created by the hunger strikes, when the IRA accused him of using his influence to end the hunger strikes in a way which harmed the aspirations of Bobby Sands and the others, but he is still a nationally-respected figure. He is admired for his courage as much as anything else; simply to drive home at night with his reputation in Northern Ireland, at risk from every set of initials in the lethal alphabet soup, IRA, UDA, UDR, SAS, demands more courage than most of us possess.

Fr Des Wilson, who lives in Ballymurphy, would approximate more to the European idea of a 'worker priest' inasmuch as he shares the life of his people, running classes in Art and French and co-operative ventures of all sorts in an effort to make life bearable in that beleaguered war-torn area of Belfast. He too is known for his clashes with the authorities, including church authorities, having been severely restrained in his activities by his then Bishop, Dr William Philbin. When Dr Cathal Daly succeeded Dr Philbin, Fr Wilson was restored to an episcopal favour which continues to sit somewhat uneasily with his unabated outspokenness on issues such as prison conditions, the Anglo-Irish Agreement or 'institutional violence'.

Other signs of synthesis working out rather well between the traditions of the past and the strains of today are exemplified by the flourishing school of theology in Trinity College, Dublin run by Professor Sean Freyne, an ex-priest. When I was researching *Ireland Since the Rising*, Trinity College was a place in which a Catholic was forbidden by the hierarchy to enroll without first seeking permission of his bishop. Today several of the lecturers in its theology school are Catholic clergy.

The major Catholic seminary in the country, St Patrick's College, Maynooth, is certainly a more conservative place theologically than Trinity. But for humanity and hospitality, Maynooth would have very little competition anywhere and its professors and students are certainly fully in touch with international trends. Maynooth opened its doors to lay students in 1967 and now has more lay students, particularly girls, than clerical ones; in fact, its professor of English is not alone a woman but a Protestant, the brilliant Barbara Hayley. Sean O'Casey, who in his memoirs described the great spire of the College church as being 'like a dagger through the heart of Ireland' would have been bemused at the thought that one day the roads around Maynooth would be filled with girls in jeans hitch-hiking to and from classes. Maynooth is also a major bastion of Irish tradition in scholarship, particularly in language and history.

Along with notable clergy and nuns the Irish church has also produced some outstanding lay activists. Frank Duff, the founder of the Legion of Mary, was active during the early part of the period under review, and supporters of his are already collecting evidence to help towards the cause of his sanctification in Rome. Alfred O'Rahilly, a Professor of University College, Cork, Catholic apologist and controversialist, who ended his days by becoming a Holy Ghost priest, was also active. Amongst lay figures prominent on the Catholic landscape today, one would have to take note of the work of Brian McKeown, of Trocaire, or Jerome Connolly of the hierarchy's Commission on Justice and Peace.

But at the risk of being condemned for being unduly particularist, I would cite the work of a number of Catholic journalists as being of significance, chiefly those of the cadre who reported on the Second Vatican Council and were instrumental in bringing its winds of change to Ireland. John Horgan of the *Irish Times*, Louis MacRedmond of the *Irish Independent*, Sean Mac Reamoinn and Kevin O'Kelly of RTE, and figures such as Jack Dowling, a lay theologian as well as a writer and broadcaster, did more to enlighten the Irish Catholic public about the greater world outside that of 'traditional Irish values' than a thousand pulpits. Though religious journalism does not now have the appeal it had in Vatican II days, a figure such as T.P. O'Mahony of the *Irish Press* is still accorded authority.

In the sphere of communications, the long-running religious programme, 'Radharc', ('sight' or 'view') is still influential and popular under the editorship of Father Joe Dunn. The priests who came to notice with the development of the programme, such as Tom Stack, Billy FitzGerald and Peter Lemass, have become household names.

To paraphrase Khruschev's famous description of India, the Irish church is like an elephant — it won't run and it won't fall.

6

The Church and State

*The Contraceptive Question; Referendum on Abortion;
Pluralist Vision; Divorce Rejected*

THE elephantine motif was certainly borne out, in terms of strength, in three major political controversies during the period under review, concerning contraception, abortion and divorce.

The Contraceptive Question

The contraception controversy came to a head, if that is the correct term, in 1979, the year in which Charles Haughey succeeded in having implemented a family planning bill which he termed 'an Irish solution to an Irish problem'. The 'problem' had been growing for the previous fifteen years, public discussion on the topic having commenced during the years of the Vatican Council when, so far as I am aware, a small women's group founded by my wife asked the Irish hierarchy to press for a ruling on the issue during the closing stages of the Second Vatican Council.

Their Lordships apparently found the idea of discussing 'the pill' too difficult to swallow and little was heard of the subject until I raised it on RTE television in January 1964 in a discussion with the President of the Irish Medical Association, Dr William O'Dwyer. The resultant detonation of controversy may not have greatly enlightened the Irish public, but it did a great deal for my education on the subject of talking about Things like That on the national television station, the impropriety of which those who disagreed with me, and they appeared at the time to be legion, did not hesitate to bring to the attention of my employers, the *Irish Press*.

Over the years further publicity was generated by feminist groups like those led by Mary Kenny and Anne Harris (both of whom worked for the *Irish Press* at the time) who, having first announced their intentions to an avid media, brought a consignment of contraceptives to Dublin on a train from Belfast. Customs officers, acting on instructions, took no action against the smugglers, thereby frustrating any possibility that the prohibition on contraception might be tested in the courts. Caution on the part of Ireland's male legislators also frustrated the efforts of civil rights-minded parliamentarians such as Mary Robinson, Trevor West and John Horgan to have the law changed. The Supreme Court decided on 10 December 1973 that it was unconstitutional to prohibit the importation of contraceptives. The effect of the judgement was that contraceptives might be imported, but not sold. This decision, which was carried by a majority of four of the five judges, followed an appeal from a judgement of the High Court by Mrs Mary McGee, a mother of four children, who had been prescribed contraceptives on health grounds but had had her imports seized by the Customs. In delivering judgement in favour of Mrs McGee, Mr Justice Walsh said: 'The private morality of its citizens does not justify intervention by the state into the activities of those citizens unless and until the common good requires it'.

But in 1974 a bill to legalise the sale of contraceptives to married couples was voted down. It is true to say that until the Haughey Act Ireland officially set its face against what spokesmen for the hierarchy termed the 'contraceptive mentality', arguing that such thinking led inevitably to divorce and abortion. Unofficially, there was a huge rise in prescriptions for the pill —prescribed for 'regulation', not contraception —and the accessibility of Belfast, London and increasingly of sympathetic doctors within the Republic meant that devices such as diaphragms and coils became more and more available.

However, as the census figures show, the Irish population continued to grow, despite the fact that large families were increasingly unsupportable and increasingly difficult to care for in an era of working wives and rising inflation. One side-effect of that situation was a flourishing 'abortion trail'; some 3,000 Irish women underwent abortions in England annually, according to official statistics, and the actual numbers may have been twice as high. Certainly my private observation of the prevalence of abortion in Irish society would seem to indicate that the official figures do not tell the whole story.

Desmond O'Malley made the speech of his life in favour of Barry Desmond's amendment to the contraceptives bill, and was expelled as a result from Fianna Fail five days later, on 25 February 1985. In his speech he indicated the likely effect on unionist opinion of the bill's being defeated, arguing for legislation which took account of pluralism in Irish society and for a twenty-six county state that was 'really a Republic, practising real republican traditions'. 'Otherwise', he said, 'we can forget about the possibility of ever succeeding in persuading our fellow Irishmen in the North to join us'. O'Malley defended the right of young people in particular to the 'exercise of their own private consciences' and he faced the church/state issue squarely. He said: 'I have seen a Reverend Bishop saying that we can legislate for private morality. I beg to take issue with him . . . I do not believe that the interests of the state, our Constitution and of this Republic, would be served by putting politics before conscience in regard to this. There is a choice of a kind that can only be answered by saying that I stand by the Republic and accordingly I will not oppose this Bill'.

O'Malley's new party, the Progressive Democrats, took its slogan, 'Building a new Republic', from this speech. He formally launched the PDs at 12.00 noon on 21 December, 1985. Whether or not history will record that there was any symbolism in the fact that this was the shortest day of the year we do not know, but it is certain, Haughey factor or no, that O'Malley's new party is unique in late twentieth-century Europe for growing directly out of a church/state issue.

While the party has not fulfilled the early promise of opinion polls, it has already proved itself a significant force in Irish politics. Ironically its principal adversary, Charles Haughey, was able to proceed successfully with cuts and right-wing policies, although in a very vulnerable minority government position, because of — not despite — the emergence of the PDs. For the rise of the PDs coupled with Fine Gael's known espousal of such policies, showed that there was a secure base in public opinion for him to be able to safely ignore any would-be 'heavers' left in the party. Consequently, Fianna Fail is clearly moving from being a party of social preservation to one of social change, a circumstance that must assuredly have a profound significance for church/state relationships in the future.

Referendum on Abortion

The extraordinary thing about the abortion controversy, which divided the Republic far more bitterly than the Northern Ireland issue ever did, is that a few short years after the uproar people are already unsure as to how or why it all began.

The set-piece, visible beginning of the campaign was clear enough. In April 1981 Garret FitzGerald, then leader of the opposition, gave the Pro-Life Amendment Campaign (PLAC) a commitment (in the face of a looming general election) that if returned to government he would hold a referendum to introduce an amendment to the Constitution to prevent abortion being introduced to Ireland. Haughey followed suit.

But why was the campaign in place? Whence came the need to protect Ireland from an abortion law? The general climate regarding the subject, for the good reason of regard for life and the bad one of hypocrisy, was well summed-up for me by a convent school teacher who, having been abandoned by her lover, had once felt herself forced to take the 'abortion trail' to London. 'Most abortions', she said, 'are to save the life of the father'.

Prior to 1981 the only concerted anti-abortion effort I was aware of was the particularly distasteful one of a series of visits to girls' schools throughout the country by an American priest, who backed up his lecture with such props as foetuses embalmed in glass jars. One of my children had nightmares long after that ill-advised man visited her school.

A principal apologist for the anti-abortion amendment and also for the subsequent anti-divorce campaign was the Dublin barrister, William Binchy, of the Law Reform Commission. Even he could not say precisely when the decision was taken to press for a constitutional amendment. PLAC was already active before Binchy became attracted to its work. Dr Julia Vaughan, another principal figure in the PLAC campaign, first came to my attention one winter evening in 1981 when she called to my office. Petite, intense, at the time on a diet of 500 calories a day, Dr Vaughan left me in no doubt that her slight calorific intake bore no relationship to the force and energy which she and her like-minded medical and legal friends could, and would, display in support of her crusade. Even the manner of the meeting bespoke organisational ability — I had been asked to see her out of the blue by a priest who had taught me over thirty years earlier.

One can only speculate as to where the switch was thrown. By the Pope himself? Right-wing American church circles? Opus Dei? All that can be said with certainty is that apparently by some osmotic process during 1980 and 1981 various groups in Irish society suddenly became disturbed at the thought that abortion was about to be inflicted on the country. These included the Irish Catholic Doctors' Guild, the Guild of Catholic Nurses, the Irish Association of Lawyers for the Defence of the Unborn, The Irish Pro-Life Movement, and the most vocal Society for the Protection of the Unborn Child (SPUC). All came together in Dublin in April 1981 beneath the umbrella title of the Pro-Life Amendment Campaign (PLAC) under the chairmanship of Dr Julia Vaughan.

The pro-amendment lobby proved so powerful that a bill to permit the holding of the referendum was introduced in the Dail on 9 February 1983 by Michael Noonan, Minister for Justice, whose introductory speech admirably stated the position at the time and encapsulated the public position of the groupings demanding the amendment:

'The Bill proposes to amend section 3 of Article 40 of the Constitution by adding the following subsection —

3^0 The State acknowledges the right to life of the unborn and, with due regard to the equal right of life to the mother, guarantees in its laws to respect, and, as far as practicable, by its laws to defend and vindicate that right.

The government are proceeding with this measure in accordance with the committment in the Programme for Government that legislation would be introduced to have adopted the Pro-Life Amendment published by the outgoing government. As stated in the programme, the Parliamentary Labour Party reserves the right to a free vote on this issue.

'I think it right to refer briefly to the background. The existing statute law on the subject is contained in sections 58 and 59 of the Offences against the Person Act 1861. The effect of those sections, broadly speaking, is to make it an offence unlawfully to procure an abortion. Until recent years, those provisions were regarded as adequate but developments, mainly in other countries, have taken place that have given rise to concern amongst many people. It has become apparent that judicial decisions concerning abortion can alter fundamentally what had been accepted to be the law, even to the extent of introducing what is virtually a system of abortion on demand.'

Noonan said that a situation might arise where an Irish government might find itself pressurised by a decision made abroad — in Strasbourg, for example — into introducing legislation to facilitate abortion, or alternatively faced with a series of legal actions before the European Court. Recent developments in cases under the European Convention on Human Rights are such as to suggest that that Convention may be interpreted as conferring a right to have an abortion. 'In this context, it is necessary to think of the United States Supreme Court decision on marital privacy. That proved to be the first step on the road to what has become something very close to abortion on demand.'

The wording which Noonan proposed to introduce was Fianna Fail's. FitzGerald having led the way, Haughey would not and could not show himself 'soft on abortion' and only two days before losing power, on the eve of a confidence debate in which defeat stared him in the face, felt it necessary to issue the Pro-Life Amendment Proposal which the bishops greeted as follows:

'While no constitutional provision can of itself be a full response to the problem of abortion, the text of the proposed amendment does seem to contribute positively to safeguarding the right to life of the unborn and as such it is welcome'.

In his legal opinion, Peter Sutherland found the Fianna Fail wording: '. . . ambiguous and unsatisfactory. In particular it is not clear as to what life is being protected; as to whether "the unborn" is protected from the moment of fertilisation or alternatively is left unprotected until an independently viable human being exists at twenty-five to twenty-eight weeks; faced with the dilemma of saving the life of the mother, a doctor knowing that to do so will terminate the life of the "unborn" will be compelled by the wording to conclude that he can do nothing.

Whatever his intention he will have to show *equal* regard for both lives and his predominant intent will not be a factor. In these circumstances I cannot approve of the wording proposed.' Sutherland went on to point out that 'certain contraceptives can operate after fertilisation; then these would be abortifacient if human life commences on conception. Thus the importation, dissemination and use of such contraceptives would be prohibited and as an example, the use of the "morning after" pill in the treatment of rape victims will not be permissible nor will the use of such contraceptives in certain conditions of the health of a woman — e.g. valvular heart disease, diabetes'.

What Sutherland had proposed by way of new wording was: 'Nothing in this constitution shall be invoked to invalidate any provision of a law on the grounds that it prohibits abortion'.

In response, the hierarchy issued a statement on 29 March 1983 which said:

> 'The new wording proposed by the Minister for Justice does indeed seek to prevent abortion being introduced as a consequence of a judgement by the courts. It has, however, been acknowledged in Dail Eireann that this wording would not exclude the possibility that in the future a law could be passed permitting abortion in some form, without a direct vote of the people. Experience in other countries shows that this possibility is not as remote as it might seem.
>
> 'It is our earnest hope that, at the conclusion of the debate, our legislators will put before the people a form of amendment which will give them the opportunity to decide whether or not they wish to give unborn human life the full constitutional protection already guaranteed to every citizen'.

The Dail finally approved the Fianna Fail wording on 27 April. By then, Fine Gael had been riven by Sutherland's alternative; in fact, eight members of the party had to be given special permission to abstain on the vote lest their expulsion split the party and so overthrow the government. FitzGerald had said that there would be no free vote but the archetypal Fine Gael back-bencher, Oliver J. Flanagan, when asked by a Radio Eireann interviewer about his views on losing the whip, spoke in the authentic tones of Darkest Mountmellick (his County Laois base) when he replied that if anyone should lose the whip it should be Dr FitzGerald for his failure to keep his solemn committment and for 'his efforts to terrorise every mother, and to terrorise every woman in the country'.

On 22 August, as bitter debate raged throughout the land, the hierarchy issued a statement which contained the following:

'While some conscientiously hold a different opinion, we are convinced that a clear majority in favour of the Amendment will greatly contribute to the continued protection of unborn human life in the laws of our country. This could have a significant impact in a world where abortion is often taken for granted. A decisive "Yes" to the Amendment will, we believe, in the words of Pope John Paul II in Limerick, constitute a "witness before Europe and before the whole world to the dignity and sacredness of all human life, from conception until death".'

In a final pastoral salvo on 1 September, Archbishop Dermot Ryan issued a statement which indicated clearly where duty lay. Amongst other things it said: 'Over the last few weeks many people have been asking me for guidance. My advice to them and to all of you, is that a "Yes" vote on Wednesday will protect the right to life of the unborn child; it will not create a threat to expectant mothers; it will block any attempt to legalise abortion in this country'.

On Wednesday 7 September 1983, the nation accepted Dr Ryan's guidance. The amendment was carried by 841,233 votes to 416,136.

One coda may be added to the abortion referendum saga: on 19 December 1986 Mr. Justice Hamilton, President of the High Court, decided in favour of SPUC in an action that organisation had brought against a family planning clinic. The Judge found that, according to the Constitution as amended in 1983, it was illegal for the clinic to give women advice concerning abortion facilities in England. This judgement, coupled with the fear of what further actions SPUC might take concerning the type of contraceptives mentioned in the Sutherland reservations, has raised a serious question mark over the continued operation of family planning advice centres throughout Ireland.

Pluralist Vision

The referendum result was a personal tragedy for Garret FitzGerald, who from the early seventies had been stressing the need for a pluralism throughout Ireland. In 1971 he had written to the *Irish Times* criticising the Fianna Fail government proposal to hand over the previously non-denominational vocational schools to the Catholic church. Bravely, for the time, he said: 'We are not prepared to see the schools we have established handed over to the ecclesiastical authorities of one church'.

The following year he wrote a book in which he stated that one of the obstacles to Irish unity was the justifiable fear of the Northern Protestants, given the Republic's record, that they would be 'subjected to an authoritarian desire to enforce private morality by means of public law'. Even as the PLAC onslaught gathered force he went on radio (RTE, 27 September 1981) to say that he wanted to: 'lead a crusade, a republican crusade to make this a genuine Republic, on the principles of Tone and Davis'. He said that one of his principal motivations in politics was to dismantle the sectarian barriers the Republic had erected against the North, and criticised Haughey's 1979 family planning act: 'We expect the Northern unionists to join a state which in 1979 was bringing in laws based on the theology of one church. Now that has to change, and what I want to do is lead public opinion towards that'.

FitzGerald's diagnosis had a deal of truth in it. I remember Desmond Boal, Paisley's confidant and one of the few intellectuals produced by Unionism, telling me at the time what an unfortunate response the community schools issue elicited in his political circles.

Now, by decision of the Irish parliament endorsed by the people, the wishes of the Catholic church leadership had clearly prevailed, at a time when Garret FitzGerald was head of the Irish government. While the abortion amendment campaign was reaching its final crescendo in 1983, FitzGerald was launching the New Ireland Forum. This was supposed to result in a blueprint for a country in which there would be no fear of Catholic domination. One could hardly blame unionists for being some-what underwhelmed by the high-minded noises emanating from the Constitutional Crusaders at the Forum, while at the same time they were listening to Protestant church leaders protesting at the sectarian proposals of many of the participants in the Forum.

When one looks back on those three years of mounting unemployment, the political instability of having three general elections in a short time, the subtraction from governments' concentration on economic problems by preoccupations with the Forum and the amendment issue, the power of the Two Colonialisms can be seen manifesting itself clearly: Mother Church dictating how the referendum should go; Mother England creating both the necessity for, and outcome of, the Forum deliberations.

Rome acted on the lessons of the campaign. Dr Dermot Ryan, Archbishop of Dublin, was brought to Rome as pro-Prefect of the congregation for the evangelisation of peoples, the former Propaganda Fide. The bishop who, next to him, had figured most prominently in the campaign, Dr Kevin McNamara, was unexpectedly plucked from distant Kerry and installed in Dublin. Privately, however, Rome was somewhat unhappy at the style in which the campaign was conducted. The stridency and divisiveness were disliked, and word to that effect was conveyed to Dublin via the Nuncio, Dr Alibrandi.

Incredible as it may seem, with the enemy victorious on the field and the taste of blood still fresh on their lips, FitzGerald decided to give battle to the conservatives yet again, less than three years later. This time the issue was divorce.

Divorce Rejected

Fine Gael took a battering at the polls in the local government elections of June 1985; the party managed to secure only thirty per cent of the poll, a result which, if repeated in a general election, would have given Fianna Fail a majority of something like thirty seats. And in the European Parliament elections held in June of the previous year the party had shown an overall drop in support, and Labour had lost all of its four seats. Clearly the government was in no shape to embark on new and risky moral crusades.

However, a number of factors were at work. There was, and is, a serious problem of broken marriages in the country; the lowest figure not disproved is of the order of 70,000 and rising. Secondly Fine Gael, as part of FitzGerald's overall liberalisation programme, had been committed to ending the constitutional prohibition on divorce since as far back as 1978, and Desmond O'Malley's new party, the Progressive Democrats, had been threatening to steal FitzGerald's clothes on the issue.

The Taoiseach was finally pushed into the dangerous waters of a pro-divorce campaign by one of his own parliamentary party, Michael O'Leary, the former Labour leader, who had joined Fine Gael. In November 1985, as feelers were being put out by the O'Malleyites towards prospective defectors from other parties, O'Leary introduced a private member's bill to amend the Constitution and facilitate the introduction of divorce. A free vote was allowed and the measure was defeated. FitzGerald in turn announced on TV that he too favoured removing the constitutional ban on divorce. This caused a public clash with a leading Fine Gael conservative, the Minister for Defence, Patrick Cooney, who told the Dail that he and a majority of Fine Gael opposed divorce. Two days later on 8 December, the Feast of the Immaculate Conception, a bad date to be indulging in such controversy in Irish politics, FitzGerald felt obliged to state that he wanted no delay in removing the constitutional prohibition and that, moreover, he spoke 'for a majority within Fine Gael, whatever anyone else may say'. He was back on the same path strewn with banana-skins on which he had embarked by first accepting the proposal for an anti-abortion amendment in haste, and then spending two years repenting it at leisure.

When the Labour Party introduced its own bill, FitzGerald voted against it on the grounds that it would be wrong to change the law without first finding out the views of the churches. Catholic church representatives had already told the Dail committee on marital breakdown, which had been sitting for several years, that they were against divorce. When the Taoiseach consulted the church, he may have been depressed, but he can hardly have been surprised.

FitzGerald should now have done as was promised during the abortion referendum, and introduced various pro-family measures: family courts and conciliation services, a higher marriage age and, above all, legislation to protect the entitlements of people affected by divorce. Despite these omissions, and the fact that only eleven Fine Gael TDs had shown themselves prepared to vote for the Labour Party's bill, the government published its proposals on 23 April 1986.

Sub-section 3 of Article 41 of the Constitution, which had stood since its introduction in 1937, was to be dropped; it said flatly: 'No law shall be enacted providing for the granting of a dissolution of marriage'. The courts were to be empowered to grant divorce. Where a marriage had failed for five years, remarriage was allowed for if there was no reasonable prospect of a reconciliation, as long as any dependent spouse and children were provided for. Legislation was to provide for a variety of questions related to marital breakdown.

The opinion polls initially favoured FitzGerald's initiative. Fianna Fail did not officially oppose the proposals, but many TDs campaigned privately against them and Michael Woods, a former Minister for Health and a member of the Dail committee on marital breakdown, said that the introduction of divorce would unleash a 'Frankenstein's monster' on the land.

Fine Gael deputies divided publicly on the issue. Patrick Cooney returned to the attack as did a number of others, so many that it may be true to say that more of the Fine Gael parliamentary party opposed the measure, or did not campaign for it, than actively supported it.

Church opposition was more restrained than in the abortion controversy, the official line being contained in a communication from the four Roman Catholic archbishops which termed the government's proposal 'the most unrestrictive form of divorce in the world today'. Only a few bishops, notably Dr McNamara and Bishop Newman of Limerick, pursued the issue with any vigour.

The unofficial line was pursued quietly but effectively. It was well exemplified by the following anecdote told to me by a Fine Gael minister:

'I was at Sunday Mass the week before the referendum. The parish priest is a visitor to my home and the curate is a close personal friend. The curate stood up in the pulpit to give the sermon. He said that he knew people would be wondering how the church would react to the forthcoming vote. But it wasn't for the church to tell anyone how to vote. That was a political matter. They all had their consciences and they knew what was right and wrong. However, it was of course a most serious matter and the church recognised that it had a responsibility to help people arrive at a correct decision.

'Then he looked down at me and said that accordingly the following Wednesday there'd be a day of prayer followed by Mass and Communion so that everyone would have the opportunity of receiving the grace to make a correct decision.

'As I walked out of that church I could see Fine Gael supporters I had known over the years dropping away from me on every side. . . .'

The public role played by PLAC in the abortion debate was now taken over by the Family Solidarity League, and the polls reflected a similar continuing drop. Such influences, combined with the behind-the-scenes efforts of groups like the Knights of Columbanus and Opus Dei, had a potent effect. So did the supply of money and campaign advice from Catholic sources in the US.

The coup de grâce was probably administered in a brilliant TV performance on the 'Today Tonight' programme by William Binchy, a week before polling day. Earlier I mentioned the failure to put in family legislative changes before embarking on the campaign. Binchy deftly highlighted the re-marriage aspect of the issue and pointed to the lack of safeguards for property entitlements, including social welfare entitlements for the first family. As many Irish marriages, particularly in the country where land is involved, have a property component this argument, which the anti-campaigners had already been making to some effect outside the studio, had a perceptible impact even on people who favoured divorce.

In an uncertain era of rising costs and unemployment, people entered the lonely confessional of the polling booth bereft of the alibi of the congregation to confront the imagined loss of their land or their children's allowances, and in a time of frightening change and culture shock opted for the safe, the known, and the voices of childhood instruction.

The result was another disaster for FitzGerald and the government. The proposal for divorce was defeated by a majority of 935,843 against, 538,279 for.

Perhaps not surprisingly, the year closed with the Labour Party determined to go it alone in future general elections. Ideological differences apart, the two bruising defeats sustained in its referenda encounters with the forces representing church teaching were a prime reason why, for the first time in the history of the state, an outgoing administration found itself so demoralised that it did not offer itself for re-election.

Rome had won a victory but as the Church of Ireland Bishop of Cork, Most Reverend Samuel Poyntz, said after the vote, quoted in *America,* 26 July 1986:

> 'The problem will not just go away. Meanwhile suffering, unrecognised unions, and the problem for children will continue to be swept under the carpet, Irish-style. The glorious vision of the New Ireland Forum has been set aside — hopefully temporarily — and we have, for all our Republican claims, settled for a divided Ireland rather than a Christian, pluralist and united land.
>
> 'Some who have consistently backed the New Ireland Forum process and the Anglo-Irish Agreement will feel let down. A valuable opportunity to demonstrate compassion, Christian generosity, and comprehensiveness has been lost for the time being. Many will interpret the 1986 Referendum result as sending out a signal that we are not prepared to accept as of now the price of unity by consent. However, history has a strange way of righting things, and I believe perhaps within ten years, certainly before the year 2000, we will have accepted divorce. . . .'

Perhaps.

One other point should be made about the referenda triumphs of those who battled for 'traditional values' over the claims of those who either pointed North, or indicated those who went east to England (for abortions, contraceptive devices, divorce or jobs), or who lived in Ireland amidst the debris of broken marriages. It concerns the politicians' attitudes to that other central tragic, but unacknowledged, Irish theme, emigration.

Nothing was heard of this topic, of course, during either the 'heaves' which convulsed Fianna Fail, the referenda campaigns or in fact during the four general elections held between 1981 and 1987, a period during which this traditional Irish scourge manifested itself again only too clearly. The reason for the politicians' reticence was perfectly described at a seminar on emigration attended by experts from all over the country and from England (7 April 1987). The presenters of one paper, two young men from Kerry, described their response from their local TD:

'Politicians *don't* like to talk about emigration because they say if you talk about it, or propose money for projects to help the emigrants, you'll only be drawing attention to the problem, or be accused of making it worse, whereas if you say nothing, there's a fair chance that the problem will solve itself. They'll go away and maybe get jobs, and either send back money, or come back some day with money made. But they won't be costing the state anything — if they stayed at home, they'd be a terrible drain'.

Yet it is at the point of emigration (and here of course I'm talking about forced emigration) that the implications of both the Catholic birthrate and those of Ireland's fiscal, agricultural and industrial policies most tellingly come home. The 'terrible drain' the politicians indicated, that of unemployment benefits, is of course as nothing compared to this far more terrible drain of the nation's most priceless asset, her educated youth, out of the country.

7

Blinkered Industry

Workers Unite; Inept Enterprise; In the Air, On the Air;
Private Sector; Agriculture; Forestry; Fisheries; Natural Gas; Oil;
Mining

WRITING in the Irish Management Institute's journal *Management* (July/August 1984), Dr George Delafield dealt with IQ results in American and English intelligence tests and said: 'What is clear from most of the studies that have been carried out is that some of the greatest entrepreneurs in the world are Irish men and women, but this is true for the large part only for those who leave Ireland. This indicates that there's something in Irish culture which constrains entrepreneurial action'.

The 'Two Colonialisms' resulting in lack of capital, lack of self-confidence, the absence of a climate of opinion supportive of belief in one's own ability, lack of a work ethic in the Roman Catholic church, even climate, a particularly enervating force, these all play a part in explaining Delafield's 'something'.

The facts are that in a self-operated enterprise, be it business, farm or whatever, Irish economic and industrial experience has not encouraged a belief in the assured return, either in rewards or advancement, for years of hard work. 'He who tries and does his best, goes down the road like all the rest' is a belief widely held by Irish workers. Dr Delafield pointed out that American management develops strong traits of self-control and motivation. American managers work in an environment where if one has 'A' (i.e. drive, initiative) then 'B' (i.e. reward) automatically follows. Irish experience tends to be along the lines that 'If an individual believes that what he or she does makes no difference, then why bother?'

It can fairly be said that in the years 1965 to 1985 the position of the Irish trade union movement stayed the same — only worse. The proliferation (there are some 100 Irish unions), and hence the weakening of the movement as a whole, continued. The period could be said to have begun with the movement pursuing a carrot dangled for it by Sean Lemass, who needed its support for his economic policies, and who therefore ushered in the twenty-one-year era under review by conceding a wage round of 12 per cent. The National Wage Agreements which this rise initiated were hailed as a breakthrough in employer-labour relationships, unique to Ireland. They failed, however, to prevent damaging disruption in every section of the economy in which labour was sufficiently well organised to make its muscle felt: among power workers, police, teachers, civil servants . . . the list is as long as the category of unionised workers.

On one level, as the following table shows, it might be concluded that this militancy paid off, particularly in the public sector.

Percentage increase in real pay (inflation adjusted) per person 1971–81

Sector	Percentage
Established Civil Service	18.5
Primary Teachers	19.4
Secondary Teachers	25.7
Gardai, Wardens	34.3
Prison Officers	22.1
Army	13.7
Average Industrial Earnings	9.3
Growth in Real GDP	17.0

Despite the foregoing apparent gains, the workers who either formed part of or supported these categories were in fact losing out so badly to unemployment and taxation that, by 1986, the picture on both fronts was frightening.

By November 1986 emigration was rampant, 18 per cent of the workforce was unemployed, and the Minister for Finance, John Bruton, told the Dail that PAYE workers who still had jobs were paying four times as much tax on average as farmers and a third more than the self-employed. Levies and health charges deducted at source from the hapless PAYE payer were still owed by farmers and the self-employed for the previous three years: £24m in the case of farmers, £62m by the self-employed.

The Department of Finance figures released on 7 April 1987 showed that the PAYE workers fared even worse than Bruton had indicated. In 1986 the PAYE sector paid £1987m in tax; the farmers £37m, and in fact this amount was outstripped by the amount refunded to farmers in VAT repayments, £79.4m. The self-employed contributed less than 10 per cent of the PAYE figure, a total of £172.7m.

An ambassador from a country which has a number of factories in Ireland told me that he could always tell which were managed by his countrymen and which were under Irish management as soon as he got to the door. 'At the Irish-run factory, the managing director meets me — very friendly. Where my compatriots run things I am met at the door by the managing director — *and* the union representative . . .'

The low level of co-operation built up between the unions and society, represented by government, may be gauged from the statement of the Irish Congress of Trade Unions to the National Economic and Social Council (NESC Report No. 53, *Economic and Social Policy 1980*–1983): 'We reject the suggestion that pay increases in the public sector should be based on the government's capacity to pay'. Yet when the first National Understanding was signed by trade unions, employers and government, its signatories noted that: 'The success of the National Understanding depends on parallel contributions from all three parties involved .. They recognise the need for a radical change in the relationship between government and both sides of industry . . .'

Under the Irish system even a senior executive, apparently enjoying the advantages of expense account meals and travel and a pleasant home in a leafy suburb, stands in an invidious relationship to his European counterpart. His salary of £30/35,000 bears no relation to his take-home pay. Depending on the size of his family, the bottom line could be as little as one third of his taxable earnings, and is unlikely to be more than 40 per cent. Nor will the various deductions for pension, Voluntary Health Insurance, or pay-related social insurance actually cover the outgoing which may arise. There's always a shortfall.

'Free' education means nothing of the sort. At the earlier levels, apart from 'voluntary contributions' to the children's schools, the executive will have had to pay for books, travel, uniforms, sports equipment and so on. A school of his own choice which has remained outside the 'free scheme' can push up these costs astronomically. In any case, they will be astronomical when university time rolls around. Despite Scandinavian levels of taxation, government subsidies in education, as in the ramshackle health system, are quite inadequate.

Similarly the health system leaves gaps. Although dental care and spectacles are levied for, the executive will find himself paying in both cases. Where more serious health problems arise, he is increasingly likely to find himself the victim of the Irish growth in three-tier medicine. If he lives in the provinces the medical advice he receives will frequently be to by-pass the local regional hospital and its experts and seek the better treatment available from a Dublin consultant; in Dublin he is likely to find that the consultant of his choice now operates, not in an ordinary hospital, but in one of the new luxury clinics (the Blackrock Clinic or the Mater Private Hospital) which are run on American lines. Treatment here is more expensive than that ordinarily covered by Voluntary Health Insurance. Voluntary Health Insurance rates have therefore been raised considerably so that the executive, never mind the more lowly-paid white collar worker, finds one more frustration added to the climate wherein he is supposed to make his dynamic and innovative contribution to good industrial relations and the production of improved goods and services.

If, in the teeth of the foregoing, he had managed to save a little money, say £3–£5,000 in a building society, the introduction of a Deposit Interest Retention Tax on savings (DIRT) by the coalition would have caused him to follow the example of thousands of other small savers and transfer his money out of the country, to dream wistfully thereafter of following it. The 'Black Hole' is not merely an economic reality; it also consists of broken dreams and frustrations.

One of the most knowledgeable of Irish industrialists, Dr D.S.A. Carroll, governor of the Bank of Ireland and chairman of Carroll Industries, has described how the Republic got itself into its current state:

> 'Ireland's admission to membership of the EEC in 1972 determined the future for business. That future was going to be one in which the disciplines of the competitive market-place

would be the decisive influence for success or failure. There could be no unilateral protection for Irish business.

'Following a transitional period, during which we could enjoy an extremely attractive programme of industrial incentives, we could hope to have adapted our businesses finally to the disciplines of market-place competition. The variety of governmental interventions in business, whether of a restrictive or of an incentive nature, would progressively be diminished, as the survivors of our indigenous industry, and the new industries which we would attract, generated for the nation the production of enough goods and services to yield the standards of living and the levels of employment to which the Irish people aspired.

'The benefits of the Common Agricultural Policy, as opposed to the cheap food policies practised by the United Kingdom for generations, would bring new wealth into rural Ireland. This wealth could be expected to expand the volume of markets for all kinds of goods and services.

'That was what we foresaw, but it was not to be . . .'

Carroll's description contains both accuracy and a degree of *suppressio veri.* He describes exactly what happened but avoids mentioning the banks' responsibility for it. Describing the post-oil shock years he says: 'For ten years the nation and its successive governments avoided that reality and sought to sustain our capacity to consume by borrowing abroad ever-increasing amounts. As with all borrowings, there was an obligation to repay them in the future'. Agreed, the avoidance of this 'reality' was greatly aided by the borrowing policies of the banks . . .

Carroll advocated that the 'anachronistic processes and practices of industrial relations should be ended' so that labour-price determination should be subjected to the disciplines of a competitive market. He argued that the 'rights and powers of trade unions can no longer be justified'.

There is a further merit to Carroll's thesis which at first may be difficult to comprehend — he actually mentioned agriculture in his animadversion on the Irish union/employer scene. The Common Agricultural Policy was there.

I labour this point because both Carroll's views and some of the value (and valued) judgements made above, are taken from what might be termed the Definitive View of Irish Business, a book entitled *Government and Enterprise in Ireland* (Gill and Macmillan 1984) written by Ivor Kenny, for long the director of the Irish Management Institute, in which Kenny never mentions agriculture. For better, and often for worse, agriculture is nevertheless Ireland's largest 'enterprise'.

A depressing picture overall, but I feel the Carroll/Kenny critiques do help, against the Irish taxation and industrial relations backdrop, to explain Delafield's 'something'.

Workers Unite

Complicating the effect of the foregoing in the trade unions during the years under review were the retirement or death of such titans of the movement as Ruairi Roberts, John Conroy, Michael Mullen and Jim Larkin.

Of these men it could be said that they understood the union movement, the national scene and the overall economy. They had vision and a sense of history. Conroy and Mullen, who followed each other as leaders of the giant Irish Transport and General Workers' Union, had a keen interest in politics, particularly in republicanism. Jim Larkin, whose father was the joint founder of the ITGWU with James Connolly, followed in his father's footsteps and might have developed his stature further had death not cut him down prematurely. When he died he was the principal figure in the Workers' Union of Ireland, which his father had carved out from the ITGWU following a struggle with William O'Brien which split the entire labour movement during the forties.

Ruairi Roberts, whom I was consulting for this book shortly before he died in 1986, helped to shape history by founding the Workers' College to a chorus of 'Godless Colleges' and 'spreading Communism' from the right, and salvos from the Catholic press, notably the *Standard*. After his retirement as President of the Irish Congress of Trade Unions, he was sorely missed.

Donal Nevin, Secretary of the ICTU, was the ideal back-up man for both of these figures, as a fountain-head of knowledge and as an organiser for the trade union movement and the Labour Party. But, as the great names dropped out, something of a leadership vacuum formed in the trade unions. External forces came to have a major influence on the movement: Common

Market membership, the oil crisis, inflation. In these years it was apparently futile for a man like Harold O'Sullivan of the Public Services Union to call for moderation and understanding between workers and employers. Though much admired, he was unable to stem the tide of events.

The running of current budget deficits had been a feature of Irish life since the oil shocks in 1973. Current account borrowing reached very high levels by 1975 under Richie Ryan, the coalition's Minister for Finance, but income tax had risen as a result and a wealth tax had been introduced. Borrowing was reduced in 1976, but the 1977 Fianna Fail manifesto unleashed an explosion in both current and capital spending, much of it borrowed money. The economy boomed in 1978, growing by 7 per cent, but at a terrible cost. The public service pay bill exploded in 1979 and 1980, rising in one year by around 34 per cent, and the economy has been as flat as a pancake since 1980. The six billion pounds of EEC transfers went largely to agriculture, where they ensured that production of basic commodities would continue at a very crude, if temporarily profitable, level.

For a time EEC membership meant that the trade union movement did not have to concern itself with developing broad social policies. EEC legislation took care of all sorts of things, from increased public holidays to maternity pay and equal pay for women. Pay rises came relatively painlessly until the effects of the oil shock finally sank in around 1979, biting not alone into pay packets but also into unfounded assumptions, like the claim that Ireland was the 'silicon valley' of Europe. It also became clear that the country could no longer continue to neglect its natural resources, and get away with it.

Belatedly, workers began to wake up to the fact that they were weighed down by taxation and that phrases such as 'worker participation' referred to ideas that could apply to their work situation — including the fact that some of them had no work. Recession, the micro-chip and the increasing dynamism of the Pacific area were chasing men off the factory floor in Ireland. But it was too late. Trade unionists used the same conceptual approach and the same rhetoric as before, relying on their strength to push through their wage demands. There was a comforting belief that somehow the weaker would share the profits.

There was no planning for the way forward in the new circumstances, no building of consensus with the employers, no building of consensus within the movement. Three-quarters of a million people marched to protest against income tax in the great marches of the seventies, but only a few hundred ever marched to protest against unemployment. Meanwhile, of course, international competitiveness weakened and unemployment soared. The black economy flourished. In some cases, employers and workers conspired to defraud the tax man, with workers drawing both unemployment and 'nixer' money. People not entitled to benefits contrived to get free medical cards and other social assistance. The farmers by and large stayed resolutely outside the tax net, thus maintaining an unhealthy urban-rural divide in which the ever-squeezed taxpayer grew shriller and shriller in protest but achieved very little.

By 1985 new leaders and new faces were clearly discernible in the trade union movement: Billy Attley of the Federated Workers' Union, Greg Maxwell and Phil Flynn, both in public service unions, Des Geraghty and Pat Rabbitte, both in the ITGWU. These new men realised that the old ways and the old slogans were no longer effective. They tried to promote fresh thinking. But it is difficult to gain a hearing for new concepts when financial stringency means that nothing but the most hard-faced, old-fashioned trade union bargaining and browbeating can wring even the smallest concessions from either public or private employers.

Another hidden factor which does not help the union movement is the internal pressure stemming from the competition between 'Stickies' (members of the Workers' Party) and the established trade union leadership.

From the outset, the Stickies made it a policy to seek influence via the trade union movement as much as through the polls. As a result their members have gained particular strength in several trade unions and in state institutions. Apologists for the Stickies would argue that these people are there on merit rather than by infiltration, and there is a good deal of truth in this. Workers' Party members are often more dedicated than other trade unionists. They tend to be more politicised, sometimes with roots going back to membership of some branch or other of the republican movement.

In the case of Phil Flynn of the Local Government and Public Services Union there are echoes of the Provisional-versus-Stickies divide. Flynn, a vice-president of Provisional Sinn Fein, was ruled a non-person by the coalition government through much of the eighties, and it was announced that no minister would meet him or negotiate with him. Flynn refused to be cowed and instead went on a brutally punishing tour of the union's branches throughout the country, winning a huge vote of support for his leadership. Through sheer prestige and ability, he had to be accepted at the state negotiating tables, where he achieved major concessions for his membership.

This was a doubly noteworthy achievement on his part because he was at the time (1983–4) at odds with the new Northern-led Sinn Fein movement and had intended to resign from the Ard Comhairle (governing body) anyhow. He refused, however, to allow any government to dictate his policies to him and only resigned when he had confounded his critics within the union and gone on to outmanoeuvre his adversaries in various pay bargaining concessions.

Inept Enterprise

It would be wrong to suggest that the entire semi-state sector is a desert of corruption and inefficiency, but the record over the years and the failure of successive governments to instal adequate controls have certainly raised large questions about the operation of much state-sponsored activity.

It is surely significant that one of the issues in the 1987 general election was the Progressive Democrats' proposal that the semi-state sector be privatised, a process which whatever its ideological merits, involves first, shaking up companies to get rid of undeniable flaws, before daring to venture in to the cold light of day of the non-government-cushioned market place.

And in one of the first speeches he made after the 1987 Budget the Minister for Finance, Ray MacSharry, replying to Desmond O'Malley gave a broad hint that Fianna Fail was moving towards the Progressive Democrat view on privatisation. He said (on 7 April) that henceforth state companies would have to be run with the same efficiency as the private sector and that current levels of inefficiency would no longer be tolerated.

In fact, privatisation has already come to one part of the public sector — to Nitrigin Eireann Teoranta — the Irish fertiliser company.

Perhaps, though it would take another book to argue it, the real issue is: private enterprise socialism. This philosophical question is certainly at the core of much Irish semi-state and state involvement in the administration or mal-administration of Ireland's resources and services. For the purpose of this book however, I am taking a few examples of semi-state activity at operational level only, beginning appropriately enough with fertiliser. Nitrigin Eireann Teo., the state-owned fertiliser company, was founded in 1973 and in the first ten years of its existence managed to lose £153 million. Through pollution, it made of its erstwhile pleasant surroundings near Arklow, Co. Wicklow, a scene reminiscent of a World War I battlefield.

The company came back into the black in 1984 in operational terms, recording a small profit of less than £3 million. Its overall indebtedness at the end of 1984 still remained at £180 million and despite a brutal paring of the work force (down from 1,500 to nearly half that in 1985, with more to go by 1990) a very big question mark hung over the company.

Eventually, after scouring the world for a suitable partner, the Chairman of NET, Sean MacHale, a former rugby international and well-known Dublin business consultant, who had been appointed by the government in an attempt to turn the company around, contacted the British giant, ICI. A deal was eventually worked out with ICI, whereby NET and Richardson's Fertilisers Ltd, Belfast, went into a joint venture known as Irish Fertilisers Ltd, in which ICI held 49 per cent of the shares and the new company 51 per cent. Mr MacHale, the architect of the package, remained on as Chairman and NET became merely the holding company. The NET deal could well be taken as creating a headline for the semi-state sector — in order to make the company attractive to ICI, the output per worker in the pre-privatisation period rose so that the new company, Irish Fertilisers Ltd, now ranks with the top six companies in Europe, a significant development in company/union cooperation.

The other significant aspect of the move is that the deal was still not publicly announced by June 1987, some months after it was finally completed, lest Paisley began trumpeting against it, a circumstance which says much about how in Belfast tautly balanced political/economic sensitivities can obtrude, perhaps appropriately, even into the area of fertilisers.

The troubles of another world industry, that of steel, are reflected in a poor performance by Irish Steel; though it has received over £125m in state grants, it lost some £83.50m in the five years from 1980. Here again savage redundancies are slowing but not halting the haemorrhage; losses in 1985 were £17.5m, as opposed to £23m the previous year. Favourable exchange rates helped the company to a profit of £½m in June 1986, but it is on a knife-edge.

CIE (Coras Iompair Eireann), the national transport company, is the company most people love to hate, since so many are touched by its activities, or lack of them. The city of Dublin is virtually impossible, or at least very difficult, to traverse on existing routes. Queues, delays and complaints about poor services are the order of the day. I genuinely pity anyone relying on CIE to get them out of Dublin in the late evening. The bus drivers and conductors are seemingly so browned off with the company's and the public's attitude towards them that they appear to have reverted to the wartime convoy system (during which they never lost a bus) and appear to delight in leaving people standing at stops as they hurtle past, preferably when it is raining and there is no other bus for the night.

One reason for this sort of attitude is poor pay. The unions claim that the average bus driver's wages are below the national industrial wage (£150 per week as opposed to £175) but this niggardliness, if it exists (and many suspect that it is made up for by unduly high overtime payments), has not resulted in a more economical service. If wages are low, fares are high. It cost me £20 to travel between Galway and Dublin by train in January, 1986. The train, packed mainly with emigrants returning to England, had neither heating nor a restaurant car. Yet privately-run buses leaving from outside the station are able to offer a round trip from Galway to Dublin for only £8.

One of CIE's problems arose from a lack of a definite government policy on transport. The city bus services, the road freight and bus services and the railway system offer three separate opportunities and challenges, which were not adequately dealt with by being bulked under a state-run bureaucracy located in Dublin. Another major CIE problem is industrial relations; stoppages have occurred so frequently that Ishmael appears to have been adopted as the patron saint of CIE.

During the 1980s there was continual governmental discussion about dividing CIE into three separate companies (road, rail and city) and rationalising the company's operations. The coalition of 1982-7, in particular the Minister for Communications, Jim Mitchell, made several purposeful noises about this during its term. But as the government's popularity weakened at the polls so too did the political will to tackle the CIE dragon which, with 14,295 people on the pay roll and on the voters' lists, is one of the biggest state company employers. The changes in the company's structure were only announced in the last few days of the coalition's reign, when it could do nothing to see them through.

So large and powerful is the company that it has been able to get its own way despite public opinion or ministerial disfavour. DART — the Dublin Area Rapid Transit Railway System — went ahead at a final cost of £117m despite the opposition of the minister of the day (Martin O'Donoghue): it subsequently proved itself the one CIE service to live up to its projections by failing to pay its way. Devices such as 'feeder' buses are improving the numbers carried, but the government subsidy works out at almost two punts per head, per journey; current numbers carried are roughly half those CIE thought it would have. In short, the venture has worked out exactly as badly as a similar project in San Francisco which was studied beforehand. A prediction which it did not live up to was that it would reduce Dublin's appalling traffic congestion.

The company has its own method of reducing its equally appalling debts. By a feat of book-keeping legerdemain the company managed to announce a small profit in September 1986. It had adopted the device, common in Europe, of calling its government subsidy of nearly £120m a 'social service' so that instead of an astronomical loss, it recorded a profit of £6.8m. . . .

The taxpayers were enormously cheered as a result.

The state-owned freight line Irish Shipping was the only link which the nation possessed capable of supplying the country's basic needs in a time of crisis. It was valued at IR£100m and generated IR£50m annual turnover. It operated in a glow of general public esteem, tinged with a patriotic patina going back to the formation of the company in the crisis conditions of 1941 when it kept the country in essential supplies during the war. In the commercial war which hit world shipping after Suez and which necessitated a move into large, diesel-powered vessels, the company was equally successful, recording respectable profitability until 1982.

In the following two years however, the company was torpedoed by the effects of some ill-conceived charter deals. Losses for 1984 alone amounted to over 70 per cent of turnover, making a combined total of £45m for 1983–4. These charters had the effect of doubling the capacity of the Irish Shipping fleet, and began in September 1979, a year after the Chairman of the company had stated in his Annual Report that from that date some 30 per cent of the world's dry cargo ships would have to be laid up if freight rates were to achieve break-even for ship-owners. Yet the deals went ahead, nine in all from September 1979 to February 1981, while freight rates fell from $20,000 a day to only $1,500. For negotiating this fiasco with the Hong Kong-based Wah Kong Shipping Company, Irish Shipping paid another Hong Kong shipping company, Anglo Eastern Shipping, £500,000 commission.

That commission was 'earned' for an arrangement which contained a number of manifestly unsavoury features, such as rates that were grievously out of line with the going market rates, had no 'get-out' clause or normal back-to-back freight arrangements and were not sanctioned by either the board of Irish Shipping or the Minister for Finance — the largest single shareholder. In fact the first time the board heard of the deals officially was at its meeting of June 1981, although no details of the charter arrangement were either vouchsafed or asked for in any meaningful way. The general level of supervision at the time may be gauged from the fact that the Joint Oireachtas Committee on Irish Shipping issued a most favourable report on the company's activities after a cosy *pro forma* 'investigation' during which the Chairman of the committee asked whether there were 'any skeletons in the cupboard', clearly expecting the answer he got from the Chairman: 'No'.

Irish Shipping, it should be added, was set up under an Act which states that 'The Minister for Transport is responsible for the overall policy control of the company and proposals involving capital expenditure must be approved by him'. If the ministerial office was held in such contempt by the fat cats of Irish Shipping that the minister was not even consulted about the charters, why worry about a few lesser politicians on a Dail committee?

The tale points an accusing finger at the arrogance and incompetence of some of the executives involved, as well as the gross negligence of the board of Irish Shipping and the parliamentary watchdogs.

Shortly after the liquidator moved into Irish Shipping, the workers involved — trade unionists, ships' captains, the lot — were left spattered around the globe wherever Irish Shipping vessels were docked, without even their last week's pay or their fares home.

In the Air, On the Air

The national airline, Aer Lingus, exists not so much as an airline but as a variety of auxiliary activities, some of them remarkably diverse. Through subsidiaries the company manages hospitals in the Middle East, hires out flight crews and aeroplanes, distributes Japanese robots in Britain and runs the Dunphy hotel chain in the US. All this makes a profit, a record £30m in 1984. But only £500,000 of this came from its very costly air transport service.

The airline employs a total staff of fourteen thousand, five and a half thousand of whom are employed directly in air transport: if one takes the 2.2 million passengers carried in 1984, fewer than 400 passengers are carried per employee. To carry these passengers, Aer Lingus uses twenty-four aircraft at peak times such as August Bank Holiday weekends; at other times of the year the planes are leased or put into cold storage. There are three Boeing 747s, one 707, eleven 737s, four BAC I-IIs and four Shorts commuter aircraft. The Boeings are coming near the end of their service and in the next five years Aer Lingus is going to have to find some £600m in order to stay in the air. Hard decisions will have to be taken by the government.

If one looked at its balance sheets divorced from its letter-headings, the Electricity Supply Board could well seem to form part, and a large part at that, of the American space programme. Capital expenditure in the four years to the end of 1983 amounted to £825m; a major item was a new coal-burning plant at Money-point, County Clare, for which there is little or no demand and to which there is a great deal of opposition on environmental grounds. £250m went on general improvements within the sytem, £100m on a plant erected 'to take advantage' of the natural gas find at Kinsale and another £80m for an ESB station generator at Shannon Bridge.

Irish industrialists claim that their electricity bills are 20 per cent higher than those of their European competitors. By 1984 the ESB's total debt was £1.3 billion. Rising interest rates alone would have accounted for a considerable amount of the cost to industry. The company argues that much of its problem arose from listening to government views on the future demands of the economy. However, the state-sponsored Economic and Social Research Institute issued a comprehensive report warning against such assumptions. The truth is that a great deal of the ESB's problems arise because of the common theme running through all state companies, giganticism. The ESB employs 12,000 people at an average of 180 per cent of the industrial wage; it has borrowed around £1,200m to build a generating capacity which is 60 per cent greater than peak demand.

The ESB now has a particularly able Chief Executive, Patrick Moriarty, who leads a talented management team which has effected a number of cost-saving and revenue-generating innovations in the eighties. The ESB operation is very sophisticated and has a highly-developed foreign exchange dealing business which is the envy of Dublin's banking community. The company adopts a progressive attitude to looking after its staff, subsidising leisure activities and supporting a top-class pension scheme.

Radio Telefis Eireann (RTE) contains some of the most talented people in their field to be found in Europe. But there is gross waste and inefficient use of talent resulting in frustration and the deployment of creativity, not to what appears on the screen, but to outside interests and to what appears on the expense account.

And what are the political watchdogs doing about all this? The answer is that the politicians, all politicians, do everything in their power to make a bad situation worse. Let me give an example.

RTE is statutorily controlled under the Minister for Communications by an Authority appointed by the government of the day, and the station is run on an operational basis by a Director General. An outstanding Director General like T.P. Hardiman (1967–75) could and did set standards of professionalism and of resistance to governmental pressure. His tenure in office coincided with that of Dr C.S. (Tod) Andrews as Chairman of the Authority. Tod, a cultured bureaucrat who had come through both the Anglo-Irish War and the civil war to found one of the few continuously successful state companies, Bord na Mona (Turf Board), was on terms of personal friendship and respect with most of the public figures of the day, particularly those in Fianna Fail. With this formidable backing Hardiman, an engineer by profession who had come up through the ranks of RTE, did much to make RTE a power in the land, particularly through horizon-widening current affairs programmes.

However, when in 1969 a programme which made unsustainable claims about the widespread but (in the programme) unproven practice of illegal money-lending was screened, the Fianna Fail government set up a judicial tribunal presided over by a high court judge to inquire into this enormity. The tribunal lasted an eternity, cost the taxpayers a fortune and — a year later — found against RTE, with consequent harm to investigative current affairs broadcasting and to RTE's influence generally. The decline was accelerated when the government sacked the entire Authority, claiming that the station had infringed the Broadcasting Act when it broadcast a report of an interview with the Chief of Staff of the IRA, Sean Mac Stiofain, in November 1972. Hardiman's contract *was not renewed* at the end of his term, though he went on to scale the heights of banking directorships and chairmanships of important boards. RTE declined in prestige, probably its lowest point in terms of demoralisation occurring under a coalition government. The Authority had quite properly decided in autumn of 1984 to press ahead with the appointment of a new Director General as the term of office of George Waters, another former engineer with RTE, was ending in the New Year. The post was advertised and by December a list of the front-running applicants had been invited to attend for interview in mid-January. These interviews took place, an outside business consultant was engaged to run the rule over those who emerged, a final short list was again interviewed and a new Director General selected. Then, the government suddenly called on the Authority *not to appoint* a Director General. The stated reason for this intervention, as unprecedented as it was unexpected, was the government's equally unheralded decision to have a thoroughgoing review of the station's operations conducted by a firm of management consultants.

Such a review, leading to an eventual overhaul, was not out of place, but why was it introduced at such an inopportune moment, when the costly process of advertising and putting a number of interviewees through the trouble and embarrassment of the interview process had been completed? Why? a) Because the largely Fianna Fail-nominated Authority was due to be replaced a few months after the nomination was made; b) Because the coalition government did not want to find itself then with a Director General favoured by a Fianna Fail Authority on its hands; c) Its favoured candidate was Muiris MacConghail, who seemed unlikely to succeed because some of the Fianna Fail-orientated Authority had begun to make favourable noises about John Sorahan, yet another RTE engineer.

This affair culminated in the coalition duly naming a new Authority later in the year. Meanwhile, a stop-gap Director General was appointed, a better man indeed than the selection procedure warranted, the highly competent Vincent Finn, who was later confirmed in the job. Muiris MacConghail, a very able producer and the man targeted by the 'Seven Days' tribunal over the money-lending programme, had also served as head of the Government Information Service during the 1973–7 coalition. When the dust of the Director General rumpus settled he was one of those who took a golden handshake and quit the station.

The whole affair deepened the cynical attitude amongst the plain people of Ireland that whatever the consultants came up with, even in an era of satellite television, spreading local radio and unparalleled new challenges and opportunities for creativity in communications, predictability in political affiliation was more valuable than any professional competence. The consensus amongst the few committed broadcasters left in RTE had better be imagined than described, as it was expressed most frequently in four-letter words.

The station has shown signs of an improved performance

since 1985. Staff numbers have fallen by 100 to 2,148, and a profit of £3.5m was reported for 1986. Home-produced programmes are expected to rise from 37 per cent to 45 per cent of output in 1987–8.

Private Sector

Given the overall state of the Irish economy, the recession, industrial relations and the taxation situation, the surprise is not that the private sector is depressed, but that some companies do so well. However there is one drawback to the thrust of Irish industry, which by 1980 saw one major Irish company after another either being taken over, often by non-nationals, or making foreign acquisitions.

This means that a small open economy is yielding further hostages to fortune through ceding control of part of its industrial base to outside interests. In some ways indigenous Irish industry is tending to become the obverse side of the multi-national medal; it uses its Irish profits to buy abroad, but as expectations rise and cash is needed for more acquisitions, repatriation of profits back to Ireland to fund growth in the parent company takes second place to the needs of the foreign expansion.

Let us look briefly at some of the success stories of Irish industry, the top ten publicly-quoted Irish companies. Pride of place goes to the Smurfit Group, with a 1986 turnover of £915m employing 12,500 people and with pre-tax profits of £56m. Its 1986 market value was just under a billion pounds at £937m.

The Smurfit Group could almost be considered a US company with an Irish base following a series of acquisitions, the most outstanding of which was the billion dollar purchase of Containers Corporation of America in 1986. As a result most of the group's sales and profits now emanate from the US. The group started in the Irish print and packaging market, and built up a near monopoly during the 1960s. Print/packaging still forms the base of the group's business and its top executive is Michael Smurfit, whose father founded the firm.

Cement Roadstone Holdings, which in 1985 had a turnover of £530m, employs 7,236 people and in 1985 had pre-tax profits of £27.6m. Its market value is £500m. CRH has become a US-oriented firm with an Irish base, the largest of its American acquisitions being the $40m takeover of Callanan Industries in New York in 1985. Throughout 1986 the firm under its chief executive James P. Culliton (currently chairman of the RTE Authority), took over firms in Europe and America at the rate of almost one a month. In Ireland the firm still concentrates on the manufacture and distribution of construction materials. By the end of 1986 63 per cent of its profits came from abroad.

In banking, the two giants are Allied Irish Banks and the Bank of Ireland, AIB being the larger of the two. In 1985 its gross assets were £8,245m and it employed 9,000 people, with pre-tax profits of £87m for a market value of £547m. Pre-tax profits in 1987 were £102m. AIB's profit performance in recent years is also due in part to US investment, mainly in the First Maryland Bankcorp. AIB spectacularly displayed its power in the Irish community, paradoxically enough in its handling of its biggest flop. This was a disastrous investment in the Insurance Corporation of Ireland Ltd, which cost the shareholders some £90m when ICI collapsed in 1984, but will cost the Irish public even more ultimately, certainly over £100m. The bank went to the government and said, in effect: 'Bail us out or we collapse, and with us the Irish banking system'. The coalition government agreed to underwrite the losses and Fianna Fail intends to carry on with the bail-out policy.

The Bank of Ireland had gross assets of £7,000m in 1986 and employed 8,608; its pre-tax profit was £81.3m in 1986, and it had a market value of £386m.

Three old-established companies which are confronting the problems of contemporary Irish and international trends with success varying in degree rather than kind, are Waterford Glass, Carrolls Industries, and Irish Distillers.

Waterford Glass, now Waterford Wedgwood Holdings, is the most successful. Its turnover was £255m in 1985, but these figures do not take into account the effects of its £260m sterling acquisition of Wedgwood in 1986. The combined group is expected to have sales for 1986 well in excess of £400m and pre-tax profits in the region of £40m or more. The combination of two reputations which gives WW Holdings a good international position in the world market is reflected in a total market value of £620m. The group had attempted to diversify into the motor industry via garages and the Renault franchise, but disposed of this activity for a nominal £1. In return for the assets the purchaser had to take on £19m in debts and liabilities.

Carrolls Industries, with a turnover of £285m to September 1986, employs 1,305, has a pre-tax profit of £13m and a market value of £104m. Based on cigarette manufacture, it has seen its traditional tobacco market reduced in the last decade through a combination of taxation and the growing move against smoking. Efforts to diversify out of tobacco have been less than successful; a joint venture with the American towel company Fieldcrest in County Kilkenny flopped, but two subsidiary companies, Cahill May Roberts and Dakota Printing, are profitable. Carrolls has plans to establish a mail order firm in the US at a cost of over £40m, and to diversify into fish-farming in the west of Ireland. Don Carroll himself has adopted a long-term strategy of investing in Ireland; if he can succeed, this will be far more beneficial to the national interest than the current widespread policy of investing Irish profits abroad.

Irish Distillers, as one might expect given Irish drinking habits, is also highly profitable. In 1986 its turnover was £240m. The firm employed 1,550 people for a pre-tax profit of £13m, and had a market value of £131m. In recent years taxes and recession have hit sales and profitability, but profits have been maintained by growing sales in Britain and the success of the low-alcohol drink West Coast Cooler. However, Irish whiskey has not yet made a significant impact on US palates, who favour the blander Scotch blends over the Irish malts.

Three very disparate companies show what the Irish are capable of, even in adverse conditions. These are FII-Fyffe Plc, the James Crean Group and Woodchester Investments.

FII-Fyffe Plc has a turnover of £154m, employs 500 people and had a pre-tax profit of £7.2m in 1986 with a market value of £127m. The company, whose core business is importing and re-exporting fruit, has mushroomed over the past decade, capping a series of acquisitions with the £26.5m takeover of Fyffes in 1986. The company has cleverly used share sales instead of debt to raise funds for expansion, avoiding the interest charges which crippled many other Irish firms trying unsuccessfully to expand.

The Crean Group, basically a distribution company, had a

turnover of £100m in 1986, employed 1,050 people and before tax made a profit of £4.6m. Its market value is £122m. The group has a wide variety of interests, including industrial electrical goods, a wholesaling operation in the US, and minerals and confectionery in Ireland. Crean too is expanding in the US, acquiring the New York frozen foods firm, Freezer Queen, for $35m in 1986.

Flourishing despite political upheavals is the firm of Masstock, headed by Alastair McGuckian and his brother Paddy from County Antrim. This is a world leader in irrigation and food growing, particularly in Saudi Arabia, whence the Masstock firm has expanded to China and America. What the rare and valuable genius of the McGuckians has achieved abroad could be benefited from in Ireland, given enlightened government policies.

Woodchester Investments, though smaller in scale than others mentioned, is also a high-stepper which well illustrates the distinguishing characteristics of Irish industry currently. The company's basic business is office equipment leasing. Wood-chester acquired the Hamilton Leasing company in a £20m deal in August 1986, and at the same time was itself taken over by British and Commonwealth Shipping Company, which now owns 50.1 per cent of the Woodchester equity. Its market value is currently £104m.

Its entire financial success is based on the use of tax avoidance methods (all legal) which allow the owners of leased assets to offset their capital cost fully against operating profits, reducing the tax liability to zero. The only tax payable by Woodchester in recent years has been Advance Corporation Tax on its dividends; following the take-over of Bowmaker Bank in 1987, it is expected that even this will be reclaimable.

The natural resource position is equally depressing.

Agriculture

Statistics furnished by the Irish Farmers' Association (IFA) show that for 1983 national agricultural output was close to £2,400m, and agriculture's contribution to GNP was 11 per cent (the comparable average figure for agriculture in the EEC was less than 4 per cent). Direct employment on farms was 182,000, or about 16 per cent of total national employment. Furthermore, the food processing industry, which employs 42,000 people, accounted for over 20 per cent of total employment in Irish manufacturing. A study conducted by the Economic and Social Research Institute in 1983 claimed that for each job in agriculture and the food industry combined, a further job was generated somewhere else in the economy through the combined expenditure of farmers and food industry employees. Agricultural exports, including transfers from FEOGA (the EEC Agricultural Guidance and Guarantee Fund), amounted to £1,820m, or 25 per cent of total exports.

It is nearly impossible to overstress the importance of agriculture to Ireland. However, while agriculture is the backbone of the Irish economic and political system, it is also alarmingly and appallingly inefficient. Any thinking person would have to agree with the verdict of *Hibernia* when, writing about Irish agriculture's enraged response to some courageous reporting by RTE's Agricultural Correspondent, Michael Lally, the magazine said: 'Irish farmers were producing beef and dairy products that could not be sold at any price . . . the fairy godmother in Brussels was no longer prepared to pay for massive stock-piles that eventually would have to be dumped . . . Irish agriculture has been built on false foundations and on false promises. Now the October 1986 cupboard is bare, there is no more money to pay for surplus products. Irish farming was exposed on national television for what it really is — a massively laid-back lifestyle which has been cushioned and comforted for years, and which now has no hope of getting cash for the bulk of its wares'.

Yet there are honourable exceptions, examples of what might have been. A handful of large co-operatives do extremely well. Kerry Co-Op, Waterford Co-Op and Avonmore Creameries are three of the most successful businesses in Ireland. Kerry Co-op exports the milk derivative casein to the US, where it is in demand for making processed cheese. Waterford Co-op developed and marketed the top-selling Irish yoghurt, Yoplait, and Avonmore is a huge supplier of milk to the Irish market.

It is certainly permissible speculation that had governmental strategy concentrated on developing enterprises based on natural resources rather than pouring money into the maw of the IDA, things would have been far better for the country. Individual sparks of agricultural genius exist; on a kibbutz in Israel I heard praise for Irish expertise in poultry raising. This can be seen at work in the north at the Silver Duckling hatchery at Emyvale in County Monaghan, or in the south where Whitaker Hatcheries and Keoghan Developments pooled their resources to bid for a huge Libyan hatchery/breeding project; this nearly brought the country an order worth in excess of IR£100m, until the American bombing changed the political picture.

The Irish meat firm, Goodman International, claims to be the biggest meat processor in Europe. It has sales of £500m a year and six major plants in the Republic. However, one of the biggest problems with the meat business is continuity of supply. Most Irish meat plants have had to close for large parts of the year, while working overtime during peak periods. The European housewife and the big European supermarkets want value-added type products, special cuts packed individually: however, it is only possible to win such contract business if supplies can be guaranteed throughout the year. Only Goodman has been able to do it to date; the Irish meat trade has seen more than its share of disasters. Chapter 8 helps to explain why.

Forestry

Forestation has been scandalously neglected. The Irish climate is peculiarly suited to growing trees; according to official estimates, trees can be grown in Ireland 10 to 30 per cent faster than in Scandinavia. Yet the Irish land area under forestry, at 4 per cent, is the lowest in Europe.

Public attitudes play their part in this statistic. Irish land-owners, great or small, feel cheated if land is leased for forestry, never again to be put to its 'proper' agricultural use. And owning land used for either tillage or livestock carries with it a status which the Irish are loath to relinquish. There is a widespread attitude that forestry land is 'inferior', 'only fit for growing trees'. The long-term nature of the investment involved also militates against development, as does the fact that much of the forestry activity in the country is controlled by the civil service, whose commitment to regulations rather than entrepreneurship does not favour enterprise. State planning has hurt rather than helped people engaged in the industry; multi-national firms attracted by the IDA, for instance, get preference in timber supplies over small, native sawmills, which teeter on the verge of bankruptcy without such supplies.

It makes a sorry tale for a country that as late as the seventeenth century was 12½ per cent under primeval forest. The need to deny cover to native guerrillas and to line pockets as quickly as possible before the next rebellion broke out, not to mention the needs of the Royal Navy in the age of the timber man-of-war, almost removed trees from the Irish countryside by the beginning of the nineteenth century. It has taken almost two hundred years to crawl back to 4 per cent. But instead of trying to supply the EEC with the timber it wants — a demand of the same order as for oil — Irish agriculture is still geared to supplying it with milk and beef which the EEC does not want and which have to be stored in intervention.

Fisheries

At the time of Ireland's accession to the EEC the amount of negotiating time spent on fishing as opposed to farming interests was fractional. The fishermen's voices now largely go unheard and their industry is in a shambles, dominated by cartels. Ireland is allowed to land only 4.6 per cent of the Community's total catch, while Spanish, French and East European trawlers make lucrative hauls daily in Irish waters. There is a possibility of developing the industry via types of fish not covered by the EEC quota regulations: blue whiting, for example, and horse mackerel. But somehow there is something obscene about the use to which these are put — being either used as fish meal, or pumped ashore at Rossaveal in Connemara to be turned into cubes for chicken or mink-rearing, killing fish in order to be able to kill mink to make fur coats worn by people who eat chicken that tastes of fish. But with the exception of a few supermarkets and a handful of good fish shops, edible fish is comparatively scarce and expensive to buy in Ireland.

The basic education of the fisherman has also been neglected. There is a tradition along the west coast of leaving school in the early teens to 'go on the fishing'. In an era of increasing sophistication which requires a successful fisherman to have a working knowledge of electronics and marketing interest rates as much as fishing methods, it is a miracle that tradition has produced as many fine fishermen as it has along Ireland's fertile, if furious, coasts. But a modern trawler skipper, with in effect a million-pound industry under his feet, is at a serious disadvantage, educationally speaking, by comparison with a land-based businessman controlling a similar scale operation.

Lack of training in the business side of the industry has been a major contributory factor to such ills as unsuitable and over-expensive boats being purchased by inexperienced young skippers, and then repossessed when the debt is not paid. Bad handling of fish, which leads to lower prices, has been a feature of the industry, and so has the diversion of profits to another purpose than loan repayment, be it buying a house or drink, until such time as the repossession axe falls. When it does the boats are generally run down, denuded of expensive equipment and resold at a fraction of their original cost: literally a net loss to the tax-payer.

Ireland has the last fertile fishing grounds left in western Europe. Her continental shelf runs roughly from Kerry in the south-west to Donegal in the north-west some 50 miles out to sea, along a line approximately 350 miles long. The Irish Sea and Celtic Sea, which are shallower, are also fertile and exploitable; stocks of herring, mackerel, cod, whiting and other fish, although less than would be found along the west coast, are still far greater than elsewhere in Europe.

There were only 7,643 people employed in full-time and part-time fishing in Ireland in 1985. They landed some 205,000 tonnes of fish, which contributed one per cent to the gross national product and which, when taken together with the numbers employed in the fishing industry, amounted to one per cent of the labour force. How can so low a level of activity be tolerated? The answer is the bullock!

I often think that the late Oliver Cromwell did less harm to Ireland than did the bullock. In order to allow Irish farmers the luxury of exploiting this stupid four-legged eunuch, the country's EEC negotiators permitted the Irish fishing quota to be fixed at the level of catch obtaining at the time of accession to the Community. This was when the industry was still trying to make of itself something other than a subsidy for the Irish language, being principally located in the western Gaeltachts. Every sort of ill has befallen the fish industry as a result of this piscine mess of pottage. In mid-1985, 80 per cent of the 3,135 boat owners in the Irish fishing fleet were in arrears with their repayments and an aid package had to be introduced to prevent the industry collapsing altogether. Those of the boats built in Ireland were said by Bord Iascaigh Mhara to be some fifteen per cent more expensive than boats built in European yards, but Irish fishermen alleged that they cost up to fifty per cent more.

Even at sea the black economy flourishes, as fishermen who have caught more than their quota, or who simply wish to avoid the income tax man, have been known to sell their fish to east European and Russian 'luggers'. During the herring season these may be seen off Killybegs with notices on their sides advising the price they will pay for fish! Salmon poaching has been elevated to an art form, the drama punctuated by annual clashes between the state fishery protection vessels and illegal fishermen.

The drop in world oil prices and the slight easing of the recession meant that trawler skippers had relatively good seasons in 1985–6, and there are a handful of wealthy skippers to be found in Dublin, Wexford, Kerry, Galway and Donegal at any time. Overall, however, bereft of a coherent lobby, the Irish fishing industry is a disaster area which can prosper only if some way can be found of increasing that statistic of 4.6 per cent. The newly-installed Fianna Fail government has set up a Marine Department which may ultimately improve the picture, but this has yet to prove itself.

Natural Gas

Ireland has not as yet discovered any commercially viable oil fields. A friend on the National Board of Science and Technology tells me the official expectation is that it is only a matter of time and oil-price politics before oil is brought ashore, somewhere along the eastern and south-eastern coasts in a line stretching from the Kish Bank in Dublin Bay down to Kinsale.

Kinsale was the scene of a huge natural gas find in 1970. A state company was set up, An Bord Gais, to dispose of the gas to existing companies operating in the cities. Very large expenditure was involved in building a pipeline and in converting the existing fittings to natural gas. This was understandably contemplated with equanimity by the state and private sectors alike, in view of the obvious benefits to be expected from such a resource.

Equanimity has long since faded. The biggest centre involved was Dublin. The Dublin Gas company is now squarely in the middle of a national political and financial scandal. The public's first real intimation that something was amiss came in December 1983 when Frank Cluskey resigned from the cabinet in protest at a deal done by government whereby the Dublin Gas company received £125m in cash, supplies, credits and subsidised gas from An Bord Gais, but conceded to the state only 25 per cent of the company's shares in return. The company is now under the control of a receiver and Cluskey's former colleague, then Tanaiste, Dick Spring, publicly declared that he intended to nationalise the firm. It is losing money at the rate of £2,500 per hour, and sales of natural gas are 25 per cent off target. Massive redundancies loom and the company has gross debts of £124m, kept going only through the generosity of An Bord Gais. The trading loss for 1986 was £20m. Write-offs and redundancy costs are estimated to add more losses of £62m, taking the grand total to £82m: a hefty sum for a company trading in natural resources which was 75 per cent owned by private shareholders prior to the receivership and was quoted on the Stock Exchange. Hefty sums appear to have been the order of the day at Dublin Gas; as a result of questioning by Cluskey it was disclosed that one executive's pension had cost £600,000 to fund.

The actual operation of the company, in terms of supplying gas to its customers, is as bad as the figures suggest. Gas leaks are common in almost every street and suburb of Dublin and two people lost their lives in January of 1987 as a result of seeping gas which eventually exploded destroying a block of flats at Ballsbridge. Reports of leaks and suspected leaks have caused Dublin Gas to dig at least 3,000 holes in Dublin streets between January and June 1987. Gas has recently been brought to Limerick at a cost of between £15m and £25m; there are 4–5,000 gas users in Limerick, so the cost of bringing the gas to each consumer was several thousand pounds. Each was given a new free cooker suitable for natural gas (this apparently was cheaper than organising a conversion programme on the Dublin model). Fianna Fail has plans to bring gas to Dundalk and then across the country to Sligo to supply cheap power to horticulture along the east coast, which, like much else in Ireland, will be a good thing if it works.

Oil

Needless to say, the hype and ultimate disappointment which attended the efforts to profit from other forms of natural resources were displayed in all their customary unloveliness when it came to oil exploration. The distinguishing feature of the oil debacle was the frenzied nature of the share dealing it generated.

Several small Irish companies, in association with the major oil companies, have drilled without much success in the Celtic Sea since the 1970s. The shares of these performed as well or as badly as one might expect, given the fact that no commercial oil fields were discovered. But one company in particular, Atlantic Resources, proved conclusively that the fact no wealth is generated on the floor of the sea does not mean that a great deal of it cannot be generated on the floor of the Stock Exchange.

Between 1983 and 1984, Atlantic's share prices rose to £10 each, bringing the paper value of the company to some £150m. The shares were then split five times to improve their saleability. (By June 1987 these split shares were being quoted at only 15p each and there was scarcely a bank manager or an accountant in the country who did not have a tale to tell of customers, some of them widows and pensioners, who had invested savings, borrowed money, mortgaged or re-mortgaged their homes to invest.) Amongst the casualties was a well-respected firm of stockbrokers, caught off-guard at the end of a heady period with over-extended credit to its speculating investors, which was 'hammered' as a result.

Atlantic operated in association with such international giants as Gulf Oil, Union Oil and, after the others pulled out of the Celtic Sea in 1986, BP. But the glamour of the company stemmed not from its drilling associates, but the reputation of its Irish controllers, figures such as Tony O'Reilly of Heinz, the chairman of both Atlantic and Independent Newspapers plc; Vincent Ferguson, a former chairman of Dublin Gas; Gerry McGuinness, another Independent director, and a millionaire through his flourishing *Sunday World,* and fashionable Dublin solicitor, James Cawley.

Both for the manner in which they boosted the value of the Independent Group, and the short-lived burst of esteem achieved by their investment company, Fitzwilton, in which O'Reilly and Ferguson were also prominent during the early 1970s, Irish investors saw the Atlantic team as possessing the golden touch that would bring Saudi-like riches to Ireland. Atlantic's bullish approach to drilling results sustained this belief. For example on 15 November 1984 O'Reilly wrote to the shareholders of Atlantic informing them that, despite apparently disappointing results from tests on an exploratory well 49/10-1 which produced only formation water and very minor amounts of gas, 'the sum total of information received from the 49/10-1 well is both positive and encouraging. In our view the results not only enhance the hydrocarbon prospectivity of the Celtic Sea in general, but Atlantic's acreage in particular.'

The coverage by the Independent Group newspapers of Atlantic's activities were enthusiastic. In fact, when in the early months of 1984, Lloyd Smythe, an *Irish Press* financial journalist, suggested that Atlantic had hit a dry hole, the *Evening Herald* ran a centre-page spread attacking him. No oil flowed, however. Threats of legal action did (I was amongst those who got one) when the *Irish Press* and the *Sunday Tribune* tried to find out why the share prices were surging about like a run-away oil rig. We didn't find out — but neither were the actions proceeded with.

Throughout 1986, as oil share prices worsened, there was open controversy between the Independent Group and Dick Spring, the Minister for Energy. Spring claimed that a campaign of 'truths, half-truths and misleading statements' was attempting to force the government to give oil exploration companies a better deal. New and improved exploration terms were, in fact, agreed by the coalition in September 1986, even though it became known that several members of a Fine Gael committee examining the oil situation were buying oil shares.

But throughout 1986 the price of crude oil dropped on international markets and the pressure mounted on Atlantic. The blow really fell on 12 June 1987, when BP struck rock, not oil, in the Celtic Sea. That same day Atlantic had announced the placing of fifteen million shares with institutions in London and Dublin. The following Monday the placing was cancelled.

In the six years of its existence, Atlantic had raised £43.1m from investors for oil exploration which had yielded no oil of any consequence. As the share prices fell to levels at which it would not have been unreasonable to expect to find fossils, if not hydrocarbons, the Atlantic Annual General Meeting held shortly after the share cancellation was understandably a somewhat tense affair.

Another depressing chapter had been added to the saga of ineptitude that is decision-taking Ireland's attitude towards natural resources.

Mining

The largest zinc and lead mine in Europe is Tara Mines, which employs around 960 people at Navan, County Meath. The mine lost money in 1986 because of ailing metal prices, but it made £40 million profit in 1984/85. However, it has never paid any tax, royalties or dividends to the state, which owns a 25 per cent interest, because of the terms which the mine's owners secured at the commencement of operations. Tara raised borrowings of over 100 million dollars to get the mine into production, and is in the process of repaying these debts. Presumably when they have been cleared, some taxes will be paid.

The company was taken over in 1985 by Outokumpu, a state-owned company from Finland, and all its ore is exported for further processing in mainland Europe. Irish mining policy does not run to the provision of a smelter which might generate further wealth for the state.

For several years the operations at Navan were bedevilled by the relationship with Bula Mines, which came into being through securing some land in which Tara was interested, acquiring control of part of the Navan ore body. Bula is now also in the hands of a receiver sent in by the banks, who are owed £14m in principal, apart from interest. The state also paid out £9m in the mid-seventies for a 25 per cent share in the company. Not one shovelful of ore has ever been mined. The whole project got bogged down in wrangling over planning permission and then in numerous futile attempts to introduce outside partners to provide the £100m or so needed to get the operation going. Now the only bidder is Tara, which is offering a reported £5m.

If exploration for oil, gas and zinc were new, exciting and potentially profitable activities, they seemed to contrast starkly with that most traditional of occupations — farming. If success was so fugitive beneath the surface, how did we fare on the land?

8

Down on the Farm

New Money, Old Ways; The Poor Mouth; The TB Scandal;
On a London Bus

ONE thing farmers do not lack is an interest group. A good
starting point to begin looking at modern Irish agriculture, in the
context of this book's time scale, is 7 October 1966. On that day
farmers from all over Ireland, beginning at Bantry, County Cork,
set off on a march to Dublin. The march was accompanied by road
blocking and vigilante patrols (made up of stalwart farmers) to
ensure that no produce was transported from any farm for sale. It
paralysed the country for several days and culminated in Dublin,
with the farmers sitting on the steps of Government Buildings to
make their protest.

The immediate cause of the march was a humble old penny
(these were the days before decimalisation). The farmers'
leaders, Rickard Deasy, President of the National Farmers
Association, and the NFA Secretary, Sean Healy, had been called
to Government Buildings prior to pre-budget talks by the
Minister for Agriculture, Charles Haughey, and shown a portion
of the forthcoming speech in which an increase to farmers of a
penny on a gallon of milk was included.

However, in subsequent pre-budget wrangling in the Cabinet,
the penny was dropped under pressure from Haughey's colleagues, and when Jack Lynch made his budget speech as Minister
for Finance the farmers learned with a sense of anger and be-
trayal that their penny would not be forthcoming. The huge
protest eventually followed.

The protest had the short-term effect of wrecking Haughey's

prospects of becoming Taoiseach when Lemass retired a few weeks later, but a number of lasting developments also followed. There was, and still is, another important farmer lobby group, the Irish Creamery Milk Suppliers' Association, particularly strong in the Munster area. The NFA leadership saw the ICMSA as largely a commodity association devoted to the interest of milk producers. Apart from this, personality issues and the tendency of organisations to be self-perpetuating, developing their own infra-structures and power bases, have combined to keep the two bodies separate since then.

At the time of the protest the NFA leaders argued that the ICMSA did not properly appreciate the country's agricultural potential. For instance, going back to the days of the economic war with Britain in the 1930s, when calves were slaughtered for two shillings and sixpence in old money, many of the older milk producers saw no value in calves — the only way they believed they could make money out of a farm was from a milk-producing cow. However, the IFA leaders, with one eye on the prospect of EEC membership looming distantly on the horizon, had more fundamental changes in mind. At the time of the protest, for example, the normal thing was for the UK buyer to come to Ireland to buy his bullocks. The newer breed of Irish farming leader intended to break this pattern by going out to look for markets in Europe. 'Marketing' was very much the vogue term.

The *fons et origo* of Irish agriculture is the cattle trade. The 1966 milk producers sold their milk to co-ops, managed by men who might or might not have taken one of the courses in dairy science available in University College, Cork, but equally possibly had taken over the job from their fathers or uncles. These men could be called upon to test milk and to produce butter very reliably, but not much else. The idea of marketing agricultural produce, as the NFA envisaged, was foreign to them. It was also foreign to the people who controlled the cattle trade. The 'jobbers' had matters tied up, either for themselves or for a handful of big buyers, through a network of cells touching every fair in Ireland, and they wanted things left as they were. Moreover, these jobbers and cattle dealers cut across party lines and were able to make their views known to all politicians so powerfully that the government turned down the idea of 'a marketing board with teeth', as the demands of the time phrased it.

Another powerful influence at the time was the advice emanating from the Agricultural Institute under the tutelage of the independent-minded, forceful Dr Tom Walsh, who preached that the emphasis in the future would have to be on quality.

Walsh's influence, the governmental turn-down, and the new spirit amongst farmers in the wake of the protest march culminated in the farmers setting up their own marketing structure, or system of marts. The old picturesque (but foully unhygienic) fairs, in which country towns were taken over by cattle, sheep, pigs and horses for a day or two at fixed intervals while jobbers and 'tanglers' moved through them making deals directly with the farmers/owners, were abolished. In their place concreted, railed-off marts were set up at which cattle were publicly auctioned.

Initially the farmers, showing an unusual degree of solidarity in their actions, put up £2½m for the NFA to fund the scheme. The first big venture was Cork Marts IMP (Irish Meat Packers), a direct answer to the march demand which, as Sean Healy put it, was 'to break out and to break in', i.e. to break out of the jobbers' grip and break into a market other than the UK.

New Money, Old Ways

At the time the NFA were beginning to make contacts with European groups such as the Boerbond de Belge and the International Federation of Agricultural Producers, so that the general 'European' mood gripping the country was faithfully reproduced in the farming world. In the late sixties and early seventies moves were afoot because of looming EEC membership and the pattern of world trade.

Land prices began to rise, going up steadily from around £100 an acre for good agricultural land in the early fifties to a peak of £4,600 prior to the oil shock of the mid-seventies. This was dearer even than land prices in Holland, with its long history of agricultural and horticultural development; a Dutch farmer on average can rear almost twice as many cattle per acre as can his Irish counterpart. Many Irish farmers bought English farms far cheaper than they could buy land in Ireland, on the proceeds of the Irish boom — an ironic way of 'breaking the UK grip'.

Banking competition increased; old-established banks began

to merge into large conglomerates. The Provincial, Royal, Munster and Leinster banks merged into a single monster, Allied Irish Banks, to rival the hitherto dominant Bank of Ireland, which itself merged with the National and Hibernian Banks and increased its efficiency by bringing in American experts to modernise itself. The Ulster Bank associated itself with the British giant, National Westminster, and a host of new financial houses were set up in Dublin.

The Irish banks then proceeded to mislead the Irish farmers in much the same way as did their American counterparts the American farmer. Sitting in their altitudinous, marble-walled, thickly-carpeted offices looking out over a city whose rape they largely facilitated by fuelling a property speculation boom, which they began and ended with equal ruthlessness, it became fashionable for decision-taking bankers to tell each other that, as one bank director put it to me, they were 'under-exposed in the agricultural sector'.

This filtered back down the directors' lift and out into the various branches and sub-offices until it became commonplace for bank managers to visit clients on their farms urging them 'to take advantage of the credit facilities available'. Roughly translated, this meant 'now is your chance to get up to your hocks in debt'. And get into debt they did.

Many farmers are now undoubtedly in a bad way. Land prices are a third of what they were in the boom years. The Common Agricultural Policy (CAP) is drying up under the assault of the British and Germans in particular, and the IFA is desperately negotiating with banks and such bodies as the Agricultural Credit Corporation on behalf of farmers in danger of having their land seized, having to repay borrowings at a time when incomes are down by perhaps as much as 40 per cent. The other side of the lending coin was, of course, the fact that, if farmer Murphy was refused a loan at his friendly neighbouring branch of Irish Predatory Ltd, all he had to do was trot down the street to the competing branch of Mohaired Carnivore Ltd to be given anything he wanted.

Any visitor to the Spring Show or Horse Show in Dublin was struck by the enormous array of huge, costly and complex farm machinery on sale, from hard currency countries such as Sweden and West Germany — all of it selling merrily, mostly on credit.

The purchase of some of this machinery could have been justified on a co-operative basis, but farmers preferred to buy for themselves, arguing that if they went into a co-operative venture the machinery might be tied up with a neighbour when they needed it at some crucial period such as harvest time.

New farm buildings went up. Costly home improvements were effected. The eating-out habit spread and overdrafts mushroomed.

The benefits to the farming community of EEC membership have undoubtedly been enormous. Successive Irish Ministers for Agriculture have wrested huge sums from EEC coffers; a total of £5½ billion in all went to the farmers. In 1986 the farm support mechanism gave Irish farmers 100 per cent higher prices than those obtaining on the world market. Farmers' incomes rose by 400 per cent after Ireland joined the EEC. However, underneath the patina of prosperity and modernity old habits and attitudes persisted. It became fashionable to talk of 'agri-business' but farm business methods remained rooted in the past.

It was possible to go to a co-op meeting at which two hours would be devoted to wrangling over whether or not to build new lavatories, but the approval of a £2,000,000 expenditure on equipment, which few present understood, went through on the nod. The simplest thing to produce on a farm, and the most lucrative, was a bullock. All a farmer had to do was to glance at the beasts every day, take a few elementary precautions such as dosing and ensuring provision of fodder, and he made money. Why bother with the exhausting uncertain business of planting vegetables?

If he did bother he often had that ingrained rural Irish attitude that contracts and fixed prices are dangerous snares set by the purchaser to trap the poor producer. If someone offered a better price for his crop, he blithely sold at the eleventh hour, thereby disappointing either a wholesaler or a vegetable processor who might go bankrupt or at least go elsewhere next year. This would leave the farmer with the following year's crop on his hands, and created boom/glut situations in which many farmers washed their hands of vegetable production altogether. As a result, a steady tide of Israeli, Cypriot, Dutch, Portuguese, Polish and even Canadian and American vegetables, including potatoes, found their way into Irish shops and supermarkets. Since the end of the

1970s shoppers have been able to riffle through countless packages of West German and Dutch chips and frozen vegetables in the freezer compartments of Dublin supermarkets without finding any Irish brands.

The early EEC aspirations about marketing and quality grading did not extend as far as vegetables. Beef, mutton and pig products could in the main compare effectively with their European counterparts. Vegetables lamentably failed to do so. Potatoes, for example, were (and often still are) sold in sacks made of thick, brown paper. These, when opened, revealed muddy, ungraded potatoes. Often, under a layer of large tubers, were many small ones which ought to have been fed to pigs. The European counterpart was and is made of mesh or plastic, so that the shopper can see the properly graded potatoes on offer.

The entrepreneurial class amongst the farming community which might have been expected to encourage developments such as pates, yoghurts, imaginatively-packed butter, or processed vegetables, like chipped potatoes, simply didn't exist. Most vegetable growing co-operatives went bankrupt through bad business methods.

The Poor Mouth

The Chairman of the co-op could well be the local parish priest. Certainly the committee would be trained in habits of deference to authority and to suspicion of initiative. In the early EEC era, co-op meetings were held in local schools, often begrudgingly lent for the purpose by elderly parish priests who grumbled about the dangers of boys and girls being brought together in this way, and could be seen shaking their heads and muttering that a little education was a dangerous thing.

The impression that Brussels was a gravy train of limitless proportions encouraged the feeling that Dublin, the centre, was a place of 'them', not 'us', from which public money could be extracted by a combination of direct action on the lines of the great protest of 1966 and of the traditional 'beal bocht', the poor mouth. This attitude was summed up by the cartoonist who depicted one farmer talking to another in a field and saying, 'I was ruined last year and I was ruined the year before but I was never so ruined as I was this year'.

The cartoonist did not exaggerate. During the bad summer of 1985, in which much flooding occurred during July, I heard a farm economist on radio soberly assess the damage at £30,000,000, a not inconsiderable sum and a genuinely powerful argument for the farmers' case that they should be given some government help to make up their losses. However, the economist was followed on the programme by a farmers' leader who spoke of the position in apocalyptic terms and placed the damage at £300,000,000!

In the event the farming community were disgusted that year when the government rejected demands that the farmers be paid grants to help them buy grain to replace lost crops and to feed their cattle. The government supplied them directly with grain, not money! Yet by the year's end it was a demonstrable fact that much of this grain had been resold by farmers at a profit because they had not needed it in the first place, and that the Republic had made record sales of hay and straw to British and Northern Ireland farmers.

There are other ways in which Irish farmers make money from the border and from England. Irish farmers are no more corrupt than their continental counterparts; they simply avail themselves of what is available. At the Berleymont building, for instance, you will hear that apparently the Vatican State (which is not in the EEC), imports so much butter annually that it works out at over one thousand tonnes per Cardinal! This sort of thing is made possible by the network of EEC subsidies which cushions exports to 'third countries'.

Under this system, if an Irish dealer sells a bullock to Colonel Gadafy for £500, Gadafy will have to pay only £250. The EEC makes up the rest. There is enormous smuggling throughout Europe. Lake Geneva at night (with obvious Swiss connivance) sees vast quantities of Swiss produce move across the water. These at least are actual items produced by the Swiss; in the case of the Vatican State, the butter does not exist. West Germany feels itself perfectly entitled to allow an enormous flow of unchecked East German products into West Germany and hence the Common Market. Yugoslavia too is known to take advantage of EEC regulations on a grand scale.

So why should Irish cattle and meat exporters be stigmatised for taking advantage of an opportunity to sell into intervention meat which can turn up in a Dublin hotel? The East Germans, the Yugoslavs and the Italians all avail themselves of the opportunities offered by a border . . . 'red diesel culture' in excelsis.

In the Irish case the advantage stems from the fact that the Republic of Ireland is a *disadvantaged* area in EEC eyes, one of the benefits secured in the negotiations prior to accession. The results can still be seen along improved Irish roads, where signs record that they were 'built with the aid of the European Community's Regional Fund'.

The North of Ireland operates under rules applicable not to Dublin but to London, so that cattle crossing the border from the Republic qualify for EEC subsidies. An enterprising haulier or cattle owner can make a fortune by crossing the border at Point A, doing a U-turn up the road, recrossing at Point B and going back in again at Point C to collect new subsidies on the same cattle. This is a commonplace occurrence. It would of course be easier, with the services of a corrupt customs official, to make money by crossing with a lorry load of non-existent cattle (like the Vatican State butter). In the absence of such sophistication in Ireland, most smugglers have to make their money the hard way, by actually crossing over the border with their cattle and back again.

The TB Scandal

While the case can be made that having gone to Europe with a begging bowl, the Irish did no more than get up to a few of the fairly harmless tricks normally associated with beggars, the same cannot be said of what the Irish agricultural sector has done to the rest of the population, particularly to the taxpayer. Apart from using its muscle to avoid paying much income tax, health charges, or a land tax, the farmers actively conspired, with the connivance of a professional body and a large section of the civil service, to defraud the taxpayer of vast sums of money.

As the cattle trade is of such importance to the economy, the Department of Agriculture has been allocated very considerable funds to ensure the eradication of tuberculosis from cattle. By March of 1985, according to the Minister for Agriculture, Austin Deasy, the scheme had cost £1 billion since its introduction in 1954. This money was intended to enable vets to test herds so that diseased animals could be identified and slaughtered. During the euphoric sixties (again!) it seemed as if the scheme was working as it was intended to. Ten years after it was introduced, a predecessor of Mr Deasy (Charles Haughey) declared that the country was 'almost attested', that is virtually free of bovine TB.

However, somewhere along the line things slipped backwards. The autumn and early winter of 1981 were enlivened in farming circles by the publication, and subsequent controversy in the *Farmers' Journal*, of statistics which showed the disease was still far from eradicated. Speaking in the Seanad, Dr T.K. Whitaker said that the way the scheme was being, and had been, operated was 'the greatest financial scandal in the history of the state'. That was in 1981, when the figures for the previous year showed that there had still been a TB prevalence in herds of 2.10 per cent. However, despite Whitaker's onslaught and the publicity attending the *Farmers' Journal* revelations, nothing substantive was done to correct matters. Indeed, as a fine piece of investigative journalism by Willy Kealy (*Sunday Independent*, March 1986) showed, things had got worse.

In 1984, when for some strange reason only a half round of testing had been carried out, TB prevalence was up to 3.04 per cent. The previous year, in which a full round of testing had been carried out, the figure was as high as 4.54 p.c. This was a sorry state of affairs for a scheme directly employing over 2,000 people — 1,300 civil servants and 550 vets. It had cost more than £1,000 out of the pockets of every tax-paying worker in the country to create a situation where, in layman's language, there was four times as much bovine TB in the Republic as in Northern Ireland!

The loopholes in the scheme which allowed this to happen were: (a) The scheme allowed the farmer, not the Department, to nominate his own vet; (b) The Department paid not the vet who did the testing, but the practice which employed him. This resulted in a buddy-buddy relationship between the farmer and the man who owned the practice. A tip-off to a farmer that early testing had showed up reaction in his herd enabled him to dispose of it to an unsuspecting customer — a butcher, say, or another farmer — before the follow-up testing could be carried out.

The customer does not even have to be unsuspecting. I know of a case where a farmer, stricken to learn that he had bovine TB in his herd, informed his neighbour of the fact out of courtesy and to warn him that the Department of Agriculture would be examining the neighbour's herd next day. When the vet showed up, the neighbour refused to allow him on his land without a court order and bought time, using his existing certification, to transfer his herd (at midnight) to a farmer friend in another part of the country, who eventually sold the cattle to a butcher for sale to the housewife. This was a case where contaminated meat was sold knowingly. It can happen unknowingly also, because some farmers and vets fail to notify neighbouring farms of the proximity of the TB.

In certain instances the disease, *often* it is said carried by badgers or by cattle drinking from contaminated streams, quickly reached epidemic proportions. Such epidemics occurred in Counties Kilkenny and Waterford, not long before Kealy conducted his investigation. And in November 1986 it was revealed that epidemics had swept County Longford to a degree which had raised the level of disease to 12 per cent of the country's herds, an appalling statistic in itself, and in what it threatened for its neighbours — including northern neighbours, whom the Republic is politically at least attempting to convince of the benefits of a closer relationship with the south. Moreover, the actual testing procedure was often deficient, because as the money went not to the actual vet who carried out the testing, frequently the most junior member of the practice and only receiving half or less of the Department's money, the young vet, lacking incentive and supervision, often carried out his testing in a sloppy and inefficient manner.

The Minister for Agriculture is now trying to reform the scheme by having a named, state-selected vet appointed, and paid to carry out the testing, thereby bringing both accountability and incentive into the scheme. But as half of the country's veterinary income is derived from testing, the stakes involved for those with practices are very high, and reform will not come easily. The Minister is being opposed strongly by the Vets Union, though the major farming associations — whatever about the greed of individual members — support him.

However, less has been done to clear up this disgraceful mess by the public watchdogs than by journalists like Willy Kealy. Before stern necessity started rattling skeletons out of cupboards, it was official Department of Agriculture policy *not* to let the public know what was happening — on the grounds that it might damage the image of Irish meat! The fact that it might also have damaged the livelihood of 1,300 civil servants was not adverted to by the Department or by those responsible for it, the politicians in Dail Eireann.

On a London Bus

The salient facts of the foregoing warts-and-all picture of Irish agriculture are two. First, the concentration on cattle grew as a result of EEC membership to the neglect of 'down-stream' activities such as food processing. The Irish farmers did not get into the EEC agricultural market — they got into intervention. Secondly, the number employed in agriculture went down steadily from 48 per cent in 1948 to approximately 17 per cent in 1987.

A similar trend exists world-wide, of course, but for Ireland, depending as it does so heavily on agriculture, the flight from the land has put appalling pressure on the cities, noticeably on Dublin. It has wasteful consequences both in terms of human resources and of the money invested in those resources.

Sitting on a London bus one September Monday in 1986, I fell into conversation with a group of young Irish people ranging in age from 21 to 23. Judging from their holdalls and rucksacks, they were either going camping or emigrating. In fact, they were emigrating. All six had just qualified as civil engineers and they had with them the previous Sunday's *Sunday Press*, which carried a large picture of their graduating class — of the 47 beaming young faces in the photograph, only one had a permanent job in Ireland, two had temporary work, and the other 44 were emigrants. Very few, initially at least, were working as engineers. My six had worked as labourers, temporary barmen, whatever they could get, in some cases at jobs lasting only four or six days each. They had just managed to scrape up between them, largely through the efforts of one girl who had been working as an engineer throughout the summer, £1,400 to pay eight weeks' rent in advance for a house in Golders Green.

They had been doubling up in friends' bedsitters, sneaking into hostels after hours with illegally-held keys, and generally subsisting in a variety of ways never envisaged by themselves or their parents as they worked their way through sixteen difficult, costly years of education. Of course, the pity about the sort of improvements I am advocating in natural resources, fishing, forestry, vegetable growing and so on, is that not alone would these come too late to benefit the young people I met in Golders Green, but that having begun they would be very costly and slow to show a return — not the sort of prospect which a political system notoriously prone to the 'quick fix' is likely to embrace with either alacrity or enthusiasm.

Nevertheless, for reasons which I trust I have made clear, these improvements will have to be set in train sometime. For me at least, the time to begin is now.

9

Foreign Affairs

Neutrality; Keeping the Peace; American Emotions;
Establishment Friends; A House Divided

Neutrality

Irish foreign policy has two major preoccupations: first, to keep out of trouble (expressed as 'neutrality') and secondly, to help other nations to stay out of trouble also (a policy called 'peace-keeping'). Foreign policy also aims at getting the best deal it can out of the EEC, improving Anglo-Irish relationships, and helping the country to expand its links with the Middle East. It is not altogether clear what we think we are doing in the US. An indication of the importance of Anglo-Irish relationships may be gleaned from the fact that, apart from incessant ministerial and diplomatic contact, there were twenty-one meetings of Irish and British prime ministers between 1971 and 1984.

The most curious aspect of Irish foreign policy is 'neutrality'. This was appropriately described by Dr Patrick Keatinge[1] in his book on the topic as a 'singular stance'. The general attitude of the Irish public and its politicians was well summarised by the then Taoiseach, Dr Garret FitzGerald, in an interview with the *Irish Times* on 5 February 1983, in which he said: 'I think that the Irish people have a very strong attachment to the situation in which we are not a member of a military alliance. The word neutrality is used by different people in different ways, and gives rise to a great deal of confusion. But something to which our people are so firmly attached is inevitably firmly embedded in our foreign policy'.

1. P. Keatinge, *A Singular Stance,* Institute of Public Administration, Dublin 1984.

Speaking as an Irish prime minister in this vein, FitzGerald knew that for once he was on assuredly safe bipartisan soil, grounds which since de Valera's assertion and practice of neutrality had been similarly defended by all parties; 'neutrality' in the Irish context is a little like Lewis Carroll's 'it means exactly what I choose it to mean'. Jack Lynch, for instance, in extolling the virtues of EEC membership in the Dail in February 1969 observed correctly that Ireland had 'never been ideologically neutral!', i.e. in effect between America and her allies, and Russia and its associates.

However, the distinguished Irish soldier Lt General Carl O'Sullivan, on retiring as Chief of Staff, pointed out in an interview in the *Irish Times* on 2 February 1982 that the Irish stance was meaningless in the east-west conflict. 'Internal aggression is about all the army could deal with at the moment; if we faced external aggression we are not equipped to face even a minimum attack from outside. We haven't the ships, the planes, the artillery, the armour'.

General O'Sullivan said: 'Ireland would need to spend over £500 million annually to handle an attack from outside, to back up the claim that Ireland is militarily neutral. We are in a crucial position in the North Atlantic. The threat in the last war came from Europe and the UK. The Soviets have a strategic fleet sited in Murmansk. They have airborne divisions in the Kola Peninsula which pose a threat to the North Atlantic, and Ireland is in a crucial position there'.

East-west considerations did not weigh with Charles Haughey when America's closest ally was involved in hostilities some months later. During the Falklands war he was smarting from his treatment by Thatcher during the hunger strikes and saw to it that Ireland abstained. He said in the Dail on 11 May 1982: 'Ireland is not afraid to stand alone on the issue of peace, or to reassert our traditional policy of neutrality'. Ireland had supported the UN resolution calling for Argentina's withdrawal from the Falklands, and a separate EEC action which applied sanctions. After the sinking of the *Belgrano,* the government announced that it would table a resolution at the UN which would be less favourable to the British case, and also withdraw from the EEC sanctions. Haughey said that Ireland found herself: 'moving into a situation which would seriously endanger our traditional policy on neutrality. We were being seen to be and obviously could fairly be interpreted as being associated with a serious escalation of military activity'.

The Irish abstention meant, in effect, as James Prior told myself and Aidan Hennigan (the *Irish Press* London Editor) later that year, that Mrs Thatcher regarded the Irish UN activity as 'working on the side of the Argentinians', with all the consequential coolness one can imagine this brought in its wake — a coolness which I know from private conversations was regarded with acute alarm by the Irish Embassy staff in London at the time.

Other arguments advanced by the Irish against abandoning neutrality are the existence of partition — because to join in NATO with Britain would be to accept the existing frontiers, including the border — and the need to enlarge the EEC. Sweden and Austria, for example, could be urged to join the EEC without abandoning their neutrality because of the Irish example, Peter Barry told me in November of 1986. A counter-argument put to me by American Embassy sources is that Ireland should follow the French example. This view is accepted by the vast majority of the Irish Army officer cadre, and expressed by General O'Sullivan: 'France is not a member of NATO, but . . . she plays a crucial role in the defence of Europe . . . France has an external association with NATO who, while she pushed all NATO bases off her soil, involved her in keeping about 40,000 men in Germany; she is not a "free-loader" where defence is concerned'.

But it was neither the soldier nor the politician who concentrated Irish minds on the neutrality issue as this book was being written but an agricultural economist, Dr Raymond Crotty, who successfully petitioned the courts that the Single European Act was in conflict with the Irish Constitution.

The Single European Act was signed into law by President Hillery on 24 December 1986, but injunction proceedings brought by Crotty the day before delayed the Irish government's ratification of the Act. The Act envisaged an EEC of unencumbered frontiers through the elimination of existing fiscal, technical and bureaucratic barriers. The loss to Ireland of the principle of unanimity voting (which, though little used, in effect gave member countries a kind of veto *in extremis*) in favour of a qualified majority vote, which obviously lessened the clout of smaller countries, was held to be greatly outweighed by the fact that the Commission had recommended that the funds available to the less developed regions be doubled. In fact, this last consideration propelled Ireland to the forefront of those European nations which actively campaigned to get the EEC to espouse the SEA. It would have been a complete reversal of years of Irish policy to have rejected the Act — if for no other reason than that most of those who did so would have driven to the polls over the roads built by the EEC in the first place!

However on 9 April, when the Supreme Court delivered its verdict on the appeal against the High Court injunction, it found, in the words of Mr Justice Henchy, that if Ireland ratified the SEA it would be bound in international law to engage actively in a programme which would 'impinge progressively on Irish sovereignty'. It was really not an Act, but a Treaty, which would bind Ireland to act in a way which would be 'inconsistent with the Constitution'. Yet another referendum had to be held to amend the Constitution; held on 26 May, it passed by 755,423 votes to 324,977.

Fine Gael had hesitated to hold a referendum on the issue at a time when the Act might still have been changed and all the agreements about neutrality might have had some relevance to the actual wording of the Act, but they feared that Haughey might enmesh the issue with the divorce referendum, which was already sending danger signals to the government about tampering with 'traditional values'. These fears were not without foundation; when the SEA Referendum campaign got going, some of Haughey's former supporters campaigned against ratifying the Act, not on the grounds of sovereignty, but on the grounds that it would enable abortion to be introduced to the Republic! Haughey himself, now in power and committed to a 'yes' vote, had the mortification of seeing his speeches on the SEA made in opposition now being circulated for use against him by the 'no' campaign.

The SEA controversy and the problem of illegal emigration to the US illustrate an Irish governmental problem that I adverted to earlier when citing how the preoccupation with Sunningdale distracted attention from the economy. Preoccupation with the Anglo-Irish accord is similarly cited in political circles as the reason why the Irish Foreign Minister, Peter Barry, was not prompted to seek an exemption for Ireland which would have got over the constitutional difficulty and which, it is averred, would at that stage have been readily available from the Europeans.

A similar claim is made by Irish diplomats in relation to the 1965 American Immigration Act which set up the quota system that led to the present disadvantaged position of Irish immigrants in the US. It is averred that at that time Speaker Tip O'Neill was ready and able to secure exemption for Ireland, 'had a phone call come through from the Irish Embassy — but the phone call never came'.

In 1965 the government policy, under Lemass, was that the bad old days were over and emigration was a thing of the past. In fact, as late as 1986 when the sixtieth anniversary of the founding of Fianna Fail was being celebrated, party sources issued a map of Ireland showing the achievement of Fianna Fail in each county. The legend for 1965 proclaimed 'emigration ended'!

The SEA and US immigration issues illustrate that though Ireland is internationally-minded, her concentration is not always geared to watching where she is heading internationally.

Keeping the Peace

The high-water-mark of Irish foreign policy efforts to save the rest of mankind from disorder probably occurred in Moscow on 1 July 1968, when the Treaty for the Non-proliferation of Nuclear Weapons was signed by the members of the United Nations, including the man who had first proposed and nurtured the UN resolution, the Irish Foreign Minister, Frank Aiken.

The Treaty remains today the only instrument for the limitation of the weapons of Armageddon. It owed its origin to the high ideals of Frank Aiken himself and of Eamon de Valera in upholding a special kind of Irish moral position in world affairs which had existed since the foundation of the state and had been promoted by the pioneering work of early Irish ministers such as Patrick McGilligan and Kevin O'Higgins.

After July 1968, Irish foreign policy became more concerned with European and economic questions than with broader international issues or neutrality. The question of joining the EEC dominated everything else and the country duly attained its goal, being admitted on 1 January 1973, and taking up its first presidency of the EEC in 1975.

The early euphoria over membership, born out of a combination of beliefs that Ireland would make a fortune out of farming, become more independent of England, more European-minded and somehow help implement the vision of such European giants as Monet and Schumann, soon faded. Paudeen didn't exactly diverge from the statesman-like Aikenite position to one of exclusively scrabbling in the greasy till, but overall the Irish public became less concerned with the United Nations, which of course also declined in importance in the same period, and more interested in concentrating on Europe.

The following table sums up why in a nutshell:

In 1972 — 51 per cent of Irish exports went to Britain.

In 1985 — only 25 per cent went to Britain.

In 1972 — 17 per cent of Irish exports went to EEC countries.

In 1985 — 40.77 per cent went to EEC countries.

It was difficult to get a constituency in which to take up moral stances in the face of those trade developments but Ireland did become more overseas-conscious. The country won golden opinions from European commentators for the way it handled the Irish presidency of the EEC in 1975, 1979 and 1984. In 1970 Ireland had a grand total of eighteen embassies abroad, three permanent representatives in the EEC (Brussels), the United Nations (Geneva) and the United Nations (New York), and five consulates. By 1986 Ireland had twenty-nine embassies and, in addition to their representations and consulates, three development corporation offices, with a fourth envisaged.

The expanding circle of world contacts in Dublin — a total of thirty-four accreditations at the time of writing — included Russian and Chinese embassies, unheard of in the mid-sixties. Meanwhile the Department of Foreign Affairs has grown in size from 366 staff in 1970 to 805 in 1986.

Irish diplomats showed themselves as able as their European counterparts in negotiating major treaties, such as that governing entry to the European Monetary System. All the diplomatic activity did mask some failures in political foresight — for instance Ireland, with its incredibly fertile fishing grounds, accepted limitation of its fishing catch to 4.6 per cent of the EEC total.

It would not be altogether true to say that idealism died with the Aiken era; though Ireland is a signatory of the Lomé Convention which channels EEC aid to Africa, the country likes to take individual initiatives as well. Ireland has therefore established overseas aid offices in Lesotho (1978), Tanzania (1979) and Zambia (1980). In these countries and in the Sudan, the Irish have done some valuable work for development, the bill for which went up steadily from £1.5m in 1974 to £44m in 1986. Accordingly, Irishmen are found engaged in all sorts of activities from cross-breeding Arab and Connemara ponies in Lesotho to showing the Tanzanians how to run county councils, helping Zambia become self-sufficient in cement production, and helping the Sudanese to instal a water supply. All this is of course additional to the missionary efforts in which Irish men and women play so large a part.

The major continuing hangover from the time when the United Nations rather than the EEC was central to Irish foreign policy is that of peace-keeping. UNPIC (United Nations Peace in Cyprus), established in 1964, saw some 9,000 Irish soldiers pass through Cyprus although the operation has now been scaled down almost out of sight. UNEF (United Nations Emergency Force), set up in 1973 as a consequence of the Arab-Israeli situation, continues to be an Irish Army care. More particularly, so does UNIFIL (United Nations Interim Force in Lebanon), which has seen some 13,000 Irish troops pass through its ranks. The Irish lieutenant Aengus Murphy, who was killed in August 1986 was only the latest in a long list of casualties (not all of them fatal, admittedly) sustained as a result of the unclear position regarding the United Nations mandate and the local antagonisms which have sometimes led to tension between the Irish and the Israelis. The Irish relate better to the relatively easy-going Arabs than they do to the Israeli regular army who, unlike the civilian reserve, often appear to be arrogant and overbearing.

The Irish diplomatic effort abroad is on the side of tolerance. In the United Nations Commission on Human Rights, the country is particularly active over religious intolerance issues — as well it might be with Belfast in its backyard — and they will tell you with quiet pride in Iveagh House that the Hillsborough Agreement of December 1985 between Ireland and England is a prime example of this. *Peut être . . .* !

American Emotions

One area of Irish diplomacy which has consistently met with a mixed reception, and which interacts directly with Hillsborough, concerns the Irish in America. At census time some 40,000,000 United States citizens give their origins as 'Irish', and the Irish are reckoned to be the best educated and wealthiest ethnic group in the country.

Yet, as they will tell you at the Irish Embassy in Washington, the corresponding Irish-American input to Ireland is minuscule when compared to that of the American Jews to Israel. What enrages some Irish-American activists about this approach is its casuistry. A principal contributory factor to the lack of concerted Irish-American action on the Northern Ireland problem is the policy pursued so actively by those same Irish diplomats. This in effect boils down to telling one large section of the Irish-American community that it is doing wrong and is in error, while giving no very clear-cut indication of what is actually wanted. Apart, that is from support for some vague platitudinous aspirations about 'peace by consent', which in the real world of what happens in Belfast or Crossmaglen is like having a preacher explain his church's attitudes in terms like: 'our position on motherhood is we're for it; on sin, we're against it'.

There are other reasons for this disunity. The Irish were traditionally organised in the service of the church, not of Ireland. The Roman Catholic church in America owes a debt to Ireland that would be hard to compute, and so to a certain extent does the Democratic Party, but the old specifically Irish involvement in politics and organisation once symbolised by Irish dominance in the trade unions, Tammany Hall or the New York police force is long gone. The very success of the Irish assimilation into American society, winning through in the upward mobility stakes and challenging the WASP (white Anglo-Saxon Protestant) element, meant that they inevitably left Irish affairs behind them.

Interest in Irish politics, Irish music, or Irish games remained strong in circles such as the Irish county associations (the Kerrymen's Association, the Galwaymen's Association and so on), the Ancient Order of Hibernians and outcroppings of the Gaelic Athletic Association like that to be found at Gaelic Park in New York. Everybody became Irish once a year for St Patrick's

Day. Green carnations, green beer, and drum majorettes moved through an orgy of marching and booze, typified by the St Patrick's Day Parade in New York, where for most of the years under review the Chairman of the organising committee, the iron-willed Judge Comerford from County Kilkenny, stoutly refused the efforts of New York's traders to have the parade shifted off Fifth Avenue.

But by and large, the consciousness of being Irish remained a tourist concept. The activities and concerns of the 'hidden Ireland', away from mainstream America, were reported not in the major newspapers but in the Irish-American press such as the *Irish Echo* of New York or the *Irish American Herald* in San Francisco. However, as the Northern troubles erupted, the strains and tensions observable in Ireland between constitutionalists and the supporters of physical force were reproduced in America.

The Irish in America had traditionally been the fertile source of funds for revolution in Ireland. In the days of the Anglo-Irish War, de Valera followed in the footsteps of leaders such as Parnell and John Redmond to obtain support amongst the Irish emigrants. This vein of Irish-American support withered away as the tide of revolution ebbed, and when the troubles erupted in 1969 there was not a great deal of specifically Irish organisation anywhere in America. However, old memories and old traditions came speedily alive. Irish Northern Aid, led by Michael Flannery, an ex-IRA man from County Tipperary, and Martin Galvin, an American civil servant of Irish ancestry, found willing new recruits to the old colours. The Irish-American oil magnate Emmet O'Connell (50), describes the situation as follows:

'The older generation that fought in the Anglo-Irish War or the civil war is almost gone now. You don't have the letters in the beautiful handwriting coming across the Atlantic giving the news of home.

'That generation gave Dev legitimacy as the leader of the Irish both at home and in America. They often disagreed with him. I still remember the day in our house in the States when we got a letter with the news of the IRA men being executed by Dev; boy, he certainly got some stick that day! But still, he was seen as being basically sincere on the reunification of the

country. He had the stature and there was a belief in Fianna
Fail. But after Dev that legitimacy was withdrawn. The Irish
Americans don't see the leadership of the Irish race as coming
from Dublin'.

There are some pockets of exception to this — fairly sizeable
ones at that. It would not be true of Irish figures on the American
scene who are active socially or commercially in Ireland. It would
not be true, for instance, of the extraordinary Tony O'Reilly, who
is not alone the Chief Executive of the Heinz Corporation of
America, but also has extensive business interests in Ireland,
including Independent Newspapers, nor of the sort of person
who has his or her horses trained by Vincent O'Brien and delights
in attending the Irish Derby. Nevertheless, my observation of the
Irish-American scene based on more than a dozen visits to the
States over the last twenty years and continuous regular contact
with the Irish-American community largely bears out
O'Connell's analysis.

It should be remembered that a high percentage of the Irish
emigrants now slipping through the US immigration net are
disaffected young nationalists from Northern Ireland, who most
emphatically do not concede 'legitimacy' to 'Dublin' or to any
grouping connected with Ireland save the IRA, and who devote a
high percentage of their energy and ingenuity towards furthering
the cause of that organisation.

In Congress, Senator Mario Biaggi, an Italian-American, has
supported the cause of Irish unity, setting up an 'Ad-hoc' committee on Capitol Hill. This soon claimed the support of eighty-
four senators and congressmen, but has been viewed warily in
Dublin as being too close to the physical force school. The same
reserve was extended to Father Sean MacManus, whose brother
had been prominent in the 1956–62 IRA campaign and who
established an efficient lobbying operation in Washington, the
Irish National Caucus. Almost from the outset this was
considered suspect in Dublin as altogether too pro-IRA. As the
conflict mounted, the Department of Foreign Affairs (partly
under the influence of John Hume) took a little-publicised but
far-reaching decision to work not with the existing Irish-
American organisations but with establishment political leaders
instead. Figures such as Senator Ted Kennedy, Tip O'Neill,
Congressman Tom Foley, William Buckley of New York and
Hugh Carey were 'in'.

Noraid of course was definitely out and the Ancient Order of Hibernians, the largest Irish-American organisation, was looked upon at best with condescension. At the Irish Embassy at Washington they would argue forcibly that the Irish groupings were riven by petty feuding and electorally counted for little. At the same time, the Embassy sought to influence these groups' activities. As a result, considerable resentment built up; I have often heard Irish-Americans utter the complaint, 'All they do is say "don't support the IRA". We're not in favour of violence but we want to do something about what's going on. What are we supposed to do? All the Irish government seems to want is to get our dollars for IDA investment and tell us to shut up'.

The classic example of this animosity in the bitter years of the hunger strikes (1980–81) was a tactic adopted by Judge Comerford, Chairman of the organising committee for the New York St Patrick's Day Parade. On the sumptuous green programme he listed the names of the participating dignitaries, — but deliberately noted only the title of the Irish Ambassador, omitting the name Sean Donlon.

The old warrior had too much respect for the country not to invite the official representative, so he acknowledged the office whilst laying a marker on the man. Donlon, for his part, had a more energetic St Patrick's Day than the other dignitaries, because every time a Noraid banner approached he stepped down off the stand!

Establishment Friends

Establishment spokesmen point to the success of Irish diplomatic activity in securing such tangible recognition of the Irish situation as the Carter Initiatives of August 1977. These promised economic help for Northern Ireland if a peaceful settlement could be reached. Aso quoted is the Friends of Ireland Declaration of 1977, signed by 'The Four Horsemen' — Buckley, Carey, Kennedy and O'Neill — pledging support for a peaceful solution to the Irish problem. Above all, there was the endorsement of the Anglo-Irish Agreement by Reagan and Tip O'Neill in November 1985 which resulted in Congress approval for an aid and loans package to help create support for the Agreement.

Whether these advances were solely attributable to orthodox

diplomatic activity or were partly the result of lobbying by Irish-American activists, coupled with the worsening nature of the crisis itself, is debatable. The probable truth about Irish-American political support is that all these factors and personalities played their part.

Dublin-US political contact is not always smooth. When President Carter said during his election campaign (in October 1976) that the Democratic Party was committed to the unification of Ireland, that the US could not remain idle over the issue and that an international commission on human rights should be set up for Northern Ireland, the Irish National Caucus promptly called for support for 'Jimmy Who'. Unionists and other groups objected to his remarks; so did the Irish government which, in the time-honoured diplomatic phrase that indicates and conceals displeasure, called for 'clarification' of his remarks. Carter subsequently communicated with Garret FitzGerald, then Minister for Foreign Affairs, disclaiming any support for violence and stressing his interest in human rights and a negotiated settlement.

Not long after the Carter hiccup, Fianna Fail had its US/Dublin 'incident'. Jack Lynch, in 1978, criticised Mario Biaggi when he visited Ireland at the request of the Caucus; Lynch said Biaggi associated with 'the men of violence'. The Dublin coolness towards Biaggi had its effect in Washington that year also when prominent Irish-Americans, led by Senator Kennedy and responsive to the Dublin line, opposed a plan put forward by Biaggi to hold a peace conference on the North in the Capitol.

Hugh Carey had better luck with Dublin the following year when he proposed peace talks in New York between the south's Minister for Foreign Affairs, Michael O'Kennedy, and the Secretary of State for Northern Ireland, Humphrey Atkins, with himself in the chair. Dublin said yes, London no. Carey was somewhat out of favour with London at the time, anyhow, through having stayed away from a dinner for Prime Minister James Callaghan the previous year in protest at British policies in Northern Ireland.

Senator Kennedy's position illustrated the cross-currents of Irish-American opinion and of Dublin-Irish-American relationships. Kennedy, as the head of a star-crossed Irish-American dynasty, has always taken a deep interest in Ireland and in the early days of the struggle took a strong 'Troops Out' position, supporting a Congress motion to that effect in 1971 and bracketing this position with attacks on internment and discrimination against Catholics. After the fall of the power-sharing Executive he moved towards a more centrist position, developing a friendly relationship with John Hume, whom he admired greatly, warning against support for the IRA and urging Carter to promise economic aid to the province, paving the way for the Carter initiative of 1977. Kennedy takes a day-to-day interest in Irish affairs and has been known to phone the British Ambassador when some aspect of British policy displeases him.

Tip O'Neill, Speaker of the US House of Representatives, is the father-figure of Irish-American politicians. With his wife Millie, he was conferred with honorary Irish citizenship by Garret FitzGerald in March 1986 for his continual support for Dublin. Jack Lynch in his time also praised him, calling him a 'true friend of Ireland'. During a visit to Dublin in 1979, in a typically forthright comment, he attacked British politicians for making a 'political football' out of Northern Ireland at Westminster and brought down torrents of abuse on his silvery head from Callaghan, Thatcher and the unionists — which did nothing to lessen his commitment to Ireland. He set up 'The O'Neill Trust' in 1978 to canalise money from private American investors into employment-generating projects in Ireland.

In Irish-American politics he is a strong opponent of Mario Biaggi. 'What's an Italian doing in Irish affairs?' he asks. He is a strong critic of the IRA. Both he and Dublin hoped that President Reagan would appoint him Ambassador to Dublin as his career as Speaker neared its end. In the event the appointment went to a Republican, Margaret Heckler, who has strong Irish links.

Both Kennedy and O'Neill were involved in an extremely unusual and damaging controversy which broke out around Sean Donlon. Charles Haughey made an unsuccessful attempt to remove Donlon from Washington during his first period as Taoiseach (1979–81); the move followed a visit by Neil Blaney to the US in 1980 during which he became aware of the depth of feeling in some Irish-American quarters against 'the Embassy'. He communicated his feelings to Haughey, and Haughey moved to shift Donlon. In Ireland the move was represented by Haughey's opponents as a victory for the IRA. Donlon was one of the ablest men ever to join the Irish foreign service, a special protége of Jack Lynch, and made an impact in Washington out of all proportion to the size of the country he represented, switching points smoothly between Carter and Reagan when the Republicans succeeded the Democrats and having both as guests at the Irish Embassy. I attended a St Patrick's Day lunch there at which table companions included Reagan, Tip O'Neill and Edward Kennedy.

When Haughey made his move figures such as Kennedy, O'Neill and John Hume conveyed to Haughey the sense of 'regret' which would be felt in Washington should Donlon return home in these circumstances. Similar sentiments were conveyed to Haughey on behalf of Donlon's colleagues in Foreign Affairs; mass resignations were hinted at. Eventually Haughey backed down and Donlon stayed put despite the known wishes of his prime minister, an unparalleled state of affairs anywhere. It was an illustration, personality considerations apart, of the different approach of Fianna Fail on Northern Ireland from that of Fine Gael. Fianna Fail traditionally would have far less difficulty in accommodating to the style of the 'Hidden Ireland' America (while not actually pursuing a substantially different policy!) than would Fine Gael.

Donlon went on to become Secretary of the Department when Garret FitzGerald became Taoiseach.

As the possibility of Haughey returning to power loomed on the political horizon in January 1987, Donlon became the first departmental secretary to retire from the civil service and take up a post in industry.

Out of office, Haughey gave more thought to Irish-American affairs, and set up the Friends of Fianna Fail as a fund-raising and 'feed-back' organisation. At the first dinner of the Friends, in New York on 1 March 1985, he said:

'There has been a major failure of communication in recent decades. Conflicting and confusing signals have been coming from Ireland to the Irish in America. There has been no clear message on policy: no specifically enunciated national objectives behind which all right-thinking Americans could rally and to which they could give their unambiguous up-front support. More often than not the official message was negative, condemnatory and critical.

'Americans who wished only to offer genuine support and encouragement were met with suspicion, rebuff and disapproval. The time has come for all that to change and change radically. Where there was antagonism and suspicion we must now create a whole new atmosphere of constructive dialogue and cooperation as the basis for an effective, powerful Irish-American voice arrayed in legitimate support for clearly defined Irish national objectives — political, economic and cultural. Irish-American public opinion is a sleeping giant that must be awakened and fully motivated with a clear understanding of, and support for, Ireland's real and urgent needs.'

A House Divided

The division in the Irish-American community has been debilitating. I have spoken to decent first and second generation Irish emigrants who simply want to lobby on their country's behalf to get a settlement on the northern issue based on a British withdrawal, in the same way that they see representatives from other ethnic groups lobbying on behalf of their nationalist interests. They speak of the 'tyranny' of the Embassy network. This is obviously an overblown term, given the relatively tiny resources available to the Irish diplomatic effort in the States, but it does show the impact of Dublin on parts of the Irish-American community.

The Embassy is so active that when a speaker on an Irish issue has passed through a given area the Consul will have the organisers in for a debriefing. If the answers are not to the officials' liking, small but significant sanctions are administered. Access to Irish newspapers in the Consulate, for instance, is withdrawn, as are invitations to official functions. It becomes known throughout the community that the person or group is out of favour.

However, as the consciousness of being Irish grew in the wake of Bobby Sands such tactics began to backfire. Some people did not want to be seen at the Consulate, and more and more Irish-American activists went their own way independently of official channels. In New York, for instance, the civil rights activist Paul O'Dwyer mobilised support amongst his fellow lawyers. He founded the Brehon Law Society, which took up the cases of individuals who ran foul of American law because of the troubles, and helped with extradition proceedings, gun-running charges and so forth.

James Delaney, a Chicago-born entrepreneur who lives in San Antonio, set up his Irish-American Unity Conference (IAUC) in 1983 as an umbrella organisation for groups of all persuasions within the Irish spectrum, from Noraid types to stockbrokers and trade unionists whose interest in Irish affairs had heightened since the hunger strikes. The Noraid component makes Delaney 'iffy' in the eyes of the Department of Foreign Affairs. Even Pat Goggin, of the non-partisan Irish Forum of San Francisco, found on a trip to Dublin during 1984 that because while on a fact-finding mission to the North he and his group had met with a Sinn Fein spokesman, a planned conference with the Taoiseach was cancelled.

Noraid is unqestionably the fastest-growing Irish-American organisation, embracing a wide variety of socio-economic classes and displaying a high degree of professionalism and organisational abilities. Many of its activities are devoted to raising funds to help defray the legal cost of Irish fugitives in the US sought on British extradition warrants.

The 86-year-old Mike Flannery, whose election as Grand Marshal of the St Patrick's Day Parade in New York was a source of nationwide controversy, is a much respected figure within the Irish community, despite his pro-IRA views. He is an archetypal figure of the daily Mass-going, good-living Irish-American Catholic. His influence will not go away just because Dublin, Whitehall or the 'lace-curtain' Irish element would like it to. Flannery represents something very deep in the Irish-American tradition.

There has been some evidence of rethink in Dublin circles about the unhealthy divisions which have been allowed to fester. These divisions are not all Dublin's fault; some of the rhetoric used by the Irish-American groupings is of a virulence that would make rapprochement under any Dublin administration extremely difficult, and there is the perennial difficulty, existing for over a century, as to who controls Irish-American policy, the Irish in Ireland or the Irish in America. The Americans are not always overly understanding of the limitations on Dublin's freedom to manoeuvre. Some better way forward is obviously desirable in Irish-American affairs.

The Biaggi/MacManus elements managed, in the teeth of opposition from the influential Reagan-O'Neill-Foley element on Capitol Hill, to force the addition of a rider to the aid package which the American Congress passed in March 1986 to support the Anglo-Irish Accord. It stated that all aid would be contingent on President Reagan or his successor giving assurances each year to the Congress that human rights were respected in Northern Ireland. This of course is impossible in real terms, given the supergrass system, Diplock courts, discrimination in employment and so on. Away from Capitol Hill it also had an important symbolic significance; it represented a triumph for Nobel and Lenin Peace Prizes winner, Sean MacBride, whose 'MacBride Principles' seek to enforce fair employment practices. These principles are increasingly becoming a rallying point for Irish-Americans outside the Embassy circles, and have had their effect among would-be American investors in Northern Ireland.

Both the aid packages and the 'MacBride Principles' are important in themselves. The tragedy is that the currents they represent should be in mutual opposition, making yet another chapter in the long history of the Irish tendency to fall out with one another, the 'split' syndrome. Together they indicate the amount of good will amongst Irish-Americans available to be harnessed should someone find the magic formula.

There is a tendency in Ireland to portray the Irish in America as out-of-touch sentimentalists who drool over 'the old sod' and drink green beer on St Patrick's Day. In fact it is quite remarkable how much first-hand knowledge and voluntary effort is put into Irish causes by Irish-American activists, people like Dr Eoin McKiernan in Minnesota, Pat Goggin in San Francisco, Jim Delaney in Texas, or figures such as Jim Roche, a former president of the AOH who now devotes much of his energy to Delaney's IAUC.

Roche was succeeded in the AOH post by Nicholas Murphy, manager of US Treasury operations for the giant ITT Corporation, a position in which he handles funds of $300 million a day for ITT. In an interview with the *Irish Times* he said: 'The Irish-American market is vast — the AOH can't tackle it alone. We need a local organisation which would give us leadership and offer us a working relationship with the Irish government. There is no continuity in the Department of Foreign Affairs: the people they send us don't have a permanent commitment here. They just articulate the policy of the government of the day and move on to Japan or Saudi Arabia'. As Murphy was born in Kerry and grew up there, his criticism cannot be dismissed as being out of touch.

This theme is universal amongst Irish-Americans who take an interest in the old country. Denis P. Long, President of the giant Anheuser-Busch Corporation which sponsors the Budweiser Irish Derby, making it the richest race in Europe, was named Irish-American of the Year by *Irish America Magazine* for 1986.

In the course of an interview with the magazine, in December 1986, Long pointed to the fact that over 30 per cent of the top American corporations are led by people of Irish descent and indicated the enormous potential which exists for tapping this economic reservoir in conjunction with the IDA.

'But', he said, 'to be effective, Irish-Americans, including myself, need to be led by those in Ireland . . . Irish-American politicians need to do more to use their power to benefit the economy of the Republic of Ireland . . . but there has to be some kind of a plan, a way to touch these people [corporation chief executives] and get some action out of them, for them to be encouraged to ask, what can we do? The struggle up the corporate ladder is still under way, and time is precious. We need direction'. That direction is conspicuous by its absence. Long has now resigned from Anheuser-Busch.

Eoin McKiernan for the entire period under review has run the Irish Cultural Institute in St Paul, Minnesota, producing an excellent journal devoted to Irish studies, *Eire/Ireland*. He arranges the funding and organisation of a variety of literary awards, and every year brings out a team of Irish experts in everything from archaeology to traditional music to lecture audiences coast-to-coast on tours that last anything from a month to six weeks. The Institute also runs a summer school in Ireland for American students. It relies for financial support on a network of subscribers throughout the States.

The Institute thus differs from the official Irish-American cultural organisation which was set up jointly by President de Valera and President Kennedy as a result of Kennedy's visit to Ireland in 1963, the American-Irish Foundation. This solicits its funds from a few wealthy donors and provides incentives for cultural, scientific and educational projects in Ireland. The

Literary Awards Committee, of which I am a member, gives money prizes to Irish writers, sometimes quite substantial sums, of the order of $10,000 each, yet the Foundation never quite made the impact it should. Kennedy was murdered soon after its inception, before he had had the opportunity of launching the foundation in a major way via a White House dinner for wealthy Irish-Americans. It was not until a former American ambassador to Ireland, the distinguished journalist and historian, William Shannon, came to the fore in its activities that the organisation began showing signs of life; after only five or six years of activity it was merged in 1987 with Tony O'Reilly's Ireland Fund. The new body may yet become the force in Irish-American affairs envisaged by the two presidents.

Tony O'Reilly has hosted hugely successful fund-raising dinners in Boston and New York. With the money thus raised he has aided a variety of projects in Ireland, from ballet to a hostel for rehabilitating drug addicts on the Aran Islands. He bailed out the Wexford Festival when a reallocation of grants by the Arts Council threatened to force cancellation of the event in 1986. The new body very much depends for its existence on the drive and genius of Tony O'Reilly himself and is viewed with dubiety by the more extreme wings of the Irish-American spectrum.

Pat Goggin's Irish Forum has brought out speakers on the Irish issue as diverse as James Prior, Sile de Valera, Peter Robinson of the DUP and myself. He has also organised the valuable converse of that operation, by bringing groups of interested professionals from the Bay area to Ireland.

Irish-American scholarship is highly regarded; one thinks of figures like John Kelliher of Harvard, whose courses in Irish literature were a beacon light throughout much of the period under review. Among younger men there is the work of Dillon Johnston for Irish poetry through Wake Forrest University Press, Emmet Larkin of Chicago University and Don Jordan teaching history in Berkeley. The list is as lengthy as it is illustrious, without even discussing the work of Irish-American writers such as the novelist William Kennedy or journalists like Peter Hamill or Jimmy Breslin.

Irish-American journalism has greatly improved in the period under review. Apart from Irish-American papers in New York, Boston and San Francisco, there is Neil O'Dowd's fine monthly

The Irish American, devoted to Irish-American affairs. Politicians interested in Irish-American issues are well briefed and through their Irish contacts are in touch with Dublin, Belfast and London frequently. The explosion within Irish-American circles of Irish awareness since the hunger-strikes cannot be overstated. I was in New York the day Bobby Sands was selected as a candidate in the Fermanagh-Tyrone by-election. The news received one paragraph down-page in the *New York News.* By the time he died, it had taken over the front page and the *News* was calling editorially for a British withdrawal, while at the same time every major American network had several television crews in Ireland.

Much of this immediate interest has since died away, but sparks from the media explosion are falling yet, and the Irish government has made a poor job of either putting them out or of deriving comfort from their warmth.

There is one problem on which every shade of Irish opinion could co-operate, with mutual benefit to both America and Ireland, north and south. Since the 1965 Emigration Act the Irish have increasingly come shoaling into the States on tourist visas and then staying on illegally to work. They can be met in the traditional Irish centres in New York, Boston, Chicago and San Francisco, working in bars and on building sites — some with MAs and PhDs but without social security, job security or residential security. They are at risk if they come home for a funeral or a wedding because their tourist visas may not be renewed in Dublin, and they continuously run the risk of employer exploitation. They nevertheless feel that it is better than living off the dole in Ireland, particularly living through a rural Irish winter.

While I was writing this book one charter flight took off from Shannon with over 300 passengers aboard, mainly from the Leitrim area, ostensibly accompanying two GAA teams to the States. Eighty of those passengers did not come back when the charter returned. Some increase of the Irish quota would be an obvious target for concerned Irish-American effort. President Reagan claimed that the Irish quota was some 20,000 annually, but the criteria are set so high that President Reagan himself, should he be coming from Ireland today, would be unlikely to get in. In fact, fewer than 500 employment visas have been conceded each year, and the Immigration Bill passed in October of 1986 contained such penalties for employing illegal aliens ($105,000 each) that it could mean that something like 75,000 to 100,000 emigrants are facing enforced repatriation.

Regularising the immigration position would also benefit America. If the young Irish could be allowed to work at the jobs for which they are qualified, rather than work illegally as waiters and so on, it would be an obvious plus for the American economy given the known track record of the Irish in America. It would make for a better type of immigrant if screening rather than automatic illegality were the order of the day. Instead of having to put up a bond and be sponsored by a relative or friend, many of today's 'wet-backs' come over with drink or drug problems and either buy a Social Security Number and/or a Green Card on the black market, or else live in a subterranean world. Many of the young immigrants sent back by the FBI were informed on by older, more strait-laced members of the Irish-American community who could not equate their behaviour with notions of being Irish.

Will the co-operation between Dublin and Irish-American organisations and politicians materialise? Who knows? It was truly said that Ireland, like Texas, is a State of Mind, and nowhere is this more true than in the land wherein Texas lies — America itself.

10

Artistic Voices

Abbey Theatre; National Gallery of Ireland; National Concert Hall; Concerned Writers; Rock, Trad and Film

VISITING journalists, a species whom the Northern troubles brought to Ireland in great numbers over the decades under review, are unanimous that Dublin is worth visiting for three institutions, the National Concert Hall, the National Gallery and the Abbey Threatre.

Abbey Theatre

The Abbey, having been founded in the most controversial circumstances, has managed to attract with the accretion of years all the criticism and controversy that one would expect of a national goldfish bowl. Its problems stem from a variety of causes: it is a state institution with state-appointed directors and is bedevilled by rising costs and the fact that the vein of Irish artistic endeavour on which it was founded appears to have dried up.

It is quite extraordinary that an Irish rebellion which has gone on almost continuously since the troubles erupted in 1968 has not produced an outstanding writer; so far as one knows, there is no Behan or O'Casey in Long Kesh. Even if one appeared, he would probably be very much out of favour in the Republic. Traditional Irish revolutionary artists come to the stage (or publisher) via prison or armed rebellion; they would not find today's Abbey the place to put on their first productions. It tends to rely heavily on revivals, although fine productions of leading contemporary playwrights such as Brian Friel, Frank McGuinness, Thomas Murphy and John B. Keane have been staged. However, its experimental theatre, the Peacock, has given many Irish playwrights an opportunity which they would not have had otherwise.

True, the Abbey is not afraid of some forms of controversy. Frank McGuinness's excellent play, *Observe the Sons of Ulster Marching Towards the Somme,* brought homosexuality to the boards, which for the Abbey was something of a feat.

One could not point to a contemporary 'Abbey School' of playwrights. The rays of the Celtic dawn have grown dim and the Abbey can now be depended on to provide a reliable, well-acted, well-designed production, either of one of the quartet mentioned above or of a play from the comfortable stock repertoire of the giants of the past: Synge, perhaps O'Casey, Lady Gregory. There might also be competent, middle-range, middle-class-appealing talent such as that of Hugh Leonard or Bernard Farrell, but no-one to bring the shock of the new. In this the Abbey reflects the rather abstracted and distracted cultural atmosphere of the period.

Politically, there are some similarities between the Abbey and the national television station Radio Telefis Eireann (RTE). The latter finds itself forbidden under Section 31 of the Broadcasting Act from transmitting interviews with people of the physical force school and this de-natures much of its news coverage by comparison with that of the BBC or ITN. The modern Abbey Theatre tends to disapprove of the sort of thinking that grouped itself around the burgeoning consciousness of being Irish which the early Abbey generated; no contemporary poet will have reason to agonise, as did Yeats after 1916, whether a play of his sent anyone out to get shot. There are good artistic, political and commercial reasons for this. The risk to the artist of becoming contaminated by the breath of the Yeatsian 'foul mouth' (nationalism) on either level is well put by Seamus Heaney in his perfectly titled 'Whatever you say, say nothing': 'We tremble near the flames but want no truck with the actual firing . . . We're on the make as ever. Long sucking the hind tit cold as a witch's and as hard to swallow, still leaves us fork-tongued on the border bit'.

Focussing on the Abbey in this way to the exclusion of the fine work that can be seen at the experimental Project Theatre or in the Gate Theatre is of course as unfair as it is incomplete. The

Gate in particular, under the influence of the talented Michael Colgan, has become the most exciting theatre in Dublin with, amongst others, landmark productions of established successes such as Sean O'Casey's *Juno and the Paycock* and new work like Frank McGuinness's *Innocence* (1986) which treated Dublin audiences to the spectacle of a homosexual Cardinal without ill effect to either party.

The visiting journalist should not fail to take note of the sterling work done by the Druid Theatre in Galway under the directorship of Garry Hynes. Among other achievements, it has staged Thomas Murphy's *Bailegangaire,* which afforded the late first lady of the Irish theatre, Siobhan McKenna, the opportunity for her last towering performance. She had, of course, begun her career in Galway's other famous theatre, the Irish-speaking Taibhdhearc. And it would be unjust to overlook the contribution of the Belltable Group in Limerick, which deserves considerable praise for the manner in which it has expanded Limerick's rather limited cultural horizons.

National Gallery of Ireland

In the last twenty years, the National Gallery, under two outstanding directors, James White and Homan Potterton, has become a force in lifting standards of visual appreciation in Ireland. It was extended in 1968 with government funds and has been assisted since 1960 by a bequest from George Bernard Shaw, enabling it to purchase works which would otherwise have been outside its range. The Gallery includes works by Rembrandt, Fra Angelico, Louis David, Poussin, Goya, Claude, Reynolds and Gainsborough, and its collection of old masters' drawings, including sketches by Durer, Cezanne and Watteau, was exhibited in the National Gallery in London in 1985 and taken on tour in the United States.

At home its exhibitions of Osborne (1984), Lavery (1985) and a particularly fine collection of Irish impressionists (1985) have attracted attendances of between sixty and seventy thousand people each. While the recession has curbed its activities somewhat, it has managed to maintain a flourishing publishing programme with its posters, reproductions, catalogues of exhibitions and so on, which have helped to bring in revenue and to sustain interest in the National Gallery — incidentally one of the most popular and inexpensive places in which to eat in Dublin.

The assumption, often made, that Ireland being for so long a nation on the run could not therefore develop skills in painting, sculpture, tapestry or mosaic, could very well have some validity. The growth in the number of small private galleries and in the attraction of an institution such as the National Gallery itself would certainly not appear to bear out this theory.

The favourite whipping boys of those who complain that the Irish have no sense of visual appreciation can literally be seen all over Ireland. These are the products of a piece of initiative by the Irish architect, Jack Fitzsimons, who in the year 1971 published privately, for the modest sum of £1, a book called *Bungalow Bliss*. Fitzsimons subsequently must have felt a bit like the French doctor who gave his name to the guillotine, which he had devised on humanitarian grounds in the hope of sparing victims of death sentences the agonies which other forms of execution used to inflict.

A prosperous generation fell on *Bungalow Bliss* for its notion of what new housing should be. It enabled purchasers to by-pass costly architects and made up for the fact that there were no local government plans available for cheap private housing.

Bungalows went up without regard to either aspect or prospect or to such improving features as trees and shrubs, though comfortable enough on the inside. (Examples could be given of bungalows built in the early seventies for as little as £2,400 later selling for £40,000.) These bungalows, which often seem to have been built with a view to achieving the worst possible clash with the surroundings, now stand as a breeze-block testament to the lack of Irish architectural tradition.

Fitzsimons himself, whom I spoke to, was horrified at the uses to which his publication was sometimes put. He had only intended to provide a guide to cheap, functional housing for those in need of it, not to cover Ireland with 'little boxes on the hillside'. He would favour some sort of 'Irish' style, but so far no architect has produced a distinctive Irish idiom which would replace either the old thatched cottage or the once familiar two-storeyed farmhouse.

National Concert Hall

The National Concert Hall, which opened in September 1981 in the reconstructed premises of the National University at Earlsfort Terrace, has introduced thousands of Dubliners to the joys of concert-going. Since it opened with a seating capacity of over 1,200, the concert hall has staged performances by the symphony orchestras of both Washington and the USSR, the Vienna Philharmonic, the US Marine Band (lent especially for the occasion by President Reagan) and concerts by international performers such as Rostopovich and Yehudi Menuhin. It has given a tremendous fillip to Irish music, both traditional and contemporary, by putting on groups such as The Chieftains, Makem and Clancy, The Wolfe Tones, The Furey Brothers, The Dubliners, De Dannan and Clannad, and solo performers like the gifted Christy Moore. The hall also provides a base for the RTE Symphony Orchestra, whose concert series it stages several times a year, and for many performances by the smaller RTE Concert Orchestra. An evening with any of the foregoing is sufficient to reassure one, at least temporarily, that in the face of such verve and talent, Ireland's problems can and will be overcome.

Interestingly enough the traditional Irish music movement has also had a beneficial spin-off on the early music movement. 'Silent' libraries have been searched for medieval, renaissance and baroque music of the pre-1750 period, and once-dead music is now performed so regularly in Ireland by people like David Milne that the country now occupies a central position in the early music movement.

Dublin's College of Music is a noted centre for introducing young children to the joys of composers like Monteverdi, and groups like 'Musica Reserata' bring not alone composers of another era, but old instruments such as the clavichord to audiences all over the country.

Ciaran MacMathuna, one of the best known radio voices in Ireland, has for decades been travelling the country recording traditional airs and preserving songs and music which, without him, would have been lost.

Concerned Writers

Supergrasses, hunger-strikes, the IRA, and all the rest of the border bit' are not quite kosher where literary Ireland is concerned. Very few of the calibre of UCD's Professor of Literature, Seamus Deane, would wish to be seen to empathise with his pithy description of what makes them take to the streets of Derry:

> The unemployment in our bones,
> Erupting on our hands in stones.

It is, of course, essential for the artist to keep his or her vision as unadulterated as is humanly possible. Art should not be required to serve Long Kesh any more than the state. The important question to be asked of contemporary Irish writers remains: 'how true can be the vision that is continuously averted?'

Some Northern writers are making the effort, notably the Field Day Group involving Brian Friel, Seamus Heaney, Seamus Deane, Tom Paulin and Stephen Rea. The first and most successful of its plays was put on in September 1981, Brian Friel's *Translations,* dealing with the difficulties of communication between the Irish and the English. Field Day also staged Thomas Kilroy's highly successful *Double Cross* (1986), a different form of analysis of Anglo-Irish relationships, dealing with the contrasting and conflicting careers of two brilliant Irishmen, Brendan Bracken and William Joyce. The Derry-born Friel is the outstanding playwright of the period under review. Of his considerable body of work his study of rural Irish attitudes and the loneliness of emigration, *Philadelphia, Here I Come!,* would by itself mark him as an artist of stature.

Field Day's founders all share a belief that new analyses and appraisal of Irish opinions, political and cultural, are necessary in the face of Northern Ireland violence. Put another way, they seek to prove that Irish literature has survived the impact of Yeats and deserves to be considered as something of worth and substance in its own right — Irish writing, not Anglo-Irish writing. They took up an interesting new/old idea in the furtherance of their aims by resorting to pamphleteering to examine questions of identity, including Irish Protestant identity, and bringing in some of the best brains of the younger school in Irish academia as contributors, notably Declan Kiberd, who lectures in English at University College, Dublin. Amongst the pamphlets is Seamus Heaney's *Sweeney Astray,* a version of an Irish satirical folk tale, from which I published extracts as a work in progress in 1984 in an anthology which I was editing at the time.[1]

Field Day are frequently attacked from the intellectual left, not for being merely a group of 'toffs against terrorism' but partly at least, I suspect, for the reasons that Stalin married Nationalism to Communism. Nationalism, cultural or political, is an ally, or, in the case of the Irish left, an adversary, which prevents other 'isms' from taking hold.

There is a certain inevitability about Field Day's development. The set of pamphlets which Field Day issued in September 1986 all dealt with repressive legislation, north and south of the border, occasioned by the Northern situation. As one of the pamphleteers, Patrick J. McGrory, pointed out, by definition the Irish identity of a nationalist in Northern Ireland does not exempt him as a juror from taking an oath that he will fairly adjudicate 'between our Sovereign Lady the Queen and the prisoner at the bar'. Nor, if he is a defendant, from perhaps finding himself promising the court 'that he will keep the peace and be of good behaviour towards all her Majesty's subjects'. It is no mere coincidence that a set of analyses beginning with questions of language and identity should, in the Ireland of the eighties, inevitably lead to Special Courts and twists in the laws of evidence.

Perhaps Francis Stuart's *Black List, Section H* should be considered in the context of these relationships. He wrote this extraordinary novel (published in 1971) as his apologia for the notoriety incurred through being imprisoned after the war for making broadcasts from Berlin. Like Samuel Beckett, the greatest living Irish writer, Stuart believes that the artist's integrity can be preserved only through alienation, but goes further, deliberately courting disgrace in order to preserve his isolated vision.

There are at least four outstanding contemporary novelists, John McGahern, Brian Moore, John Banville and Benedict Kiely. Kiely gained a new lease of creative life with his novel *Nothing Happens in Carmincross* (1985), in which he sets his face against his ancestral Tyrone nationalism. Moore, too, has turned from his native Northern Ireland in the sense that he now lives in Canada and his themes have expanded from analysis of the

1. T. P. Coogan, *The Arts in Ireland*, London, 1985.

miseries of Belfast to explorations of the Catholic conscience and
depictions of life amongst Canada's early settlers. McGahern has
returned to live and write in his native County Leitrim, maintaining with works such as *The Pornographer* and *High Ground* the
pre-eminence amongst contemporary Irish novelists which he
established in the sixties with his studies of Irish sexuality and
loneliness, *The Dark* and *The Barracks*. The Wexford-born
Banville, now living in Dublin, left his job as chief sub-editor of
the *Irish Press* to become a full-time writer after the success of his
novels *Dr Copernicus, Kepler, The Newton Letter* and *Mephisto.*
Banville's work has expanded the horizons of the historical
novel. The youngest of the group, he is also the only novelist of
stature to emerge since the seventies.

That familiar landmark of Irish writing, the Big House, was of
course also to be met within the past twenty years, through the
work of Aidan Higgins, Jennifer Johnston and Molly Keane.
Johnston forsook this time-honoured well-spring to write
Shadows on Our Skin, a study of working-class Derry caught up in
the North's agonies.

Where the short story form is concerned, although activity
abounds, no contemporary Irish writer could be said to challenge
the pre-eminence of Mary Lavin, born in 1912, and still
flourishing merrily. It is also appropriate to mention the weekly
'New Irish Writing' page in the *Irish Press,* which was initiated
in 1968 by David Marcus. I had not long been appointed editor of
the *Irish Press* when he put the idea to me of running what was in
effect a literary magazine in a newspaper. From then on until the
success of his novel, *A Land Not Theirs,* prompted him to turn to
fulltime writing at the end of 1986, Marcus published the first
work of every young Irish writer of worth for close on twenty
years. Short stories and poetry extracts from work in progress
appeared without interruption and at an astonishingly high level
of quality, as he launched literally scores of writers on a literary
career. The new editor of the page is Anthony Glavin, whose
early short stories were first published by David Marcus.

The list of contemporary poets is seemingly endless. At the
beginning of this book's time-span Austin Clarke, Patrick
Kavanagh, Richard Weber, Pearse Hutchinson, Valentin
Iremonger, Thomas Kinsella, John Montague and Richard
Murphy were all writing. Weber and the last three are still

Church leaders grew closer, but religious divisions remain far from healed.

Women came to public prominence. Two of the most outstanding were Gemma Hussey as a Minister for Education and Sister Stanislaus Kennedy as an energetic campaigner for the underprivileged.

What we have we hold: images of Ulster Unionism.

Traditions maintained? The same
generation but different traditions:
community divisions remain in
Northern Ireland and these two
young people were being moulded
for the future in 1987.

The Stardust in Dublin and the Betelgeuse in Bantry were disasters that between them claimed 98 innocent lives.

flourishing, and have been joined by Seamus Heaney, Derek Mahon, Paul Durcan, Michael Longley, Tom Paulin and Paul Muldoon. One could keep adding to the list almost indefinitely. Why leave out Brendan Kennelly or Desmond Egan for instance? Irish poetry is remarkable for its vitality and for the fact that so much of it is written by men, though Eavan Boland, Nuala Ni Dhomhnaill, Medbh McGuckian and Nuala Archer are women poets of the first rank.

Seamus Heaney, who, apart from his poetic gifts, has been blessed with a personality, presence and melodious Northern accent that make him a remarkable public performer, has acquired a status in Dublin society more usually associated with that of the poet in Moscow. His pursuits of themes of race, place and religious sensibility has earned for him the position of pre-eminence in contemporary Irish poetry once held by Patrick Kavanagh: some of his admirers would go so far as to say by Yeats.

Thomas Kinsella, having begun his career as a lyric poet, has developed, or retreated, into less penetrable forms so that I now think of him as the Poet of the Obscure. One of his undoubted achievements was his co-authorship with Sean O'Tuama of *An Duanaire — Poems of the Dispossessed,* a translation of the poets of the invaded, disrupted Gaelic Ireland from the seventeenth to the nineteenth centuries. Kinsella edited the new *Oxford Book of Irish Verse* in 1986, producing a volume in which the omissions were more notable than the inclusions. Not lacking in the volume, however, were copious examples of Kinsella's own translations from the Irish!

One might turn to other poets in English for many different reasons, to Murphy for his Western saga 'The Last Galway Hooker', or to John Montague for his long 'Rough Field', a moving evocation of Northern events benefiting greatly from the poet's own empathy with the subject. Of the younger school of Northern poets trying to make sense of their discordant surroundings, Tom Paulin can be found in the forefront of the Field Day concern to analyse present-day politics. Paul Muldoon retreats in the midst of the din to ponder the significance of both the poignant and the private, as in reflecting on the death of his own father; he now lives in Kerry. One can wince with Durcan in his evocation of a failed marriage, share with David Hammond his depiction of a vanished culture in 'Rathlin Island', or retrace one's way through bloody history with Brendan Kennelly in his long poem 'Cromwell'. All of these merit respect for their talent, their industry and the articulation of the authentic which has made poetry Ireland's liveliest literary art form today.

In the Irish language the Cork shoal (rather than school) of young poets, including Michael Davitt and Liam O'Muirthile, is still striving after the lyric perfection of Sean O'Riordain, whose death deprived Ireland of a major poetic voice in Irish. There has been little in recent years from the pen of other Irish language poets such as Maire Mac an tSaoi and that great Aran veteran, Mairtin O'Direain, but among the younger poets Davitt and Tomas Mac Siomoin clearly lead the field. In prose, a new talent seems to be emerging from the north in the person of Seamus Mac Annaidh, whose tale of a man who acquired a dual personality in hospital, *Cuach mo lon dubh buí,* attracted a great deal of critical acclaim. But it is hard to see anyone emerging of the stature of the three major Irish novelists who died during the period under review: Mairtin O Cadhain, whose novel *Cre na Cille,* in which the dead speak to each other in a graveyard, is a classic; Eoin O Tuairisc who, apart from a large body of other work, will certainly be remembered for his novel *L'Attaque,* set during the 1798 Rebellion, and the novelist and playwright Diarmuid O Suilleabhain.

The outstanding Northern-based playwrights writing today, Martin Lynch, Graham Reid, and Stewart Parker, appear to trace their lineage from Sam Thompson, who dominated the mid-fifties with his study of sectarianism in Belfast, *Over the Bridge;* they write about long-standing, deep-rooted, working-class prejudice rather than exploding out of any 'Celtic Dawn' lit by a sudden flowering of nationalist and class consciousness. The hunger-strikes produced only one play, written in Dublin by Peter Sheridan who has no connection with either Northern Ireland or the physical force school. Like O'Casey, one could argue that Reid and Parker are Protestant and imbued with the attitudes of the Protestant working class, but the resemblance ends there. No Citizen Army or IRA involvement brought them trembling, however temporarily, near Heaney's flame.

Anne Devlin, from the Catholic tradition like Lynch and McGuinness and a daughter of Paddy Devlin, the former civil rights activist and minister in the short-lived Sunningdale executive, has emerged as a different sort of Northern witness. She is the feminist looking at her sisters caught up by Northern turmoil. Devlin, now living in Birmingham and married to a BBC producer, wonders, looking back on her development, whether she did the right thing in backing one side against the other during her early civil rights involvement. She has the familiar unease of Irish writers at getting mixed up, as she puts it, 'with the tribes'. Her play, *Ourselves Alone,* based on the experience of a group of Belfast women caught up in the troubles, won several awards in London when performed by the Royal Court Theatre. Devlin herself, a devotee of O'Casey, describes it as 'my *Plough and the Stars'.* Her other exemplar is Brian Friel, so perhaps subliminally the traditional nationalist themes do cast their spell. Unionism still awaits an interpreter from its own 'tribe', but the outstanding dramatic explanation of the unionist and Orange mentality to date is the Catholic McGuinness's *Observe the Sons of Ulster Marching Towards the Somme.*

Rock, Trad and Film

In popular music Irish artists have shown themselves capable of attracting and holding international audiences. In the world of rock and roll, there is the now-established U2, there was the late, tragic Phil Lynott of Thin Lizzie, and more will be heard of the up-and-coming Feargal Sharkey. The success of traditional Irish music groups such as The Chieftains, Clannad and De Dannan, or of ballad groups like The Dubliners and The Wolfe Tones has also been phenomenal. The enthusiasm which traditional music has always elicited in Ireland has also brought local fame and international recognition, if not stardom, to such groups as Stockton's Wing, The Bothy Boys, Na Casaidigh and a host of others who attract a respectable following, particularly in Germany where Irish music is very popular.

This music detonation has been dominated by U2, one of the great rock bands of the world. It is not taking from the achievement of the musicians themselves to say that a principal factor in the group's success is their manager, Liverpool-Irish-born Paul McGuinness, who boasts of a Kerry mother, a degree in philosophy from Trinity and a knowledge of history imparted at Clon-

gowes Wood College by a Jesuit who came into the class one
morning and told them: 'You're a bright lot. You should be well
able to do some extra study on the side, so read this,' — and
handed each member of the class a copy of *Ireland Since the
Rising*! McGuinness was actually working in the theatre when a
friend on *Hot Press* magazine, who knew that he had achieved
success managing a group called Spud, suggested that he take on
U2, who appeared to have unusual talent. Bono and the others
were just then emerging from their teens, and their average age is
now 24. Bruce Springsteen, who came to Irland at the ripe old age
of 35 to give a memorable performance at Slane Castle, reckons
that they have a long life ahead of them.

There is a famous anecdote concerning the group which illustrates the sort of influences that can inhibit Irish artistic
development, particularly where the North is concerned. While
the group were preparing to launch a performance of Bono's
single, 'Sunday Bloody Sunday', during an American tour, a
rumour circulated that a brother of Bobby Sands intended attending their concert. Had he done so the record, which went on to the
top of the charts, would in all probability never have been played
on the BBC, and the band might have been given a crippling IRA
tag. In fact the song belies its title and is not in any way Republican or related to the civil rights march that ended in tragedy in
Derry in 1970.

The difficulty is not alone artistic, it is also political. A leading
Irish-American political intellectual, Senator Joseph Bidden,
analysed the problem of Irish-American and British relationships in an interview with *Irish America* magazine in April 1987:
'We have never — I am going to get myself in real trouble here
—come to grips with our relationship with Great Britain. There
is an overwhelming admiration and awe for the British jurisprud-
ence system, a phenomenal respect for British majesty and
power. In the sense that the Irish are ambivalent about the IRA,
we have been ambivalent about Britain. We have fought them
and we have loved them. As they are in the twilight of their
position as a world power, we are reluctant to take issue with
them . . .' Bidden, who was talking about an extradition treaty
with Great Britain which Mrs Thatcher wanted, to cope with
Irish political offenders, went on to say of Britain's role in
Ireland, 'It is something that is not inappropriate to have on the

agenda when the United States is dealing with what is a true, faithful and legitimate real ally'.

Such considerations are far more important than is often realised, not only in England but in America, where so much of the style is British. The influential WASP element inclines towards its British exemplar either for holiday tours of Scottish castles, clubbing in London or shopping in Harrods; at home it vies with the rest of decision-taking Washington for a seat at a Prince Charles and Princess Di banquet. At the State Department decision-taking diplomats favour tweed over worsted, take tea rather than coffee and regard the Court of St James as *the* foreign posting. In New York more young people came out on the streets to mourn when John Lennon was shot than appeared for John F. Kennedy.

And beyond these stylistic matters there lies an enduring truth concerning American-British-Irish relationships that will ultimately always influence American attitudes towards Ireland. That truth was well expressed in a CIA paper published in 1949, quoted by Sean Cronin in his *Washington's Irish Policy 1916– 1986: Independence, Partition, Neutrality:* 'Strategically, the denial of Ireland to an enemy is an unavoidable principle of United States security'.

One is aware of these things of course, but sometimes one gets a fresh perspective on how carefully constructed the Irish cultural mould has to be for international marketing. I once became friendly with a talented young woman whom I met on a visit to a prison to which IRA activity had led her. In time-honoured Irish fashion she proceeded to develop her considerable talent as a writer and eventually, prison and the IRA well behind her, she sent me a copy of her very interesting autobiography for my criticism. Had it been published it would certainly have attracted considerable attention, but it still reposes in a drawer of my desk in the *Irish Press*.

Why is the manuscript desk-bound? Because the girl married a prominent Irish actor whose career, not alone on the British stage, but on TV and film also, would have been severely damaged had producers or casting directors realised that he had married an ex-IRA woman!

One art form which surprisingly seems to have eluded contemporary Ireland is that of film, despite the readily available supply of writers and actors and some heart-stoppingly beautiful scenery. The state film company in Ardmore, County Wicklow, proved itself no more successful than did state enterprise in other walks of Irish life. Closed in 1981 after almost thirty years, the studios, which have now been bought by the American Mary Tyler Moore company, showed an unremitting dedication to losing money rather than to the tapping of a source of Irish film genius.

One can cite the Ardmore production of *Excalibur* by John Boorman, or the fact that *The Purple Taxi*, with Peter Ustinov, had a success in France, bringing many tourists to Ireland as a result. But very little else happened, apart from the fact that the studio did attract a reputation for excellence amongst its technicians. The money seems to have either gone to the wrong hands or to have been frittered away on second-rate productions — that is, when third-rate ones were not available.

Ardmore apart, there were a number of cinematic swallows which have yet to make a summer, such as *Cal*, a story based in contemporary Belfast, or *Pigs*, a study of being down and out in Dublin. The work of Neil Jordan with *Angel* and later *Company of Wolves*, and in particular his 1986 *Mona Lisa*, may yet help to literally change the picture.

There was also *Eat the Peach* in which John Kelliher, a former RTE producer, directed an all-Irish cast in an occasionally very funny account of an attempt to build a wall of death in the middle of a bog. Not yet on release are two potentially popular works directed and shot by Paddy Barron and Vincent Corcoran; the Barron work is a musical biography of Tom Moore, singer and composer, in which Moore's melodies are sung by Niall Murray, the opera singer, and Corcoran's is a literary tour of Ireland. As I have written the scripts for both and narrate the Moore film as well, I may fairly be regarded as being at worst prejudiced, at best an interested party. But I can at least assure the reader that my opinion is shared by all those who have seen the previews — the scenery is lovely!

11

Crucible

*Discrimination; The Faces of Unionism; 'Our Country Also';
Constitutional Nationalism; The SDLP; A Revolutionary in the
Making*

UNQUESTIONABLY the most momentous — and bloody —
happenings of the 1965–87 period were those connected with
Northern Ireland. Beside the tale of horror unfolded there all else
pales into insignificance. Memories like McGurk's bar or the
Abercorn restaurant now float but dimly in the history of many
places where people met in conviviality only to be blasted to
death or to be crippled for a lifetime by no-warning bombs. In
Derry 1972 began with Bloody Sunday, when thirteen lives were
lost, and Bloody Friday, later that year, left eleven dead. Thirty
people died in the 1974 bombings in the Republic. In 1976 the
New Year began with a series of sectarian murders of Catholics in
the South Armagh area, which ended when Catholic gunmen
lined up ten innocent Protestant workers and shot them all dead.
How many died in the Miami Showband attack? . . . And so the
horrible litany goes.

In 1965 all that seemed to be happening, however, was that an
historical mould was being broken. For the first time a southern
Prime Minister, Sean Lemass, went North to meet a North of
Ireland Prime Minister, Captain Terence O'Neill, who in turn
came south to repay the Lemass gesture. True, the tradition of
having an IRA campaign in every generation had sputtered into
life, briefly, during the 1950s and had shuffled ingloriously into
history with a few dead and a few more imprisoned, but the
excitement of Vatican II, the approach of the EEC, young blood

coming into politics and the spread of optimism as a degree of prosperity became general were enough to diminish those memories.

Northern Ireland itself was spoken of as the fastest-growing region in the UK, with industrial output double that of Great Britain and major construction work under way in the province, including a new city, Craigavon, a new airport and a new motorway in Derry.

However, in one of the brooding back streets of Belfast two young Catholics, Peter Ward and John Scullion, were horrifically attacked in 1966 by the founders of the recreated Ulster Volunteer Force. This murderous remnant of the once-mighty force that had defied Home Rule earlier in the century had been reborn in response to the nationalist celebrations for the anniversary of the 1916 Rising, but the working-class UVF of the sixties were far removed socially and economically from the landowners, the industrialists and the professional classes of the 1912 UVF.

The killers of the young Catholics were caught. Beyond the horror of the deed itself and the fact that one of them had a funny name, Gusty Spence, no one thought much more of old passions. People chose to believe that the physical force tradition had at long last gone to ground and that the gun was out of Irish politics.

New currents were stirring in Northern Ireland, particularly on the Catholic side. A new breed of well-educated activists was coming to the fore, not so much in politics, still trapped in their old mould of virtually one-party domination from Stormont, but in groupings like credit unions or the circles radiating from the activities of Dr Con McCluskey and his wife in Dungannon, County Tyrone. It was there that the first civil rights march was held on 14 August 1968. It was the McCluskeys who first had the idea of moving away from the nationalist versus unionist rigidities and concentrating on civil rights issues — housing, jobs and discrimination generally.

Discrimination

From the setting up of the state of Northern Ireland to the founding of the Civil Rights movement in 1967, the unionists had complete political authority in the area, and political responsibility also. Both were exercised disgracefully.

The results of the 1965 General Election were as follows: Unionists 37 seats, Nationalists 9, Northern Ireland Labour Party 2, Social Republicans 2, Liberals 1, National Democrats 1. Plural voting had been retained in 1929, and proportional representation abolished. The unionists had a majority of 70 per cent of the Stormont seats. At Westminster, following the General Election in 1966, Gerry Fitt (Republican Labour) took one seat in West Belfast, but the unionists held the other eleven in Northern Ireland. The fact that the pot of the Education Acts was coming to the boil, throwing up new elements, raised the decibel level on behalf of the Catholics but not their political clout. Gerry Fitt, who thought of himself primarily as a Labour politician, would one day be forced from his seat and his city by those who thought other forms of 'clout' were called for. I have heard him remark, 'I came in to politics to get a house for the wee woman or a job for her son. I thought at first "Rep Lab" was just a ghost of the past'. To illustrate the ambivalence of such ghostly aggravations and how policies changed from Fitt's early days it should be noted that the third partner to this conversation, Senator Paddy Wilson, was stabbed to death by a loyalist assassin.

When partition was first introduced by the Government of Ireland Act, 1920, Derry City, being predominantly nationalist, returned a nationalist for the City parliamentary seat and continued to do so until 1929. Then the predominantly Catholic South City Ward was joined to the Foyle constituency, which had a Catholic majority, but the City's electoral division was extended into the county of Derry. The net effect of this gerrymander was that the Derry City constituency ceased to return a nationalist and the seat went to the unionists. The blatant unfairness of this may be gauged from the fact that in 1964 the City of Derry had a Catholic majority of 36,049 Catholics to 17,695 Protestants. The unionists were also (in the absence of a body such as the Westminster Boundary Commission) able to manipulate constituency sizes so that they varied from as many as 43,000 electors to as few as 7,000.

Electoral discrimination brought its most blatant consequences in local government. On a province-wide basis, with 66 per cent of the population, the unionists controlled a staggering 60 out of a total of 68 Councils and the Corporations of Derry and Belfast. By 1964 nationalists had so lost faith in the system that only 6-7 per cent of the seats on County Councils were even contested. None of this was done as a matter of abstract desire to see the Union Jack fly and the Protestant religion exalted. It was done under the banner of these causes for several practical reasons, such as the retention of a grip on the allocation of housing and employment.

It is worth looking at the town of Dungannon for a moment. The civil rights cause received a fillip here through the McCluskeys' campaign for social justice which was used by a young Catholic activist, Austin Currie, to hold the first sit-in of the troubles. This took place at nearby Caledon, where the teenage secretary of a local Orange politician had been allocated a house, prior to getting married, over the heads of Catholics with large families who had been on the housing waiting-lists for periods of up to fifteen years. Dungannon's housing allocation was highlighted in a report published in 1968 by a survey team led by Austin Currie which found that between 1945 and 1968 Catholics had beyond question received an unfair share of housing allocations. Catholics comprised 52.1 per cent of the population, Protestants 44.5 per cent. The percentage of all houses allocated broke down as 55.5 per cent Protestant, 44.5 per cent Catholics. Not so bad on the surface, it might seem, until one analysed the percentage of new families getting houses: 35.4 per cent Catholics, 64.6 per cent Protestants.

In 1956, Westminster had laid a statutory obligation on local authorities to re-house families living in conditions unfit for human habitation. Before that the percentage of new families allocated houses had been Protestants 71.1 per cent, Catholics 28.9 per cent, so it is clear that that statutory obligation helped Catholics to get houses they otherwise would not have had. But it also introduced another noteworthy element, the ghetto creation factor. Sixty-one per cent of all the houses allocated to Catholics in Dungannon were found by the Currie survey to be located in the Coalisland district, and eighty-one per cent in the rural areas of Dungannon were allocated in the six electoral divisions where there was already a huge nationalist majority. In other words, they got houses where their voting strength would not threaten the unionists.

Catholics in Dungannon occupied some 83 per cent of the area in which they got houses, with the result that it took as many as

1,328 Catholics to elect a nationalist Councillor but only 473 Protestants to bring in one unionist. In the adjoining county of Fermanagh, the town of Enniskillen (56 per cent Catholic) allocated only two houses to Catholics out of 1,777 built in four housing estates in the period 1948–64.

Employment was also a major area of discrimination. The number of Protestants at senior levels in the civil service, from the grades of Staff Officer upward, was found to be unchanged in 1959 from the position in 1927, a staggering 94 per cent.[1] Local authority employment was not much better: Catholics, who formed 34 per cent of the population, got eleven per cent of the jobs in 1951.[2] The Campaign for Social Justice found in a 1964 survey that out of twenty-eight public service boards (the Agricultural Wages Body, the Fire Authority, the Transport Authority, etc.) Catholic representation was only 11.1 per cent. Of fifteen departments controlled by Derry County Council, the heads of *all* fifteen were Protestant! In the lower grades there were 145 Protestants earning salaries worth £124,424 annually, as against 32 Catholics earning only £20,420.

In private employment it was taken as axiomatic that each side should look after its own, with the Protestants, who held the vast bulk of the wealth, being in a far better position to do so. However, it is worth recording that the Barret/Carter survey notes that, though the Catholics were complained of by unionists in this regard, there did not seem to be the same systematic pattern of discrimination.

The Faces of Unionism

Captain O'Neill's policy of rapprochement with the Republic, stemming from his meeting with Lemass and his gradualist attempts to liberalise discriminatory laws, met with increasing opposition in the late sixties from within the hierarchy of the Unionist Party. Figures such as Brian Faulkner and Bill Craig were particularly critical, and on the wilder shores of unionism Ian Paisley was becoming a power in the land who would have to be reckoned with.

Part of the revolt against O'Neill, who was forced out as Prime

1. Barret and Carter, *The Northern Ireland Problem,* Oxford University Press, 1962.
2. Frank Gallagher, *The Indivisible Island,* Gollancz, London, 1959.

Minister on 28 April 1969, represented the increasing strength of the entrepreneurial Presbyterian streak of Unionism represented by Brian Faulkner. This stood at a distance from the land-owning Anglicanism represented by Captain O'Neill himself and his cousin, Major Chichester-Clark, who succeeded him as Prime Minister. Chichester-Clark lasted for two years, being replaced on 24 March 1971 by Faulkner, who went a year later to the day after Stormont itself had fallen.

In the south, Paisley was regarded as some sort of isolated freak. However, he can trace his ranting lineage through Ulster history to great bigots such as the Reverend Henry Cooke, or the Reverend 'Roaring' Hannah, who left an indelible stamp on the nature of Ulster Protestantism. A strain of so-called Free Presbyterianism developed, fundamentalist, puritanical, profoundly anti-Catholic, and equating Godliness with being British, white and Protestant in a world menaced by treacherous, over-sexed Catholics anxious to breed and, if possible, vote or bomb them into the arms of the Communist-dominated IRA. All this was part of a Popish conspiracy preached daily from pulpit, platform, and in particular from Paisley's own *Protestant Telegraph*.

At the time of the Lemass/O'Neill meeting the Orange Order was no more than the organiser of colourful parades, which it was felt in some liberal quarters would look wonderful when they would be held in O'Connell Street, Dublin to mark an occasion such as St Patrick's Day or even, as I heard a former Taoiseach speculate, to commemorate the Rising of Easter Monday! 'Sure, why not?', such expectations ran. 'Isn't it the era of ecumenism, hands across the Border, the breaking down of old barriers and concentration on the things that unite us rather than divide?'

It was like that to an extent at official Dublin-Belfast level, but to me, at any rate, the underground reality was symbolised by a bogus 'Sinn Fein Oath' which appeared in April 1967 in Ian Paisley's *Protestant Telegraph* claiming that, amongst other things, the IRA swore to murder Protestants with the approval of the Pope, using all methods including 'the dagger and the poison cup'.

There is no such 'oath'; the IRA volunteer merely signs a brief declaration of fidelity to the organisation's aims. But incredible as it may seem, the 'oath' was in fact used by the British Army in a handbook produced to acquaint the youthful Tommies with the 'realities' of what confronted them. The bogus 'oath' was withdrawn from the handbook, after I discovered its inclusion and publicised the fact in the *Irish Press.* Over thirteen years later, however, Paisley's Democratic Unionist Party was still making effective use of that 'oath' in election literature.

Constitutional Unionism today wears many hats. At the outset of the period under review it wore only one, that of the Ulster Unionist Party, which glossed over left/right divisions in its much-trumpeted fidelity to the maintenance of the Union. This resulted in the holding of ten out of the twelve Westminster seats and the direction of the affairs of the province, secure in the possession of a large majority through the operation of a type of 'Big House' network which had largely disappeared from the political landscape of the Republic some fifty years earlier.

After the fateful Lemass/O'Neill meetings, the party suffered blows from the emergence of Paisley's more populist working-class unionism, along with the Ulster Vanguard movement led by William Craig, the Reverend Martin Smith and Captain Austin Ardill. Vanguard was openly supported by the para-military Vanguard Service Corps.

The United Ulster Unionist Council was created in January 1974, based on the good Irish principle that the word 'united' generally indicates a split. By then the Unionist Party had split into three wings, the 'Official Unionists' headed by Harry West, an opponent of Brian Faulkner, the Democratic Unionist Party led by Ian Paisley and the Vanguard Unionists led by William Craig. After the Sunningdale agreement collapsed in May 1974, there was also the Unionist Party of Northern Ireland, led by Brian Faulkner, which continued the 'Big House' tradition (though led by the businessman Faulkner) through having itself represented in the House of Lords by Lords Brookeborough and Moyola (the former Northern premier, James Chichester-Clark). Another United Ulster Unionist Party, led by Ernest Baird, appeared during the Council elections of May 1977. There also appeared the United Unionist Action Council, which organised vigilante activities and tried, without much success, to reproduce the Ulster Workers' Council strike of 1974 which had brought down Sunningdale. The targets of the stoppage were Direct Rule and the need for better security, but it failed because it didn't get the support of the power workers, though it did get that of Paisley and Baird and some help from what was left of the Ulster Workers' Council.

At the time of the Lemass/O'Neill meetings the Unionist Party was very definitely a white collar, pin-stripe affair, with political meetings held midweek, a time when working-class unionists neither attended nor were expected to appear. That phase of unionism died the death in September 1971 at the hands of Ian Paisley and Desmond Boal, who founded the Democratic Unionist Party. Boal had been expelled from the Unionist Parliamentary party; he was then, and for many years after, not alone the province's leading barrister but what might be termed ·the theoretician of Ulster Protestantism. Paisley, prior to the founding of the DUP, had delivered two hammer-blows to Official Unionism, winning Terence O'Neill's Bannside seat himself and seeing his colleague, the Reverend William Beattie, successful in the second of two by-elections held in April 1970. Paisley continued to be the dominant figure in unionism. The European elections in June 1979 saw him take 8 per cent more than the total Official Unionist Party vote for two candidates, coming out with a grand total of 170,000 votes, or 30 per cent of the first preference votes cast in the election.

His first two contributions to Europe a month later consisted of a protest that the Union Jack was flying upside down outside the Parliament, and interruption of a speech by Jack Lynch (who was at the time President of the European Council) on the Republic's refusal to sign the European Convention on Terrorism. He was appointed a member of the Energy Committee. That is one quality he cannot be accused of lacking. The Scarman Report, while absolving Paisley of any blame in the sense of being a party to any act of violence in the 1969 rioting, found that 'his speeches and writings must have been one of the many factors increasing tension in 1969'.

Paisley went further than speeches and writings in his assaults on the power-sharing executive, when he and his Loyalist colleagues sat in the Stormont chamber and Paisley had to be carried out by eight police. His reward for this came a month later when his North Antrim constituents increased his majority from 3,000 to 27,000. Paisley, Faulkner, Craig, Baird, Boal, all those who opposed the Lemass/O'Neill type approach weakened the links of the union they claimed they wished to preserve and helped to create the circumstances from which the Provisional IRA were to profit.

'Our Country Also'

The essence of unionism is based on supremacy: 'what we have we hold'.

A member of the Ku Klux Klan in America's Deep South, a Boer from South Africa or a white supremacist Rhodesian would feel instantly at home at an Orange Lodge gathering in Northern Ireland amongst a group of landowners discussing the local situation. Such terms as 'niggers', 'Kaffirs' and 'IRA' would be immediately interchangeable. In 1977 Ian Smith thanked Portadown's branch of the Democratic Unionist Party for its message of support. The political philosophy of unionism tends to produce an attitude that is anti-feminine (to a degree that often suggests repressed homosexuality), and embodies racialist and bigoted attitudes to the Roman Catholic church. The proponents of these views will generally be, philosophy apart, people of friendliness, hospitality and upholders of family tradition.

Culturally, unionism is a desert. Ulster unionism has not produced a poet or a playwright worthy of the name. It is idle to the point of ludicrousness to suggest, as some unionist protagonists will, that either W.R. Rodgers or Louis McNeice should be regarded as unionists. They were not. Such writers should be thought of, like the poet John Hewitt, as belonging to the Ulster Protestant tradition invoked by Hewitt himself: 'For we have rights drawn from the soil and the sky; the use, the pace, the patient years of labour, the rain against the lips, the changing light, the heavy clay-sucked stride have altered us; we would be strangers in the Capitol; this is our country also, nowhere else; and we shall not be outcast in the world'.

How in fact the unionists behaved towards their Catholic compatriots in the exercise of their 'rights, drawn from the soil' has already been illustrated. The fact is that unionists are 'outcast in the world' of public opinion just as are Mr Botha's Boers, and neither is likely to alter course because of unpopularity. Paisley strikes a chord that has a serious resonance for many of the people who support him: 'He says out what we think'.

But the Paisleyite supporter feels there is an economic reason as well as a philosophical one for supporting 'the Big Man'. Granted there is a neo-pornographic appeal to his followers in some Paisleyite ranting such as 'The Church of Scotland drunk with the wine of its fornication with the Roman whore'. But centuries of threats from, and actual conflict with, the vengeful brooding Catholics from whom they took the land in the first place has bred into them a deep-rooted insecurity and an equally deep-rooted possessiveness. They took the land and they held it against all resistance by the natives.

Drink with a seemingly mild-mannered unemotional Protestant farmer in County Down and listen to how the attitudinal onion skins peel off during the night and you begin to understand Protestant fears. To them, fair words in peace are just the obverse side of the medal of force in war, blandishment instead of blow. Distilled, their arguments run as follows:

'Trying to get by "Civil Rights" what you failed to get over the centuries! Civil Rights! What about Protestant Rights? "For we have rights drawn from the soil and the sky . . .". We have our fierce uncerebral pride — what we have we hold. The Protestant martyrs are real to us (and the IRA attacks add to their number, of course). We won't be thrust under Dublin. We are loyal to the Crown. But the Crown is disloyal to us, Britain rewards Fenian murders by trying to force an "Irish Dimension" down our throats. We are Protestant but the Archbishop of Canterbury is betraying the Protestant people by following a Romeward path. Our forefathers fought for the freedom of religion. It's our fight and we'll fight it too if anyone tries to push us under Dublin Rule'.

Bossuet referred to the 'alienations of Protestanism'. 'Who the hell is Bossuet?', your 'thinking' unionist will reply. 'Read Kipling, there's the man who said it all'.

> We know the war prepared
> On every decent home,
> We know the hells declared
> For such as serve not Rome —
> The terror, threats and dread
> In market, hearth, and field —
> We know, when all is said,

We perish if we yield.

Believe, we dare not boast
Believe, we do not fear —
We stand to pay the cost
In all that men hold dear.
What answer from the North?
One law, one land, one throne.
If England drive us forth
We shall not fall alone.

This is a feeling shared by respectable prosperous farmers, shopkeepers, businessmen, 'yuppies' and unemployed 'Billyboys', the well-doing housewife who turns out her children so tidily that she gives rise to the Northern Ireland term of approval, 'a bit Protestant-looking', and the back-street assassin. The unionist's impulse springs from a strong desire to preserve what he sees as his hard-won supremacy, and any 'concession' to democracy in the matter of housing or fair employment would send him down a slippery slope to Rome. If he resisted the first step, one-man-one-vote, he trusted that he would never have to witness the last, Catholic Supremacy.

Even the unionists themselves began to realise early on in the eruption of the Northern conflict, when Catholic apologists like John Hume began running rings around their lumbering opponents on television, that something would have to be done about their image. The Paisleyite wing of unionism in particular, rather in the manner of certain American fundamentalist preachers such as Gerry Falwell, grasped the importance of the television camera and the computer and were first out of the trap in a new style — which, significantly, saw the *Protestant Telegraph* quietly fold up. So it came about that the traditional unionist voter, whether of the rural or urban sort, could nod approvingly at Paisleyite candidates on television, such as Mr Peter Robinson, 'saying publicly what we feel' attired in the most 'with-it' of clothing and trendiest of hair style. Robinson later distinguished himself by leading an invasion of masked, cudgel-waving men into the village of Clontibret, County Monaghan, in the early hours one morning in August 1986, allegedly to show up the Republic's security deficiencies. It was widely said at the time that the real reason for the invasion was because Paisley was away in Canada and Robinson was seizing the chance of limelight. Whatever the reason for the ploy, the subsequent costly riots before and after the various court proceedings, for which the Republic's taxpayers paid, left Robinson with an anonymously-paid fine and the dubious distinction of being the first Westminster MP to lead an invasion of the Republic.

Constitutional Nationalism

Political commentators sitting in the comfort of their armchairs in Dublin far from the conflict of Northern Ireland sometimes talk about the 'advance' made by constitutional nationalism as the outstanding phenomenon in Northern Ireland's political life over the last two decades. These advances are in fact more imagined than real and have more to do with the media's regard for some of the SDLP figures, in particular John Hume, than for tangible results on the ground.

Yet this media attention and the widespread regard in which Hume is held in the Republic are quite understandable. Hume's logic, his persuasiveness, his forceful articulation on TV, have made of this former Maynooth seminarian, teacher-turned-politician, such an admired figure that he could be probably assured of winning a seat were he to stand in almost any southern constituency. He was described by a lawyer in a manner with which few people in the Republic would disagree when he appeared on RTE's 'Late, Late Show' to support the argument for divorce during the Divorce Referendum: 'Not alone are you very well known, Mr Hume, but you are the most admired politician in the country'.

John Hume was born to Sam and Annie Hume in the Bogside, Derry, in 1937. Sam Hume was an unusually able and talented man, much in demand as a letter-writer and adviser to his neighbours, but as he was a Catholic the system allowed him no recognition of his gifts. When John was a boy he shared the experience common to Bogsiders of his father and brother sleeping two in a bed in one of their two bedrooms, the women —his mother and three sisters — doubling up in the other. Understandably, housing was to become one of Hume's top priorities.

The British eleven-plus system sent him, via St Columb's of

Derry, along an educational path which led to a period of study for the priesthood in St Patrick's College, Maynooth, and then, the cloth forsaken, to a series of teaching posts in and around Derry. His principal subject, French, was to stand him in good stead with the European media when his native Bogside erupted in 1969, and subsequently when he became a Euro MP, but his principal political formation lay in the Credit Union movement which a group led by himself and Paddy 'Bogside' Doherty, seeking to improve the lot of Derry working-class Catholics, introduced to the city, mainly to enable them to buy houses. His travels throughout the province building up a knowledge of social conditions impressed ineradicably on the young Hume the belief that the major task facing a *political* activist on the nationalist side was not an end to partition, but reform within the system.

Hume, from the outset, was in the mould of Daniel O'Connell rather than Wolfe Tone, and his sojourn in Maynooth deepened his pacifism and aversion to violence. He sought by logic, persuasion and organisation to change the system and, if he has a political Achilles' heel, it is the belief that reason and logic must prevail. He said to me once, 'We can't cooperate with the unionist while he has a foot on our necks, but once the foot is off, then we can cooperate to make a normal society'. But Northern Ireland is not a normal society. Expecting the unionist to see reason painlessly is like expecting a South African Boer to stop misbehaving towards the blacks because Nelson Mandela said so. Unionism is aimed at 'keeping the foot on the neck' of the nationalist and the philosophy has over a century of discrimination, riots and pogroms behind it to prove the point. Yet Hume and early civil rights activists like Ivan Cooper and Michael Canavan believed at the outset that a paradoxical policy of setting aside the old sterile mould of nationalist anti-British phobia and the partition issue, while at the same time appealing to British public opinion, armed with facts and figures, would effect progress and keep the thorny question of Anglo-Irish relations out of the debate.

In fact, the climate created by the build-up of agitation by such fiery socialist orators as Eamonn McCann both heightened unionist fears of being thrust out of the Union and kindled republican hopes of catching a tide that would sweep away the Union altogether. It is to Hume's credit that he maintained both his non-violent principles and his commanding position on the Northern scene in the maelstrom released by these conflicting currents of expectation and dread.

The election of February 1969 launched Hume on his political career. He was returned as an independent ahead of the old-style nationalist leader, Eddie McAteer, and Eamonn McCann, whose socialist agitation had been a principal factor in creating the climate in Derry in which Hume triumphed. His ally, Paddy Doherty, alienated as many others would be in the future by Hume's ego, dropped off the vine, going on to become a legend in his own right for community development in Derry.

After the election, talks began almost immediately on the formation of a new political party from amongst the opponents of unionism who had emerged at Stormont, figures such as Paddy Devlin, Austin Currie, Ivan Cooper, Gerry Fitt, Paddy O'Hanlon and, of course, Hume. But the events of the year delayed the process. Rioting in August, in both Derry and Belfast, began when the authorities, fearing to be seen to be giving into the Catholics, gave permission for the Apprentice Boys March to take place on August 12, although every nationalist leader in the North had warned of political catastrophe if this traditional display of Protestant triumphalism were allowed to take place through the now simmering Catholic Bogside. The march went ahead. Derry duly erupted. Belfast followed suit, Lynch went on TV, and the troops went on a shortlived honeymoon as the deliverers of the nationalists from the threat of loyalist pogrom. These circumstances overshadowed the formal birth of the Social Democratic and Labour Party in the Errigal View Hotel, Bunbeg, County Donegal in July 1970.

The first British soldier was killed in February of 1971. Hume led the SDLP out of Stormont over the failure to set up an inquiry into the shooting of two Derry teenagers on 8 July 1971, and the following month the British introduced internment at the unionists' urgings. The SDLP launched into a Rent and Rates strike in protest and the province erupted into rioting; the coup-de-grace to any hopes of a return to Stormont was administered by Bloody Sunday, 30 January 1972. (See Chapter 12).

Through all this welter of events and those that followed —the Sunningdale Agreement, the New Ireland Forum, the Anglo-Irish Agreement — Hume's star rose steadily.

He was always the principal architect of the Social Democratic and Labour Party and its obvious logical leader from the start, but Gerry Fitt, who had also come into politics seeking reform within the system, was literally ahead of him, both in representing a Belfast constituency rather than one in Derry, the second city of the province, and in the influence which he wielded in Westminster, and was elected leader. Hume was and is greatly assisted in his career by his wife, Pat, like himself a teacher, who subsequently gave up her teaching career to further her husband's aims and presented him with five children. Had Hume been born in the Republic, ego, ambition, lucidity and formidable debating skills would have carried him to success in any constituency he chose to stand in. His political philosophy was very much that of Daniel O'Connell, yet its impact was diluted by a movement which came to be led by a man whose early political involvement was almost identical to Hume's, in his preoccupation with social issues such as housing, but who followed instead Wolfe Tone's path. Gerry Adams's career, as we shall see, highlights the significance of the 'hidden Ireland' of Northern Ireland political life.

John Hume was a motor force only at a visible, national and often international plane. Like a boat bobbing above treacherous stormy seas, his course was frequently to be affected by the fierce currents often swirling beneath the surface, but nevertheless guiding or misguiding progress.

The SDLP

The SDLP, since its inception in 1970, has had to weather onslaughts from both unionist and nationalist foes. It reached a high point in May 1974 when its leader Gerry Fitt, along with Hume, Paddy Devlin and Austin Currie, all had cabinet minister status in the doomed power-sharing executive which emerged from the Sunningdale talks. These men and other figures such as Eddie McGrady and Ivan Cooper (a Protestant) had emerged from being civil rights marchers to the status of responsible political figures.

As early as 1971 the SDLP had begun to foster the idea of a British and Irish condominium to run Northern Ireland, but after the fall of the executive at the hands of the unionists, and in order to withstand the 'Brits Out' message of Sinn Fein, the party adopted a straightforward British withdrawal policy. It tempered and veered by, with, or from this position until the New Ireland Forum and later the Hillsborough Accord. By then Hume was both a Euro MP and a Westminster MP. His colleague, Seamus Mallon, was soon to become a Westminster MP also. The party held a seat in Seanad Eireann through Brid Rogers and had 101 Councillors throughout the North.

Along the way the party had shed stalwarts whose disappearance mirrored the tensions with which the SDLP had to contend. In 1976 a prominent member, Tom Donnelly, resigned over the party's refusal to give full recognition to the RUC. The memory of Castlereagh interrogations, supergrasses, the existence of a shoot-to-kill policy in Armagh and later, the Stalker affair, would continue to make it impossible for the SDLP to make this commitment without losing out heavily to Sinn Fein, despite the fact that in Dublin the coalition government had publicly urged Catholic support for the RUC as part of the Sunningdale Agreement.

In 1977 Paddy Devlin was expelled from the SDLP because he felt that the Labour component of the party's title was being neglected in the pursuit of Irish unity; he felt the party had become 'too middle class and too close to the Catholic Church'. Ivan Cooper, who generally sided with Devlin, departed a year later, as did Gerry Fitt, who shared some of Devlin's attitudes, spiced with his own personal resentment towards John Hume who succeeded him as leader. After the Anglo-Irish Agreement was signed in 1986 another prominent member of the party, Paschal O'Hare, also resigned, because he felt the pendulum had swung too far away from unity and British withdrawal.

By 1986 the party was still intact, and represented just over half of the nationalist voters, although it faced a new threat. The dawning hostility between Haughey's Fianna Fail and Hume's SDLP did not augur well for the future. Haughey's view of the Anglo-Irish Agreement as a sell-out would be far closer to that of Paschal O'Hare than to that of John Hume.

The SDLP commands the type of Catholic voter who lives in the leafy suburbs of Belfast, and Sinn Fein those who live in the ravaged red brick of the Falls Road — wherein there bubbled, and continues to bubble, the brew of hostility, discrimination, prejudice and violence out of which Sinn Fein flowed, securing some 42 per cent of the nationalist vote.

To understand why so many nationalist Catholic voters in Northern Ireland should deliberately withold support from the revered figures within the SDLP and bestow it instead on an organisation which actually supports violence, it will be instructive to look at the early career and developing opinions of the man who more than anyone else both represents and controls Sinn Fein, Gerry Adams.

A Revolutionary in the Making

The story of Ireland from 1969 onward cannot be told without reference to the IRA which Sinn Fein supports. On the face of it there should be little hearing electorally or otherwise for that story. The IRA has blown people to smithereens without warning, and used punishments which included kneecapping and pouring tar over the shorn heads of girls whose 'crime' was to date a British soldier. Yet it survives, underground illegally and overground, with Sinn Fein, legally, and its support constantly threatens that of the SDLP. How? Why should people vote for a movement with a background of such activities?

A study of the career of Gerry Adams may not supply the full answer, but it should have an illuminating effect, taking place as it did against the backdrop of bigotry, injustice, anger, poverty and ghetto creation, indicated by the discrimination statistics I quoted at the beginning of this chapter.

Growing up on the Falls Road, Belfast, the young Gerry Adams knew he was a Catholic and had a strong sense of identity, a consciousness of being Irish, formed by race and place. There were some nationalistic memorabilia in his own home and the 'kitchen houses' of the Falls Road, where he visited, but he remembers nothing of an IRA nature being discussed during his childhood days. He did not realise that his uncle Dominic Adams was in the IRA (a temporary Chief of Staff during World War II) until he read my book on the IRA. If he felt any sort of political awareness it was through his grandfather, William Hannaway, a stern patriarchal figure who wore laced black boots and had been a friend of James Connolly, a full-time Labour official in Belfast and an agent for de Valera in the 1918 election. He was dimly

aware that uncles of his had been involved in republicanism and
that an uncle, Paddy Adams, had spent most of the war years
interned in the Curragh while another uncle, Alfie, was in Belfast
Prison. It was only when the troubles blew up that the
importance of his mother's brother, Liam Hannaway, one of the
major IRA figures of the early sixties and seventies, came home
to him. His preoccupations were those of a typical working-class
Falls Road family of ten children, in which money was always
short but laughter and school books were in plentiful supply.

The events that took some of the laughter out of the situation
began for the youthful Adams during the 1964 Westminster
election campaign for the West Belfast seat. The dingy election
headquarters in obscure Divis Street displayed a small tricolour in
its inconspicuous window, and Paisley made his first major
appearance in the headlines by leading loyalist protest marches
from East Belfast to have the flag removed, using the fact that the
Flags and Emblems Act rendered the tricolour illegal. After days
of Paisleyite-inspired rioting, during which the sight of the first
car burnings on TV shocked all Ireland, the RUC removed the
flag, not Paisley, and in so doing poured bitter drops on the
seedbed of republicanism.

Adams joined the republican movement, but he was conscious
that this was largely a symbolic organisation; while over 20,000
men marched in the Easter Commemoration of 1966, there
would not have been thirty of them equipped to fight. His
interests were Sinn Fein and studying James Connolly. Much to
his parents' disgust, when he finished school, where he had been
regarded as a scholarship boy certain to win a place in the
University, he went to work in a bar.

He was interested but unimpressed in the theories being
advanced at the time by Roy Johnston that republicans should get
involved in joining trade unions and in making contact with
unionists. Adams could see no point in this; the Catholics were in
unskilled work, if they had any. The casual dockers, for instance,
were traditionally Catholic, the permanent workers Protestant.
Sectarianism reigned supreme.

He became interested in the activities of the Dublin Housing
Action Committee, and formed a similar association in the Falls
Road district of Ballymurphy and New Barnsley, agitating over
such mundane issues as pedestrian crossings. A Protestant child

had been knocked down in New Barnsley, and all sections of the community were well pleased with Adams and company when their efforts resulted in the provision of railings at the pedestrian crossing. However, continuous Protestant agitation drove everyone back into their ancestral ghettos; Protestants were evacuated from New Barnsley after sectarian feeling had provoked riots.

Another campaign in Adams's early years was that against the building of the Divis Flats complex. These high-rise flats on the Falls Road, apart from the various problems which high-rise buildings anywhere create, have since become world-famous as a breeding ground for violence, and were known at one time as the 'Planet of the IRPS' because the Irish Republican Socialist Party (IRSP) which spawned the Irish National Liberation Army (INLA) had a stronghold there. However in the mid-sixties churchmen and political leaders welcomed them because they prevented the dispersal of Catholic votes and strength to other parts of the city. Because of his involvement in this and other campaigns, Adams at one stage faced a grand total of fifty-four summonses for breach of the peace and illegal entry. His first television interview came as a result of a squat in Divis Flats.

Adams went on to work in a famous Belfast pub, The Duke of York. 'The atmosphere was heady with ideas. There was a sort of effervescence in the air'. Part of it was from reading, and some was from the exchange of ideas with the clientele of the pub —writers, journalists, politicians and actors. 'The Duke of York was a great old pub', Adams recalls nostalgically. He read everything he could lay his hands on concerning Irish history and literature, but interestingly neither he nor his friends ever discussed or read Marx. Adams and his associates are instinctive socialists. Adams's principal political colouration was a common one at the time — a consciousness of being Irish, fuelled by the growth of Fleadhanna Ceol (traditional Irish music festivals) and by Ronnie Drew's Dubliners, who revived ballad singing for the young people of the period.

Their favourite songs included such old Ulster airs as 'My Lagan Love', political ballads like 'James Connolly', and more potently a song on the death of a young IRA man in the 1956 campaign, 'Sean South of Garryowen'. It is nearly impossible to convey in words the importance of these songs. One would have to attend a ballad session in a republican club or a loyalist one to understand the fervour and the sense of empathy which the ballads arouse: the camaraderie, the drinking, leaving the hostile 'them' outside.

A branch of the Civil Rights Association was founded in the International Hotel in Belfast on 29 January 1967. Amongst the groups it embraced was the Wolfe Tone Society, of which Adams was a member. Here he broadened his 'Duke of York' contacts. 'You met all sorts of "hues and views",' he remembers. The Northern Ireland Civil Rights Association (NICRA), based on the British National Council for Civil Liberties whose secretary, Tony Smythe, attended its first meeting, included trade unionists such as Noel Harris, Ken Banks and Betty Sinclair (a life-long communist), Jack Bennet, a founder member of the Wolfe Tone Society, John Drumm, a Liberal, Dr Con McCluskey, father of Northern Ireland Civil Rights, Robin Cole, Chairman of the Young Unionist Group, and Paddy Devlin of the North of Ireland Labour Party.

Among republicans, Adams and the younger men were in confrontation with older leaders such as Liam McMillan and Jim Sullivan. In the older men's view the civil rights movement could lead to reform within the system. The younger generation argued that unionism was not capable of democratisation and favoured a destabilisation, out of which a new, more democratic state would grow. They despised the unionist philosophy rather than feared it. So far as Adams and his companions were concerned the effete, decadent, loyalist politico-philosophical culture was a colonial creation of Britain's which Britain could manipulate at will, orchestrating or quelling the backlash factor as it suited the policy of the hour. As Adams saw it, the potential backlash factor was not 'loyalism' as such but the armed and well-equipped RUC, impelled by motives of fear and score-settling. On the backlash factor Adams's views remain unchanged.

12

The North in Flames

Eruption; The Provos Emerge; From the Maze to Chelsea

Eruption

PUBLIC attention was drawn by the civil rights marches, notably those at Derry on 5 October 1968, at Armagh on the following 30 November, and a march by students from Queen's University Belfast, led by the People's Democracy movement, to Derry on 4 January 1969. This last march was ambushed at Burntollet Bridge, the marchers were driven into a river and their leaders, Bernadette Devlin and Michael Farrell (now an *Irish Press* journalist), were injured by stones and by blows from clubs with nails driven through them.

Both the PD march and that through Armagh were actively opposed by Paisley and his henchman of the time, Major Ronald Bunting. Paisley and Bunting arrived in Armagh during the early hours of the morning with scores of cars and supporters carrying lengths of sharpened piping and nail-studded sticks. They set up barricades and prevented the civil rights marchers from passing along a route previously agreed with the RUC. The police stood by and prevented neither the Burntollet attacks nor those at Armagh. The attitude of some unionist authorities to the civil rights movement may be gauged from the reaction of the Minister for Home Affairs, William Craig, to students who called to his home to protest after the October batonings by RUC at Derry had been shown on television. He called the students 'Silly bloody fools', and subsequently made a number of speeches attack-

ing the idea of an ombudsman for Northern Ireland, saying that a
Roman Catholic majority would lead to a lesser standard of
democracy and would deny Britain the right to interfere in Ulster.
This, he said, a strong Unionist party would not tolerate. O'Neill
forced him to resign the next day, 11 December 1968. He was
later given an EEC posting and put in charge of civil rights within
the Community.

In August 1969, when the civil rights demonstrations finally
provoked the backlash that led to the Bogside eruptions and the
troops were eventually sent in, all Ireland was stirred. An
emotional tape on which the veteran Derry Republican, Sean
Keenan, was heard to appeal ringingly 'For Jesus's sake, help',
struck a nationwide chord when it was played at a meeting in
Belfast by Frank Gogarty of the Civil Rights Association. As
Belfast joined Derry in flames, and Protestants invaded Catholic
areas burning out homes and triggering fierce street-fighting and
petrol-bombing, Gerry Adams quit his job in the 'Duke of York'.
He took off towards the rioting, carrying a dozen large empty
stout bottles. After all the speechifying and debate within the
republican movement, the actual armament of the IRA consisted of five handguns. Of the sixty Republicans in Belfast only
seven were actually active on 13 August 1969, and none of these
were full-time guerrillas on the lines of the Active Service Units
(ASUs) which later emerged.

It took two happenings in particular to let the genie of IRA
violence out of the bottle; these were the Falls Road curfew of July
1970, and the introduction of internment on 9 August 1971. The
Falls Road curfew was significant in two ways, firstly, for what
happened along the Falls Road on 3 to 5 July, 1970 — basically a
search-and-ransack operation in Catholic ghetto areas, designed
to seize IRA armaments. The people were restricted in their
movements and drenched with CS gas, and there was savage
house-to-house fighting in which disputed Army estimates say
either three or five people died. Sixty civilians and fifteen soldiers
were injured. No searches took place in Protestant areas, though
Protestant gun running was commonly spoken of and some
100,000 weapons were held legally (because Protestant JPs
readily issued gun licences to their co-religionists). The Catholic
population in the province as a whole was naturally outraged.

The second significant fact lay in the speed with which the

search occurred after the British general election of 18 June 1970 had turned out the Labour government which had been endeavouring to restrain the activities of the British Army on the streets, and installed the Tories, those traditional allies of the 'officer and gentleman' class and of the Ulster unionists. Paddy Devlin, then a Labour MP at Stormont, spoke for most nationalists when he issued a statement after a Catholic, Daniel O'Hagan, had been shot dead by the army in one of many stone-throwing incidents; the army were by now responding with a riot control arsenal that included rubber bullets and water cannons. Devlin said: 'The army are deliberately provoking trouble in certain selected areas where Catholics live to justify saturation of these areas by troops. The British Army are now behaving like a conquering army of medieval times. With the restraining hand of Mr James Callaghan gone from the Home Office, General Freeland is reverting to the type of general that Irish people read about in their history books'.

This impression was enormously strengthened the following year when, on 9 August, the Heath government finally acceded to the urgings of the unionist administration led by Brian Faulkner and introduced internment. Again, the blow fell only on the nationalist population, the one Protestant arrested being Ivan Cooper, the Derry-born SDLP Stormont representative. If the Falls Road had provoked a wave of reaction in favour of the Provisionals, the reaction to internment was tidal. The SDLP, NICRA and militant republicans joined in a campaign of civil disobedience. A rent and rates strike was undertaken which, together with a programme of rallies and protest marches, provided an atmosphere of turmoil in which the IRA could not have done better had they invented it. (The IRA had escaped almost unscathed from internment, being forewarned.) Worse was to come.

The year 1972 opened with British paratroopers shooting down thirteen unarmed civilians on an anti-internment march in Derry on 30 January, 'Bloody Sunday'. In the course of protest demonstrations in Dublin, the British Embassy was burned down. In March of 1972, recognising that Northern Ireland was nothing more than a hotbed of mayhem and misrule, Ted Heath, who had already transferred security control to Westminster, closed down Stormont. 'Prorogued' was the word used, but what it meant in effect was that Stormont went, never to return, being replaced by Direct Rule from London. One might have thought that this marked a spring-board for nationalist advance. Not so. Two major constitutional initiatives largely explain this lack of progress, along with a number of security initiatives, mainly associated with Labour's Roy Mason and the Conservatives' Margaret Thatcher, which I shall discuss later.

The constitutional initiatives, as the nationalists saw them consisted of one genuine effort and one bogus one. The major genuine effort began on 20 October 1972, when the Tories published a Green Paper on 'The Future of Northern Ireland' which for the first time recognised the interconnection between northern and southern Ireland, and spoke of the need for any solution henceforth to take note of an 'Irish Dimension'. In 1973 the Northern Ireland Constitution Act abolished the office of governor, introduced the idea of a periodical referendum to check public opinion on the North's constitutional status, and above all set up a new 78-member Assembly, elected by PR, with the intention of giving the minorities a bigger say.

These two steps paved the way for some Unionists (Brian Faulkner's variety), the Alliance Party, led by Oliver Napier, and the SDLP, led by John Hume, to enter discussions with Ted Heath, William Whitelaw and a government delegation from the Republic headed by the Taoiseach, Liam Cosgrave. The outcome was the Sunningdale Agreement, so called after the Berkshire civil service college where the talks were held. This agreement proposed to set up a power-sharing executive in Northern Ireland, involving both Protestants and Catholics in the form of the Official Unionist Party led by Brian Faulkner, the middle-of-the-road Alliance Party and the nationalist SDLP.

The principal features of the Sunningdale Agreement were two:

1. A fifteen-member executive of whom four were non-voting; the SDLP would hold the portfolios of Commerce (Hume), Health (Devlin) and Housing (Currie) with Gerry Fitt as Deputy Chief Executive to Brian Faulkner.
2. A Council of Ireland, modelled on European institutions, with a Council of Ministers representing Dublin and Belfast, a parliamentary tier and a permanent secretariat.

The Unionists opposed the Agreement on the grounds that

the executive, by enforcing power-sharing, was undemocratic, and that the Council of Ireland thrust Belfast under the thralldom of Popish Dublin. The whole Agreement was bitterly opposed by the Reverend Ian Paisley's Democratic Unionist Party and, more importantly, by an ad hoc loyalist group, the Ulster Workers' Council. Backed by the loyalist paramilitaries, notably the Ulster Defence Association, the Workers' Council cut off power supplies, put up barricades, indulged in widespread intimidation and thus paralysed the province into rejection of the Agreement.

The loyalists were incensed at the fact that the coalition government in Dublin, led by Liam Cosgrave, were active in drawing up the Agreement. Faulkner could not sell the Council idea to his party and resigned, being succeeded by Harry West. The Sunningdale pact had tried to reach over the heads of the extremists on both sides of the divide (basically the IRA and the UDA) by giving to the people of each tradition something of what they wanted. The Republic and the SDLP achieved recognition of the fact that the aim of a United Ireland by consent was legitimate, but the Agreement also noted that there could be no change in the status of Northern Ireland for as long as the majority decided otherwise. This latter provision was to be registered at the United Nations; nationalists had reservations about this because it amounted to international recognition of the partition of Ireland.

In the end it was not the action of the extremists or the reservations of either Orange or Green that really crippled the Sunningdale Agreement. It was lack of political will on Britain's part. During the talks Ted Heath himself presided over much of the proceedings, but the principal figure was William Whitelaw, the Secretary of State for Northern Ireland, a man of joviality and ability. The combined efforts of this pair could have made the power-sharing executive work, Loyalist Workers' strike or no, but the very day after the Sunningdale Agreement was concluded Whitelaw was recalled from Stormont to deal with the miners and was succeeded by a new man, Francis Pym. He had scarcely had time to find his feet when the February 1974 election thrust the Tories out and installed Harold Wilson in Downing Street and Merlyn Rees in Stormont. This was not the combination to force the army to face down the loyalists. That was a task for the officer and gentleman class.

Wilson's major contribution to the period was a speech which he made on 25 May that deeply wounded all shades of unionism. He attacked the strike leaders as 'people sponging on Westminster.' Pieces of sponge blossomed on unionist lapels as a result. But the Irish, both Orange and Green, who had committed themselves to the power-sharing executive wanted visible tokens of support. They wanted the army at least to clear away the UWC barricades and road blocks, but the army's approach to taking on the loyalists was summed up by one senior British Army officer: 'The game is not worth the candle'.[1] Accordingly May 1974 saw the barricades stay up and the executive come down, bringing with it a good deal of British credibility.

A lesser attempt at political settlement followed; a Constitutional Convention, first mooted in the wake of the collapse of the Sunningdale Agreement, was elected in 1975 and itself collapsed in 1976.

The bogus initiative came when James Callaghan made an unabashed effort to stay in power with unionist support. On 19 April 1978, he announced that legislation would be introduced to increase Northern Ireland's representation by redrawing the constituencies to conform to the smaller British model. Representation duly went from twelve to seventeen seats, but Callaghan reaped little benefit from the exercise; eight of the existing twelve Northern members voted against him the following March (Gerry Fitt and Frank Maguire abstained) and Labour fell by 311 to 310, losing the subsequent general election.

Fitt's abstention was crucial. A life-long supporter of Labour and Labour policies, as opposed to republicanism, he would later literally be at risk of his life from his former constituents because of his opposition to concessions to the hunger-strikers, who termed him 'Fitt the Brit'. He later accepted a peerage. At the time of the Callaghan ploy he was leader of the SDLP. Had he voted the result would have been a tie, the Speaker would have voted for the status quo and the government would have been saved. Knowing he was facing the risk of political oblivion, and after life-long Labour support, Fitt's vote indicates the depth of feeling amongst ordinary nationalists at Callaghan's stratagem.

It was under Harold Wilson that Callaghan had first gone to

1. W.D. Flackes, *Northern Ireland, a Political Directory, 1968-79*, Dublin and New York 1980.

Northern Ireland, after the troops went in in 1969, pushing through reforms in the electoral and housing areas, disbanding the B-Specials and making an attempt to reform the RUC. And in 1972 Harold Wilson (by then in opposition) met IRA leaders secretly in Dublin. Yet it was under Labour that two North of Ireland Secretaries of State, Merlyn Rees and Roy Mason, a former Defence Secretary, gave the counter-insurgents their head and did more to set in train the events which led to the hunger strikes than anyone else, with the possible exception of Mrs Thatcher.

Although the Labour Party aspires to Irish unity, the party overall is responsive to the block vote of the trade unions. This means, in effect, that the largely Protestant Scottish TUC, strongly influenced by its Northern Irish co-religionists, is a check to the party's official espousal of unity. In Ireland therefore, the party's policy often seems expedient in the extreme, rarely more so than in the time of Roy Mason, who made particularly unscrupulous use of the Peace People movement to cloak the reality of his use of repressive policies.

The Peace People were founded in August 1970 out of the horrified reaction of Betty Williams and Mairead Corrigan to the deaths of the three Maguire children, killed when a fleeing IRA gunman was shot dead by the British army and his out-of-control car mounted a footpath and struck a pram in Andersonstown. The initial peace marches were genuinely inspirational, and the TV pictures of nuns and Protestant ladies marching together through Belfast's divided streets alongside mothers pushing prams accurately portrayed the 'women together' mood of peace fervour that swept the province. Ciaran McKeown, a former civil rights activist and, at the time, a journalist with the *Irish Press,* joined the movement and became its guru, writing a peace prayer and organising marches. Williams and Corrigan won a Nobel Peace Prize, amongst many other honours.

But while media attention was focussed on these activities, and Mason and Stormont urged a public policy of 'support the peace movement', behind the scenes the brutal 'conveyor belt' policy was implemented, filling the jails and leading inevitably to the hunger strikes. Thus the British used the Peace Women's generous impulse to fill the political vacuum, incurring for them ultimately the wrath of the Catholic ghetto areas, which subsequently spread to the Protestant ones as well, when they began criticising the security forces and demanding an end to the Emergency Provisions Act.

The Tory James Prior, another British proconsul who laboured mightily but unavailingly in the province from 1981 to 1984, made an effort to find a replacement for the Stormont Parliament by setting up an Assembly; he wrestled this from the House of Commons, only to see it largely aborted because the SDLP boycotted it after the elections in 1983. The Assembly had been intended to deal with Northern Ireland matters at a level above that of county councils, but lower than that of parliament.

The hunger strikes so changed Nationalist sentiment that Sinn Fein won 42 per cent of the vote in the Assembly and Westminster elections in 1983 and threatened to obliterate the SDLP. Thus forced, as so often before in the party's history, to react not to its own policies but to those of its republican rivals, John Hume brought the SDLP down the path which led first to the Forum deliberations and then to the Hillsborough Accord. As the provisions of that Accord show, Dublin had come a long way in Belfast's affairs from the days following the Falls Road curfew, when Sir Alex Douglas Home termed an unheralded visit by Dr Patrick Hillery, the Republic's Foreign Minister, to Belfast, 'a serious diplomatic discourtesy'. Now Dr Hillery's successor is in Belfast by invitation.

The Provos Emerge

I have met people who, after Jack Lynch's broadcast in August 1969, stood out on the Falls Road to be able to tell their children that they had seen the first Irish troops arrive with bayonets flashing. The beleaguered Catholic ghettos were so short of arms that in the Protestant-encircled area of the Ardoyne there were only two shotguns. That was when the letters IRA were written large on Belfast gable walls, as 'Irish Ran Away'.

Barricades went up and the Central Citizens Defence Committee was formed to defend the Catholic areas of Belfast and to negotiate with the British. This was led by figures as diverse as Canon Padraig Murphy, a formidable, craggy-jawed parish priest, the Catholic businessman Pat Conaty, the Republican Jim Sullivan, the Socialist Paddy Devlin and the moderate Republican Paddy Kennedy, the two latter being Stormont MPs.

An IRA convention decided early in December of 1969 to contest elections, and a public split developed on the abstention issue. During the Sinn Fein Ard Fheis the following January, a walk-out led to the formation of two IRA wings. The Official IRA, led by Cathal Goulding, was initially described as IRA (Gardiner Street) to distinguish it from the Provisional IRA (Kevin Street), led by Sean Mac Stiofain. They gradually became generally known simply as Officials and Provisionals. Because the Officials used gum to affix Easter Lilies to their lapels, they were also called 'Stickies' to distinguish them from the 'Provies' or 'Provos', who because they used pins for their lilies were described as 'Pinheads'.

The Provos' armaments consisted of what could be collected by old-style republicans of the forties era who had both experience and contacts. Men like Harry White, Billy McKee and Gerry Adams' Uncle Dominic went around the country collecting arms, mainly shotguns, .22 rifles, a few revolvers and even a few submachine guns. Belfast largely went with the Provisionals who were led, apart from MacStiofain, by figures based in the south, principally Ruairi O Bradaigh and Daithi O'Connell, who had been active in the 1952–62 IRA campaign.

In the Catholic areas of Derry and Belfast barricades went up, creating 'no-go areas' to keep out not merely loyalist assassination squads but RUC and B-Special patrols, which in Catholic eyes were either scouting parties for assassins, or under cover of darkness, the assassins themselves. During the Belfast rioting of mid-August, and in breaking up civil rights marches, the RUC and in particular the B-Specials had acted in obvious collusion with Orange mobs, making no effort to restrain the rioters and sometimes actively assisting the loyalist incendiaries in burning out Catholics. Harold Wilson was amongst those who were aghast at television footage showing members of the B-Specials in the forefront of rioting Belfast mobs. Lord Hunt, the Everest climber, was invited to report on the force; as a result of his findings, the exclusively Protestant B-Special force was 'stood down' in April 1970. It was replaced by the Ulster Defence Regiment, which initially had a Catholic membership of some 18 per cent; this has now fallen to probably less than one per cent.

Despite the danger and the fear of arrest there was, in the wake of the 1969 riotings, a tremendous spirit of elation and camaraderie in Catholic areas. Schools and homes were opened up to receive refugees. Itinerants are still well regarded in some Catholic ghettos of Belfast because of their services in ferrying Catholics from beleaguered streets. Aided by the impetus of resentment following the Falls Road debacle, the Provisional IRA began to go to war.

'War' between August 1969 and February 1971 was really a matter of home-made devices such as nail bombs, or suitcases full of gelignite, often more lethal to the bombers than their targets. The traditional Belfast 'kidney paver', the Belfast cobblestone, was rediscovered and used plentifully. In homes in danger areas many slept with a 'Tipperary rifle', a hurling stick, beside them. But there was little overall co-ordination and no strategic planning. It was not until February of 1971 that a British soldier was actually killed.

It is interesting to recall that the first deaths and explosions were all the work of loyalists. The first RUC man killed in the troubles, Constable Arbuckle, was felled by a rioter in the Protestant Shankill area. It was loyalist explosions which ultimately blew Captain O'Neill out of office, in April of 1969, notably the bombing of the Silent Valley reservoir; Catholics took this as a sign that loyalists were intent on a pogrom during which there would be no water for firemen. Yet during this period the public clamour was for action against the IRA, not against the loyalist paramilitaries. Billy McKee, the OC of the Belfast Brigade, was arrested because he was known to the RUC Special Branch. Ironically McKee, a staunch republican, largely saw his role as defending Catholic areas, not attacking the British. His removal had the joint effect of removing the more cautious element from the IRA command and of leading to the establishment of an unknown tier of IRA leadership whose cover could not be blown by the RUC.

The IRA grew in areas with a special local tradition like Derry or the Falls Road, but these areas, with their barricades and vigilante policing, were not necessarily safe for guerrillas; inside the barricades everyone knew who the IRA were. One area which did not suffer from such security problems, however, was Crossmaglen in South Armagh. Ironically, in view of the reputation it would acquire, Crossmaglen was totally uninterested in IRA activities when the troubles began. The most burning wish evinced at that stage was to be allowed to get on with their smuggling activities to and fro across the adjacent border with County Louth in the Republic. Then the British Army came and its attentions grew more burdensome as troubles mounted elsewhere in the province. Around Crossmaglen today the Army can be serviced only from the air and the roads can only be patrolled in force.

What happened was that one fine day outside the Springfield Road Barracks a car back-fired and a soldier panicked, and accidentally shot dead an innocent motorist, a man from Crossmaglen. Hostility grew towards the troops, who retaliated with increased house searches. Weapons were often planted in the process (so that intelligence might be extracted in the resultant interrogations of the occupants). Standard operating procedure included stopping and beating up young men thought to be likely IRA material. They were, but not the way the Army thought of them. As a member of the Irish Special Branch observed to me, 'The Army created the IRA'.

Crossmaglen alone would serve as a microcosm of the alienation of the nationalist community of Northern Ireland. A number of other turning-points towards violence also occurred in the early seventies — the Falls Road curfew of July, internment in August of 1971 and 'Bloody Sunday' in Derry on 30 January 1972. The first gave the Provisionals an enormous infusion of internal manpower; the second created an external climate of opinion greatly favourable to their operations, and the third heightened that support to a degree that made the province ungovernable.

'Internment' had for long assumed an almost mystical significance in Republican circles. The IRA had both feared and prepared for it and on 8 August at 7 o'clock in the morning before it was due to be introduced, the word was received. The IRA activists slipped away into prepared hiding places and the Provisionals erupted centre stage from the gloom of the clouds of CS gas that hung heavily over the ghetto areas of the Falls Road.

From the Maze to Chelsea

In Ballymurphy CS gas was fired into the Adams home and Gerry Adams's younger brother, Dominic, developed a stammer. There were incessant army searches; houses would be ransacked

218 Disillusioned Decades

five and six times a night and gardens became parking spaces for
Saracen trucks. Ballymurphy riposted by fighting the British
Army for over a year without firing a shot. Every home had
basins of vinegar to cope with the CS gas. 'Bin Brigades' alerted
the inhabitants to the approach of the troops by banging bin lids
on the pavement; 'hurley brigades' either attacked the soldiers or,
using wet sacks, gathered up gas cylinders which were then
hurled back at the troops. Woe betide any platoon of soldiers
lured into a cul-de-sac: the psychological injuries from the taunts
of the women were paralleled by the physical bruises inflicted by
their menfolk.

Such was the ferocious ingenuity of the Ballymurphyites that
they once broke into the Henry Taggart Memorial Hall and made
off with the army's riot gear, jeeps, shields and CS gas, all of
which they then proceeded to use on the unfortunate soldiers.
Gerry Adams participated in these events amid a plethora of
Street Committees, Defence Committees, Welfare Committees
and Women's Committees. Like many of his kind, he was
interned on the *Maidstone* prison ship in 1972, and he was
systematically beaten up in Palace Barracks.

He recalls: 'You faced the wall for hours at a time, supporting
yourself only by your fingertips'. He remembers going for an
entire week in Castlereagh Barracks without speaking, systematically employing what he knew or guessed of the techniques of
psychological warfare to shut out his surroundings and his
interrogators. I interviewed him in a rather sparsely furnished
room in Belfast and he explained how he reacted. 'This would be a
very interesting room to be interrogated in; you see that curtain,
for instance. It's made of tweed. You could think about how the
tweed was made, where the materials came from, how they dyed
it, what sort of people worked at making tweed, what their lives
were like'. The exemplars Adams looked up to and read about in
his formative years had employed just such techniques in prison
to keep themselves sane, Fenians such as John Mitchel,
O'Donovan Rossa and Tom Clarke.

Odd kaleidoscopic memories returned as Adams talked: 'You
sat waiting the whole of the day. Sometimes they come up behind
you and drop a tray with a crash. It would scare the living
daylights out of you. A rumour went round that we were
supposed to be given truth serum. I remember when they went to

fingerprint me I was shown a blood-stained hatchet . . . When I didn't talk, this Branch man started freaking all over the place. When the interrogation period finished I made a formal complaint about my ill-treatment. Then I was taken to the *Maidstone.'*

This prison ship was moored in Protestant East Belfast, with two hundred prisoners in the bow sleeping in triple tiers of bunks. Again the kaleidoscopic recall: '. . . sewerage, claustrophobia . . . We went on a solid food strike and forced them to close the prison ship'. From the *Maidstone* the internees were taken by helicopter to Long Kesh, where to escape the opprobrium of the term 'internee' they were christened 'detainees'. As Long Kesh itself began to acquire an unsavoury reputation this too was rechristened the Maze Prison, in the best 'Windscale' into 'Sellafield' tradition.

The prison was swept with 'gate fever' in the expectation of speedy releases, but Adams expected to be kept in for the duration, whatever that might be. However, he was set free unexpectedly. He had been thirteen days on hunger strike in solidarity with a group which included his uncle, Liam Hannaway, for the usual republican prison demands: these were basically a recognition of their political status, but were also an attempt to keep alive the tradition of continuing the war in jail by means of any form of defiance available. It was a wearing practice but good for prisoners' morale. Then Gerry Adams's name was called. This normally signalled release. He thought it was some form of a trick and consulted with Liam Hannaway, who tersely told him 'get out', though he did not say why.

Outside he was met by one of the Price sisters and taken to a house in Andersonstown where he learned for the first time that a truce was afoot and that, together with Daithi O'Connell, he was to negotiate the terms. He was taken 'to a big house in Derry' where a prominent Belfast solicitor introduced the republicans to some top Northern Ireland Office civil servants. After much argument, a truce was agreed on the condition that the British would keep out of republican areas and maintain a low profile generally. The two most important achievements were the concession of 'special category status' to the jailed republicans, and an agreement, after much haggling, that a meeting would be arranged with the Secretary of State for Northern Ireland,

William Whitelaw, to discuss republican proposals for a British withdrawal. To the IRA this meeting and the duration of the truce were at that stage the central issues.

A helicopter flew the republican delegation over the Glen-shane Pass in the Sperrin Mountains to a waiting RAF plane. They were flown to London under safe-conduct to negotiate directly with British cabinet members, including William Whitelaw, in the home of Paul Channon, in Chelsea. It was the first time anything like this had occurred since the days of Michael Collins and the signing of the Treaty. It should have been a momentous occasion full of historical overtones, but Adams remembers all sorts of more mundane details, detracting from his appreciation of the occasion. His wife Colette, whom he had married on the run and with whom he had spent a one-day honeymoon in Dublin, was considerably underwhelmed by the fact that his release from jail presaged not a resumption of married life, but a whirlwind of negotiations.

Initially it was Whitelaw who seemed most nervous. He was sweating profusely and began with an 'in and out' approach, trying to make his appearance one of 'hello' and 'goodbye'. But the IRA representatives were having none of it. They refused both ploys and refreshments and made it clear that their main objective was a British withdrawal from Ireland. Whitelaw argued that he would have to put this to the cabinet (a reasonable stipulation in the circumstances!) but a substantial matter agreed on was that the truce would be extended with an undertaking that the army would refrain from carrying out personal searches, and various procedures for keeping the peace.

Adams and Bell were at the meeting as 'listeners' — making a note of what the other side said but not talking themselves. However, after a side conference when Adams did speak to Whitelaw, the pair had an exchange which Adams had consider-able reason to recall later on. In the event of certain breaches of the truce it was agreed that 'all bets were off'. The next time Adams heard those words he was in a cell in Springfield Road barracks, lying on the floor naked being kicked by a Special Branch interrogator who punctuated his kicks with the refrain 'all bets are off now, Gerry'.

The IRA delegation returned home with at least the truce to show for their efforts. But attention within the movement now swung to a new Sinn Fein policy, 'Eire Nua' (New Ireland), which had been unveiled at a press conference in Dublin on 28 June 1972. The principal proposal in the 'Eire Nua' policy was that, in order to meet the unionists' objection to being subsumed into an all-Ireland, Catholic Republic, separate parliaments would be set up in the four provinces of Ulster, Leinster, Munster and Connacht. To reassure the unionists further, Ulster would consist not of the existing six counties but of the original pre-partition nine, with three additional counties from the Republic, Donegal, Cavan and Monaghan. The proposal was rejected by the unionists, but aroused a good deal of comment in other Irish political circles — not least amongst the electors of the three southern counties concerned, about the prospects of being handed over to the unionists!

Adams became immersed in the reorganisation of Sinn Fein and was not unduly surprised when the truce broke down on 9 July over an incident in which the British army stood by as a UDA-led mob attacked Catholics, preventing them taking over houses in the previously Protestant Lenadoon Estate in Andersonstown. He pressed on with his republican activities, and was interned in 1973, promptly being appointed escape officer by his colleagues.

13

Alternative Battlefield

Special Category; On the Blanket; Feakle and After;
Hunger Strike; A New Sinn Fein; Civil Rights Now; Legal
Injustice; If it were Hong Kong?

Special Category

IT cannot be too heavily underlined that the IRA have always
regarded jails as an alternative battlefield. An IRA prisoner upon
his capture may lose his weapons but he does not abandon his
cause. He simply seeks to pursue it by any other means, jail
agitation, propaganda, defiance of any sort, which lie within his
grasp. Prisoners in the jails are traditionally a unit on their own
who elect their own leaders. Even an IRA Chief of Staff, on
entering prison, loses his rank and becomes an ordinary
volunteer; thereafter he may, or may not, be elected to officer
status within the prison. To the IRA, jail is 'The Republican
University' within which, along with insurgency techniques,
prisoners often acquire an education denied to them on the
outside. In 1986 ten times as many nationalist prisoners were
taking Open University courses as were (in percentage terms)
prisoners in UK mainland jails. Of those who had qualified three
times as many secured honours as did ordinary students on the
outside.

The British conceded IRA demands in 1972, creating what
were officially termed 'Special Category' prisoners. By 1980 IRA
prisoners in the 'cages', in compounds surrounding nissen huts
which were the first constructions to go up on the site of the old
World War II airfield at Long Kesh, ten miles west of Belfast,
were behaving like prisoners of war anywhere. They were
responsible to their own officers, dealing only with the prison

authorities through official spokesmen, wearing their own clothes and subject largely not to prison discipline but to that of their peers.

The list of concessions which the prisoners had been able to wrest from the authorities included the following:

1. Full recognition of the republican command structures (warders only to speak through OCs and staff officers to the prisoners and to address all men by their rank — Volunteer, OC, Education Officer, etc.)
2. Fifty per cent remission.
3. Extra parcels and a complete range of foods allowed into the prison — from Chinese takeaways to potted shrimps.
4. Electric cookers in each hut and raw food from the prison kitchens delivered daily; the prisoners could please themselves about when and what they ate.
5. Billiard tables allowed at the prisoners' own cost.
6. A TV in each hut, plus a radio and record player. Previously there had been one TV per three huts and this was turned off at 9 pm by the prison staff.
7. The right of the OC republican prisoners to visit each of the areas under his command once a week.
8. Full tool kits and work benches for handicrafts for the Green Cross and Irish Republican Prisoners Welfare Committee, and the right to ship these handicrafts in bulk — a van-load a time — to the outside.
9. Full control of all sports, hurling, Gaelic football and soccer, along with Inter-Compound (Inter-Company) football organised and supervised by the prisoners themselves.
10. Weekly consultation in privacy with other factional leaders in the camp — UDA, UVF etc.
11. The right to vet prison staff who would come into direct contact with prisoners, so there would be less chance of a 'flashpoint'.

This regime deeply offended the unionists and conflicted with the new prison policy which was evolving throughout the latter part of the seventies as part of an overall British counter-insurgency strategy, summed up in three words: 'Ulsterisation, Normalisation and Criminalisation'.

'Ulsterisation' was in effect the same policy as the Americans adopted in Vietnam towards the end of the war — to let the

Vietnamese do the fighting. In this case the war against the IRA was to be carried on largely by the Royal Ulster Constabulary (RUC) and the Ulster Defence Regiment (UDR). 'Normalisation' meant that every aspect of normality was to be promoted within the province so as to minimise the consequences of IRA bombing and the disruption of normal life. 'Criminalisation' was aimed at taking away the status conferred on the republicans which suggested that they were somehow different from other prisoners, 'ODCs' ('ordinary decent criminals', quoting Merlyn Rees). It came to a head with the building in the Long Kesh compounds of a second type of prison building, the H-Blocks, modern prison buildings shaped like the letter H, with the cells down either arm and connected by the bar of the administration wing.

The H-blocks owed their creation to a report by a former Lord Chancellor, Lord Gardiner, published on 30 January 1975. Lord Gardiner headed a committee set up to consider 'in the context of civil liberties and human rights, measures to deal with terrorism in Northern Ireland'. The report said: 'Although recognising the pressures on those responsible at the time, we have come to the conclusion that the introduction of Special Category status was a serious mistake . . . It should be made absolutely clear that Special Category prisoners can expect no amnesty and will have to serve their sentences . . . we recommend that the earliest practicable opportunity should be taken to end the Special Category'.

When Lord Gardiner made his report, Northern Ireland prison occupancy had risen from a total of 727 in the early days of the civil rights movement, to 2,848. As almost 1,200 of these were fully-fledged 'Special Category' prisoners, Britain had an embarrassing number of political prisoners to account for before the bar of world opinion. The government therefore decided to get rid of the terminology applied to such prisoners and the environment in which they were confined at one fell swoop — by building the H-Blocks. Despite the high-sounding rhetoric, the basic thrust of the report — to get rid of political prisoners — was not achieved. In fact, prison totals continued to rise as what became known as 'the conveyor belt system' had embarrassingly successful results. Essential components of this system were the extra-judicial Diplock Courts set up as a result of Lord Diplock's commission (20 December 1972).

Lord Diplock found that it would not be possible to get witnesses to testify in 'terrorist' cases, and proposed an 'extra-judicial process' to deal with them whereby a Judge would sit without a jury and bail could only be granted by the High Court, and then only in the most exceptional cases. Confessions made in those types of cases were to be admissable unless obtained by 'torture or inhuman and degrading treatment'. The paragraph concerning confessions was destined to create lasting bitterness throughout the nationalist community in Northern Ireland. Despite Lord Diplock's stipulation, it became an accepted fact of life that the way to get confessions out of suspects was to brutalise them.

In November 1977, the thirty solicitors who did most of the work in the Diplock Courts wrote to the Secretary of State for Northern Ireland, Roy Mason, stating that: 'illtreatment of suspects by police officers, with the object of obtaining confessions, is now common practice . . . this most often, but not always, takes place at Castlereagh RUC station and other police stations throughout Northern Ireland'. This complaint was only the tip of the iceberg.

Although Lord Compton's report, in November 1971, said: 'Our investigations have not led us to conclude that any of the grouped or individual complainants suffered physical brutality as we understand the term', Lord Compton accepted that hooding, continuous noise and enforced posture at a wall were among the techniques used by interrogators against suspects. He also accepted that suspects were sometimes deprived of sleep or food for days at a time.[1] The Compton report glossed over or discounted allegations that some detainees had been forced to run in bare feet over obstacle courses which included broken glass, and had been threatened with being dropped from helicopters, into and out of which they were bundled. The helicopter episode, said Compton, constituted a measure of ill-treatment, and the obstacle course incident may have brought to the men concerned 'some measure of unintended hardship'.

Lord Parker of Waddington's report, adopted on 31 January 1972, found that the methods *then* (my italics) in use were illegal

1. *Report of the enquiry into allegations against the security forces of physical brutality in Northern Ireland arising out of the events on 9 August 1971,* Sir Edward Compton, GCB, KBE.

under UK law, though not 'immoral', given the circumstances of the time. A minority report from Lord Gardiner held that even where terrorists were concerned such methods were immoral.

The government of the Republic brought what was generally known in Ireland as 'the Torture Case' against the British government before the European Commission of Human Rights at Strasbourg in December 1971, and eventually got a judgement from the Court of Human Rights on 18 January 1978 that a number of the techniques used amounted to 'inhuman and degrading treatment'. These particular techniques had been formally forsworn by Ted Heath in March of 1972, but others were referred to in complaints by lawyers, civil rights leaders, journalists, priests, Amnesty International and a judicial report from Judge H.G. Bennett, who found in March 1979 that: 'our own examination of medical evidence reveals cases in which injuries, whatever their precise cause, were not self-inflicted, and were sustained in police custody'.

All this was superficially successful. The Castlereagh—Diplock—H-Block 'Conveyor Belt' carried so many suspects into jail that under the Mason administration (September 1976 — May 1979) the average active service term of an IRA volunteer was cut to three months.[2]

On the Blanket

The blanket protest may be reckoned to have begun when Ciaran Nugent, an eighteen-year-old IRA volunteer, was sentenced for hijacking a van. On 14 December 1976, he swore that he would resist 'criminalisation' to the point that if an attempt was made to make him wear prison uniform 'they would have to nail the clothes to my back'. As a result, he was to spend three years living in a bare cell from 7.30 am to 8.30 pm, on a poor diet, with nothing whatever in the cell except a chamber pot.

Nugent claims, and so do the other IRA prisoners, that the actual 'Dirty Protest' began when the warders started to make a practice out of returning the prisoners' slop bowls only half emptied in the morning after the 'slops out' routine. Worse, it is alleged the warders sometimes kicked over the full bowls.

2. Peter Taylor, *Beating the Terrorists*, London 1980.

Tension between the Protestant warders and the Catholic prisoners was high already because of the blanket protest, itself a serious breach of prison rules, and because as a retaliation the IRA had begun shooting off-duty warders. After first attempting to dispose of the reeking mess by throwing it out the windows, and finding that the warders threw it back in again, the prisoners eventually began disposing of the faeces by smearing it on the walls.

Having several hundred young men living in these conditions for years on end naturally had serious repercussions on the nationalist community. Following representations from several quarters Cardinal O Fiaich, who had had several unsuccessful private meetings with Roy Mason on the issue, visited the prison and afterwards issued a lengthy statement on 1 August 1978, deploring what he discovered. He said:

'One would hardly allow an animal to remain in such conditions, let alone a human being. The nearest approach to it that I have seen was the spectacle of hundreds of homeless people living in sewer-pipes in the slums of Calcutta. The stench and filth in some of the cells, with the remains of rotten food and human excreta scattered around the walls, was almost unbearable. In two of them I was unable to speak for fear of vomiting.

'The prisoners' cells are without beds, chairs or tables. They sleep on mattresses on the floor and in some cases I noticed that these were quite wet. They have no covering except a towel or blanket, no books, newspapers or reading material except the bible (even religious magazines have been banned since my last visit), no pens or writing materials, no TV or radio, no hobbies or handicrafts, no exercise or recreation. They are locked in their cells for almost the whole of every day and some of them have been in this condition for more than a year and a half.

'The fact that a man refuses to wear prison uniform or to do prison work should not entail the loss of physical exercise, association with his fellow prisoners or contact with the outside world. These are basic human needs for physical and mental health, not privileges to be granted or withheld as rewards or punishments . . .

'The authorities refuse to admit that these prisoners are in a different category from the ordinary, yet everything about their trials and family background indicates that they are different. They were sentenced by special courts without juries. The vast majority were convicted on allegedly voluntary confessions obtained in circumstances which are now placed under grave suspicion by the recent report of Amnesty International. Many are very youthful and come from families which had never been in trouble with the law . . .'

Feakle and After

It was often alleged during the hunger-strikes that the IRA simply orchestrated them to its own ends. This is not true. The hunger-strikes would not have achieved the effects they did had they a volition of their own. Certainly the IRA fought a skilful propaganda war, and benefited from it, after the strikes broke out, but the situation within the prison was initially unwelcome and distracting to the IRA.

From the break-down of the truces which led to the establishment of Special Category in 1972, to the commencement of the hunger-strikes, the IRA was responding to differing internal and external pressures. Internally the movement began switching over from its formal Brigade structure, with companies brimming over with eager volunteers; up to ten or a dozen of these would go out on an operation for which two or three would have been sufficient, greatly multiplying the risk of capture. A cell system was set up, consisting of tiny groups known only to each other, with the leaders of the cell the sole link in the chain of command.

The movement also began a debate within itself, on how to win community support by becoming politicised and at the same time train to withstand their adversaries' fearsome interrogation techniques. The existence of the first debate, involving the cell system, eventually became public with the capture of the Chief-of-Staff, Seamus Twomey on 2 December 1977. He was in possession of documents which described the setting-up of cells as IRA policy. But the second debate remained largely secret, though it was probably ultimately the more important of the two; the fruits of this were circulated in 'The Green Book', which came to dominate the thinking of the movement in the same way that

Colonel Gadafy's 'Green Book' dominates the philosophy of the Libyan system.

Preoccupied with internal reorganisation, reformulation of policy and with another set of truce talks with the British, the IRA did not foresee where the forces contained in the H-Blocks situation would lead. This preoccupation stemmed from Britain's rather Janus-faced policy of the period. The IRA, through underground negotiations conducted through intermediaries, were convinced that a British declaration of intent to withdraw was around the corner and that the only thing at issue was the IRA's demand that this be put in writing! At the same time, the British were working towards a tougher security policy, literally building more prisons, the H-Blocks, to lock up increasing numbers of the very people with whom they were conducting peace negotiations.

The IRA for a time had reason to believe that these talks meant something substantial. Stemming from the initiative of a group of distinguished Protestant clergymen, led by the Reverend William Arlow, who met the IRA at Feakle, County Clare on 10 December 1974, a ceasefire was announced on 10 February of the following year which was accompanied by the opening of 'Incident Centres' controlled by Provisional Sinn Fein. This was a most important development. The Incident Centres were ostensibly set up to monitor the ceasefire and had a 'hot line' to the North of Ireland office at Stormont, but in fact they became political foci, providing advice and welfare and very greatly adding to the status of Sinn Fein — much to the chagrin of the North's other political parties, who felt slighted as 'elected representatives'.

However, after the IRA got their Incident Centres and were apparently led to believe they were going to get British withdrawal, the other face of Janus was revealed.[3] Merlyn Rees' speech in the House of Commons on 25 March 1976 abolished Special Category status for subsequent prisoners, though allowing those who already had this status to retain it. The prisoners who followed in Ciaran Nugent's footsteps formalised their demand for 'status' into the 'Five Demands':

1. The right to wear their own clothes.
2. The right to abstain from penal labour.

3. T.P. Coogan, *On the Blanket*, Ward River Press, Dublin 1980.

3. The right to free association (this did not mean movement
   from cell to cell but freedom of association within their own
   prison area).
4. The right to educational and recreational activities in conjunction with the prison authorities.
5. Remission restored.

The demands were not conceded and tension built up inside
the prison, with incoming prisoners going 'on the blanket', the
cells getting filthier, H-Block protests taking to the streets,
warders being shot. A score were to die before a hunger-strike
broke out in October 1980. From then on the bloody, baffling and
unfashionable Northern Ireland struggle became a priority with
American, English, Scandinavian and world TV and print organisations generally. Even in Dublin, well removed from the
Northern tumult, I was interviewed repeatedly by representatives of the international media for comment and interpretation
throughout the crisis.

Hunger Strike

Seven prisoners went on hunger strike simultaneously, led by
their OC, Brendan Hughes. As it wore on the strike became more
and more dangerous, threatening to ignite not only an explosion
of sympathy in the six counties themselves, but throughout
Ireland and in America as well. Inevitably Charles Haughey
became drawn into negotiations with the British between various
Irish groupings, including the Catholic church and the SDLP. I
came to have a peripheral, though insignificant, role myself in
these talks. An agreement was concluded on 18 December 1980,
whereby it seemed that the prisoners were allowed their
principal demands, wearing their own clothes as opposed to the
hated prison uniform, the reception of parcels and relaxation in
the supervision imposed during visiting hours.

The 18 December agreement depended for its implementation
on the goodwill of the prison officers. These were loyalists in
charge of republicans whose friends had actually murdered
prison warders in furtherance of their demands. Bitterness
amounting to hatred existed between jailers and jailed. At the
best of times a prisoner/warder relationship is a prickly affair,

and these were not the best of times. The British, moreover, privately assured loyalist leaders and prison executives that whatever agreement had been concluded, partly as a result of Haughey's promptings, there was no question of giving in to terrorism; the criminalisation policy stood. The euphoria of 18 December soon faded.

The situation came to a head when, shortly after Christmas, a test of the agreement occurred — one of those seemingly innocuous events which inside prison assume enormous proportions. Prisoners who had been on the 'Dirty Protest' now agreed to wash. The shower facilities in H-Block are, the prison being but recently built, amongst the finest available in Europe; it would have been possible to bathe and cleanse the entire English First Division Football League in less than a day. Between delays and harassment, prison staff managed to process only some twenty prisoners over the period of a day. From these and other incidents it became clear to the prisoners that the criminalisation policy still stood and that another hunger strike was inevitable.

One man who had little doubt that this would be the outcome was Bobby Sands, the prisoners' leader who would himself lead the fast to the death. In a letter of his dated 14 January 1981, he wrote: '. . . Got Comm[4] from IRSP accepting one on H/S so 'if' we go (which I think we'll have to do) we'll go with 3 Provos and one IRSP. We thought that this morning's document, i.e. Rat's statement, left some manoeuvreability, shows how wrong you can be. Yahoo!! Well that's about it. . . .' Sands had come from a meeting with the prison governor, Stanley Hilditch ('Rat') seeking clarification on a compromise proposal whereby prisoners could be simultaneously issued with prison-issue clothing and clothes supplied by their families. On receiving them the prisoners would have washed immediately, in effect ending the confrontation.

The letter makes it clear that it was the prisoners, led by Sands, who decided on the strike and its arrangements, not the IRA outside. A crucial factor in the calling-off of the 1980 strike had been the condition of one striker, Sean McKenna, who had gone blind. Sands had feared that in his weakened condition he might have been induced to come off the strike by the authorities. In

4. 'Comm': a communication. Sands' letter itself was written in tiny lettering on a rolled-up piece of toilet tissue.

Dublin those urging the British to compromise had consistently been told that there was no need for concern, because the condition of one of the prisoners was such that he would soon desist, collapsing the entire strike. To avoid such a possibility, Sands and his colleagues read everything that could be ascertained about the effects of hunger-striking, before refusing food on 1 March 1981.

Later that month, Sands was selected as a candidate for Fermanagh/South Tyrone and, as he was starving himself to death, was elected an MP. The SDLP had failed to put up a candidate, out-manoeuvred by a stratagem whereby a republican sympathiser, Noel Maguire, whose brother's death had caused the by-election and whom the SDLP did not wish to oppose, stood down moments before the nominations closed. Sands died on 5 May. He was followed to the grave by nine others, at intervals which stretched out until 3 October, 217 days later. The others were Francis Hughes, Raymond McCreesh, Patsy O'Hara, Joe McDonnell, Martin Hurson, Kevin Lynch, Kieran Doherty, Tom McElrea and Michael Devine.

Each had come from a different part of the six counties and had been a popular figure in his own area. Their long-drawn-out agonies moved public opinion, as did the life story of Bobby Sands, who could have stood as an exemplar for the lives and careers of 10,000 Catholic youths in Northern Ireland. He had been moved by the attack on the Burntollet marchers to join the IRA at the age of 18, and moved via the Conveyor Belt, and a particularly brutal six-day interlude in Castlereagh, into a three-year period in the then Special Category Long Kesh. A period of liberty yielded a broken marriage and a son, and ended with his return to 'The Republican University' in 1976, charged with a fire-bomb attack on a furniture factory.

From his writings, a voluminous collection of letters, and a newspaper, *Liberty,* which he edited up to the time of his sentence in 1976, it is clear that he had great journalistic and possibly literary potential. His position in the prison shows that he possessed leadership qualities. All these facts of his life exploded into the public consciousness when, after he had been forty days on hunger strike, he was declared an elected MP for Fermanagh-South Tyrone on 9 April 1981 — a media event of world-wide proportions.

A New Sinn Fein

Again Adams re-enters the picture, and increasingly with him the young tigers who had been privately active in the political reorganisation of the Republican Movement. They persuasively talked their way into the public consciousness via a host of interviews with the world media, who descended on the province in large numbers. They were to discover that Adams and the likes of Jim Gibney, Danny Morrison, Joe Austin, Tom Hartley, Richard McAuley and Martin McGuinness, were articulate and persuasive exponents of Sinn Fein philosophy.

The Fermanagh-South Tyrone election transformed Gerry Adams from a Sinn Fein spokesman to a national political figure. He recalls: 'It was educational for us. We learned about presiding officers, personation officers, how to campaign. It was exhilarating. Sometimes we'd come into a little town with the Catholics coralled away up at the top as usual, the Loyalists living alone the main street, with the businesses and so on. We'd have the tricolour flying, the music blaring — and the Catholics up on the top of the hills would come out to us as though we were the relief cavalry'. Throughout Northern Ireland they continued to come out for Sinn Fein. Over 100,000 people followed Bobby Sands's funeral, and later that year Northerners dominated the Sinn Fein Ard Fheis in Dublin, having earlier helped to dethrone Fianna Fail in the June general election.

Danny Morrison asked the celebrated rhetorical question, whether the delegates would object if Sinn Fein took power 'with a ballot box paper in one hand and an Armalite in the other'. This had the effect of making many constitutionalists recoil in horror but in Northern Ireland the cavalry charged on. The Armalite argument served to reassure those who thought that seeking political power meant going soft on physical force. The next year's Ard Fheis again showed the influence of the Northerners when 'Eire Nua' was buried and the Federal policy was dropped; the thinking of the Northerners was 'no sops to Loyalists'. A single unitary state was the preferred goal and towards that goal the Ard Fheis passed unanimously a resolution which read: 'That all candidates in national and local elections and all campaign material be unambivalent in support of the armed struggle'. The Armalite was clutched as firmly in the hand as any ballot paper.

The young tigers were cock-a-hoop at that Ard Fheis.

A week earlier Sinn Fein had taken just over 10 per cent of all votes cast at the Northern Ireland Assembly Elections, and the following June the party went on to win 13.4 per cent of all the Northern Ireland votes — approximately 40 per cent of the Nationalist vote — in the June 1983 Westminster election. These external changes were reflected in the internal balance of power the following November, when the Sinn Fein Ard Fheis saw Ruairi O Bradaigh and Daithi O'Connell stand down as President and Vice-President. Their stated reason was that as they were the main architects of the Federal 'Eire Nua' policy opposing Dail elections and taking seats in the European Parliament, there was no point in their continuing on. The real reason was that the hunger strike had made Sinn Fein a Northern movement led by Northerners, and Gerry Adams and his cohorts were now firmly in the saddle. Adams had defeated Gerry Fitt to become West Belfast's new MP.

Sinn Fein did not fare so well in the Republic, which was preoccupied with taxation and unemployment. The party had taken 10.2 per cent of the vote in the constituencies it contested under the H-Block banner in June 1981, but when in February 1982 Sinn Fein stood as a party in its own right its vote fell by over 50 per cent. The party won no seats and did not contest the November 1982 election. Shortly before Christmas 1983, the unloveliest face of Sinn Fein showed itself in the fatal events at Ballinamore, County Leitrim; Gardai and Army seeking to free the captured English industrialist, Don Tidey, were fired upon by IRA men and a garda and a soldier were killed. Subsequently Sinn Fein in the Republic has gone backwards, winning only 4.9 per cent of the vote in the June 1984 European Parliament election.

The ferocious behind-the-scenes debate which led to the ending of the abstention policy was hardly justified in terms of votes in the February 1987 election either. Sinn Fein polled only 1.9 per cent of the votes for its twenty-seven candidates. Adams saw the ending of the abstention policy as vital to the building up of a Sinn Fein electoral machine in the Republic, and he persuaded the IRA Ruling Army Council to endorse his position at the 1986 Ard Fheis. The move caused some dissension within Republican ranks, and those opposing the move grouped under the banner of Ruairi O Bradaigh and Daithi O'Connell to continue in the old abstentionist mould, calling themselves Republican Sinn Fein. But Adams, and those who think like him in the movement, say the 1987 election was only a beginning and that the crunch election is the next one — particularly if the Section 31 prohibition can be lifted first. All that can be said with certainty about the future of Sinn Fein in the Republic is that it is now a registered political party like any other, engaged in an attempt to build organisation, policy and a team of suitable candidates for the first time since Fianna Fail broke away from Sinn Fein in 1926.

The 1987 result has highlighted the difficulty of operating a national movement in Ireland from north of the border without good southern-based candidates standing on southern-related issues. A John Hume-type candidate could stand with a strong possibility of success in practically any constituency in the Republic, a Gerry Adams could not. Adams is quite clear, in fact, that 'intervention won't win in the wrong climate'.

But where Northern Ireland is concerned, for reasons which should now be obvious, Sinn Fein politically is an established force, with strong backing amongst Irish-Americans. Adams held off the SDLP challenge in West Belfast in June 1987. It had been widely believed that after the Anglo-Irish Agreement, a combination of Gerry Fitt's old vote and that of the SDLP's Joe Hendron would give the SDLP a comfortable majority, but the ghettoes, and especially their younger inhabitants, campaigned vigorously against the wealthier SDLP machine, making Adams an abstentionist but potent reminder for Westminster that republicans will just not go away.

Sinn Fein can justifiably claim to have undermined the Assembly and indirectly stimulated the establishment of the Forum and the conclusion of the Hillsborough Agreement. It has virtually destroyed the criminalisation policy. By December 1981, the prisoners had (de facto if not de jure) won most of the concessions for which the hunger strike was held. They were wearing their own clothes, they had 50 per cent of the full remission they had sought, and prison work was confined to around ten things they could agree to do or not to do. They had a form of 'association' and were allowed to leave their cells every night for some two hours after tea time as well as getting an hour's exercise in the fresh air during the day.

Civil Rights now

The Anglo-Irish Agreement set up an inter-governmental conference based on the Agreement of 6 November 1980 between Charles Haughey and Margaret Thatcher, to discuss political affairs, security, the administration of justice and the promotion of cross-border co-operation. The UK government accepted that the Irish government would:

> put forward views and proposals on matters relating to Northern Ireland and agree to take measures both to recognise and accommodate the rights and identities of the two traditions in Northern Ireland, to protect human life and to prevent discrimination.

Amongst the matters which the conference pledged itself to deal with were: 'legal matters, including the administration of justice'. The conference was to have a full-time secretariat:

> The Conference shall meet at administerial or professional level as requested. The business of the Conference will thus receive attention at the highest level.

The Accord thus clearly invited Dublin to share in the sovereignty of Northern Ireland though it was careful to stipulate that no changes would take place without the consent of the majority. It did, however, say that if a future majority sought a united Ireland, the UK would aid this wish, not hinder it.

As the Agreement was to receive international ratification, it was immediately challenged by Charles Haughey as a 'major set-back' to Irish unity. He said that if Fianna Fail formed the next government he would repudiate the Agreement. That was on 16 November 1985. Reality won out, however, and Haughey recognised that the Agreement was widely popular in the south and that Mrs Thatcher was not likely to change. Confirmed as Taoiseach following the February 1987 general election, Haughey declared that he would make no attempt to re-negotiate the Agreement 'with the present government. . . .'!

The Agreement has held firm so far, despite the combined Official Unionist/Democratic Unionist Party campaign against it. The RUC have stoutly contained any violent loyalist demonstrations, while Peter Barry, as the Irish minister at the

inter-governmental conference, maintained a high profile until
the coalition went out of office, raising matters of concern to the
nationalist population. However, the alienation of the young
nationalists is widespread. Is there a prospect that the Hillsborough Agreement diminishes that alienation?

The best answer one can give is: 'Doubtful', because of the
basically unsatisfactory nature of Northern Ireland society. Sinn
Fein will continue to profit from this electorally, in the absence of
any constitutional advance by the SDLP or others in redressing
Catholic grievances. A survey published in London on 4 July 1985
by the Department of Finance and Personnel referred to 'marked
differences between the Catholic and the Protestant communities
in such areas as educational background, employment, occupation
and housing'.

Amongst the findings of the survey were that in the previous
two years 36 per cent of heads of households were Catholics, with
Protestants 46 per cent (Presbyterian 27 per cent, Church of
Ireland 19 per cent). Catholic women produced an average of
three children to 2.2 for Protestant mothers. Catholics, male and
female, had the highest unemployment rates of any religious
denomination with more than twice as many Catholic men, 35
per cent, on the dole as there were Protestants, 17 per cent.
Twenty-eight per cent of Catholic women had part-time work,
compared with 35 per cent of Protestant women. Unemployed
Catholics in the previous two years, or longer, totalled 44 per
cent, compared to 33 per cent Protestants.

In the younger group, the unemployment statistics showed up
most glaringly. Only 46 per cent of Catholics in the 19 to 24
age-group were at work, compared with 64 per cent non-
Catholic. It is, of course, amongst younger Catholics that the
IRA's major recruiting field lies. The survey respondents, asked
what was the North's greatest problem, put unemployment
ahead of the Troubles as the worst scourge. Unemployment in
the province stands at 22 per cent rising as high as 60 per cent for
men in Gerry Adams's native Ballymurphy.

The comments by the Secretary for State for Northern Ireland,
Douglas Hurd, were revealing. He said that while he welcomed
the survey and promised measures for a new 'approach to full
equality of opportunity in employment' in order to make government action 'more comprehensive, convincing and effective,'

nevertheless Catholics in the North should not expect any 'early dramatic changes' in their social, economic or employment situation. This remark was perceived by Catholics as meaning that the report would achieve nothing. The Fair Employment Agency set up under Bob Cooper in 1975 to fight discrimination was intended to have forty full-time staff members, but at the time the survey was published it still had only fifteen. So far as Catholics were concerned the report was a case of: live horse and you'll get grass — if not supergrass.

Legal Injustice

A 'supergrass' is a paid informer who differs from other informers in that his evidence is both rehearsed and concocted by the police, and then accepted by the courts — uncorroborated. The use of supergrasses is a tactic grounded not in legal principles but in counter-insurgency ones, and the first fruits of the policy were seen in March 1980, when the uncorroborated evidence of Steven McWilliams put four IRA men behind bars. The system has now fallen into general disfavour; trials have collapsed because supergrasses retracted their evidence, or judges refused to accept it. Millions of pounds were spent on giving informers new identities and in putting them up in luxury hotels abroad while they rehearsed their evidence. The Chief Constable of the RUC, Sir John Hermon, claimed that what he termed 'the Converted Terrorist Process' had dealt a severe blow to the morale of both republican and loyalist paramilitaries, but the public at large, particularly the Catholic public, were more inclined to agree with Lord Gifford's assessment that the supergrass system was 'not justice' and led to 'telling lies'.[5]

Odious though it is, the supergrass system is only one of a number of malodorous components of an answer the average Catholic will give to the question: 'What do you find wrong with Northern Ireland society?'. The answer invariably is a portmanteau one: 'Plastic bullets, the UDR, strip searching, supergrasses. . .'.

The use of plastic bullets was outlawed in Britain after an incident which underlined yet again that though 'Ulster is

5. Report by Lord Gifford, published HMSO, London and Belfast 1984.

British', the 'UK overseas' is always treated differently to the 'UK mainland'. A nationalist attending a hunger-strike commemoration, Sean Downes, was killed by one in full view of American television in 1984. Nobody in Northern Ireland, even in the RUC, would argue that they are properly used. They should be fired at the ground, to make them ricochet so that they only strike their victims on the legs. Downes, like so many others, was shot in the upper body.

The Ulster Defence Regiment became operational on 1 April 1970 to replace the discredited B-Specials.

Catholics initially joined the force, but as a result of IRA attacks and the Ulsterisation policy the UDR came into abrasive contact with Catholics as frequently as the B-Specials had ever done. Several members of the force (a tactic much employed was to have members resign before charges could be brought so that the claim could be made 'no member of the UDR has ever been charged with . . . ') have been accused of serious crimes, including murder, and the Dublin government has continuously raised the behaviour of the UDR with London, though without achieving the improvements sought.

The Anglo-Irish Accord was intended to provide for a system whereby the RUC would accompany the UDR on patrol, but incidents are still heard of in which the UDR stop cars and delay and hassle Catholic drivers and passengers, sometimes even coming to blows with them, while ostentatiously waving on Protestants. But there are far more serious charges which can be brought against the UDR. One of the worst happenings of the entire ghastly era was the Darkley massacre, in which a gospel hall was shot up and several worshippers killed. This barbaric deed followed the shooting of a number of Catholics in the area, after which members of the UDR boasted openly to the families concerned not alone that they had committed the crime but that they would kill further members of the families. A family which had been bereaved in this fashion complained strongly to the RUC of what was being said, but to no avail. Then a deranged member of the family, a member of the INLA, went to the police and warned them that if they did not take action something drastic would occur. Nothing happened and the man contacted an INLA leader, borrowed a weapon from him and shot up the hall. This time arrests followed. It was in an effort to clear up this whole murky story that John Stalker, Deputy Chief Constable of Great Manchester, was appointed to investigate the 'shoot to kill' policy in Armagh. He was suddenly removed from the inquiry on 6 June 1986 having delved more deeply than was comfortable to some elements within the security authorities. An adequate explanation for this move has never materialised from a great deal of speculation.

In the case of women prisoners in Armagh and Brixton Jails, strip searching seems to have been directed solely at breaking the spirit of the women's families. Somebody in the Northern Ireland Office, apparently in collusion with the Home Office, has decided to make an attempt to undermine the powerful supportive role which women, particularly mothers, traditionally play in republican families. Complainants, including such diverse parties as the Republic's Committee of Trade Unionists against Strip Searching, or the Minister for Foreign Affairs, Peter Barry, are told that 'the practice is essential on security grounds'.

However, as a member of a tribunal set up in Dublin to monitor the situation I am satisfied that the security claim has no basis in fact. The girls are not merely stripped before or after journeys to court, which might arguably be occasions on which they could be passed messages or explosives, but at many other times. The twenty-one girls in Armagh were strip searched several times more in any given month than the total number of similar searches carried out amongst the several hundred male prisoners in Long Kesh. The two Irish republican prisoners on remand in Brixton Jail on the Brighton bombing charges, Martina Anderson and Ella O'Dwyer, complained of being strip searched daily.

If it were Hong Kong?

It is said that Ulster is British, but if the foregoing litany of events occurred on the UK mainland in say, Yorkshire or Wales, the problem would have been sorted out long ago. Moreover, had we not been discussing a situation wherein only some 3,000,000 Irish nationalists lay across the border from Northern Ireland, rather than the 800m Chinese who neighbour Hong Kong, Britain would also have long since found a solution. But having discharged her responsibilities in such a remote and faltering fashion that the IRA came back into being, and having then been forced to adopt highly distasteful methods to curb that organisation, Britain has been forced to preside over a bloody vacuum which is adversely affecting both herself and the Republic of Ireland.

The Hillsborough Agreement marked a high water mark of sorts in the progress towards finding a solution, but the solution will not come in the present framework. Britain must set a timetable and an agenda for withdrawal. The only argument against taking the 'Hong Kong Route' to Belfast is the fear of the 'loyalist backlash', but this is not a sufficient argument for Ireland and England to remain at odds. If President Eisenhower had not stood up to the bullies of Little Rock, Arkansas, the blacks would still be sitting or standing at the back of America's buses. I write as a nationalist, but I would be the first to concede that my Protestant fellow-countrymen in Northern Ireland have lived through a nightmare in which they see every attack on an RUC man or an RUC Reservist, not as an attack on loyalism, but on them.

To give an example of what the IRA campaign has meant to the loyalists from August 1969 to March 1986, consider the following casualty list for RUC, RUC Reservists and UDR. Out of a total of 2,476 killed, which included army and civilian deaths, it reads:

RUC	147
RUC Reservists	79
UDR	154

The civilian total of 1,713 deaths comprises both Protestants and Catholics, many of them innocent victims of sectarian assassinations or bomb explosions that went wrong, but the RUC/UDR figures are largely loyalist, and when one considers that over 5,500 members of the RUC and UDR were injured to a greater or lesser extent during the same period one can measure something of the scale of the onslaught to which the loyalists feel themselves subjected. They experienced this not as loyalists, but as Protestants, though the IRA would argue that it was the other way around. In a relatively small society, it is becoming harder and harder to find anyone, Catholic or Protestant, that is not in some way affected by the Troubles.

In arguing that a Hong Kong solution is the best one for Northern Ireland, I mean that it is the best one also for what are now termed 'loyalists'. These people have been led astray for too long by political witch doctors such as Ian Paisley, who told his followers that Roman Catholic Cardinals celebrate rites involving young women and altars displaying huge phalluses, and caused them to riot against a Cardinal visiting Belfast.[6] A society which exalts that type of political culture is a disaster society; the stone of history rests on it and nothing wholesome flourishes under it.

From my contacts with the north, I have ample evidence of disillusion amongst loyalists. This disillusionment was deepened by the Anglo-Irish Agreement, a 'reward', as many of them saw it, for the IRA's successful campaign of murder and destruction. After the initial outburst of wrath in which the loyalists tried to tear down the Agreement, they discovered there was nothing for them to tear, as they were not parties to it; it had been signed over their heads. The RUC proved surprisingly resolute in upholding it, and the unionist protest against the Accord backfired not alone in terms of British public opinion, but on the ground; Seamus Mallon, the able SDLP deputy leader, won a seat from the unionists in the bye-election caused by mass resignations of unionist MPs in protest against Hillsborough. Now the unionists, never the most capable parliamentarians at the best of times, have to contend not alone with Hume and Mallon at Westminster, but with Eddie MacGrady who ousted the unionist political mentor, Enoch Powell in the 1987 Westminster general election. One begins to hear comments such as those of a UVF leader: 'They should have gone the whole hog and pulled out. It is obvious now they are going to go anyhow . . .'

For all their bluster, many unionists now believe in their hearts that a full-scale British withdrawal is inevitable some time, and better that than the hate and haemorrhaging we are witnessing. Ireland is too small a country and too poor to bear the cost in blood and security, in lost investment, and in tourism. Better by far to think through the processes and mechanisms that would be needed in the wake of a British withdrawal: a community police force, acceptable to Catholics in some areas, and to the Loyalists

6. E. Moloney and A. Pollak, *Paisley*, Poolbeg Press, Dublin 1986.

in others; money now wasted on security and war costs could be diverted to maintaining those financial benefits accruing from the British link; an all-Ireland inter-governmental council on the model suggested by the Hillsborough Agreement could deal with questions of tourism, industry and cross-Border developments such as forestry and fishing.

Implicit in all this, of course, is the inevitability of negotiations involving the IRA and Sinn Fein, and the hard men of loyalism, the UDA and their cohorts.

These things are only the mechanics, once the principle of Irish unity is accepted. Whether there must be added to the ingredients items such as perhaps a temporary UN Force, does not alter the basic case for bringing the Northern agony to an end, not by a security policy solely, 'victory' over the IRA, but by a constitutional one also.

We do by doing.

It must be acknowledged that a prerequisite for any such steps is that the Republic improve both its laws and economy, so that they act as incentives rather than as now, hindrances, to the achievement of Irish unity.

All the lessons of history are that the sort of settlement within the system, devolutionary approach already described in these pages will not bring lasting peace. But, as I lay down my pen, all the indications are that in order to placate the unionists, Westminster is once more trying to cobble together some sort of power-sharing devolution package. That sort of thing is now too late.

I will conclude with the words of an Irish cabinet minister I had dinner with as I was writing this chapter: 'You know', he said 'they talk about us trying to subjugate them, wanting to take them over. The truth is that when the border goes, and go of course it must some day, Leinster House will not be big enough to contain them all — they'll be running us, and why not? We could do with their energy'.

We could indeed.

Statistical Appendix

1. Population

1961	2,818,000	1981	3,443,000
1966	2,884,000	1986	3,537,000

Increase 1961 to 1986 26 per cent.
Increase 1966 to 1986 23 per cent.

Sources: 1961, 1966, 1981 Census of Population. 1986 estimate by Central Statistics Office.

2. Employment (April)

	1961	1966	1985
Agriculture, forestry, fishing	379,000	333,500	169,000
Industry			
Manufacturing	179,000	198,000	204,000
Building and construction	60,000	74,000	76,000
Electricity, gas, water	10,000	12,000	15,000
Mining, quarrying, turf	10,000	9,000	10,000
Total Industry	259,000	294,000	305,000
Services			
Commerce, insurance, finance	157,000	166,000	209,000
Transport, communication, storage	54,000	57,000	68,000
Public administration, defence	41,000	43,000	73,000
Other services	163,000	172,000	250,000
Total Services	415,000	439,000	600,000
Total at work	1,053,000	1,066	1,074,000
Unemployment	57,000*	52	225,000
Labour Force	1,108,000	1,118,000	1,299,000
Unemployment Rate	5.0%	6.1%	17.3%

*Excludes persons looking for first regular job (36,000 in 1985).

Source: Central Statistics Office.

3. Number of Persons engaged in Manufacturing Industries

	1965	1986	% Change
Metals and engineering	32,500	58,200	+79
Food	39,000	37,500	−4
Clothing, footwear and leather	29,000	15,000	−48
Non-metallic mineral products	7,800	12,000	+54
Paper and printing	14,300	13,200	−8
Chemicals	6,000	12,300	+105
Textile industry	15,000	11,300	−25
Drink and tobacco	10,200	7,900	−23
Timber and wooden furniture	7,800	8,200	+5
Miscellaneous industries	10,600	9,900	−7
Total	172,200	185,400	+8

Sources: 1965 *The Trend of Employment and Unemployment in 1966* (CSO). 1986 *Industrial Employment* (CSO).

4. Unemployment (Live Register) (Annual Average)

1965	49,800	1986	236,400

Sources: 1965 *The Trend of Employment and Unemployment in 1966* (CSO). 1986 Central Statistics Office.

5. Consumer Price Index

	% increase over period	Average annual % increase
1960–1965 (5 years)	23	$4\frac{1}{2}$
1965–1970 (5 years)	31	$6\frac{1}{4}$
1975–1980 (5 years)	94	$18\frac{3}{4}$
1980–1985 (5 years)	74	$14\frac{3}{4}$
1986 (one year)	4	4

6. Gross Domestic Product

	% increase over period	Average annual % increase
1960–1965 (5 years)	21.0	3.9
1965–1970 (5 years)	26.5	4.8
1970–1975 (5 years)	24.6	4.5
1975–1980 (5 years)	25.0	4.6
1980–1985 (5 years)	10.3	2.0
1986 (one year)		0.25*

†Estimate by Central Bank.

7. Foreign Trade

	1965	1986
	%	%
Imports		
Britain	47	38
Northern Ireland	4	4
Other EEC countries		
Original Six	15	23
Denmark, Spain, Portugal, Greece		3
Total EEC	15*	67
USA	8	16
Other countries	26	17
Total All Areas	100	100
Exports		
Britain	58	28
Northern Ireland	12	6
Other EEC countries		
Original Six	13	35
Denmark, Spain, Portugal, Greece		3
Total EEC	13*	72
USA	4	9
Other countries	13	19
Total All Areas	100	100

†Original Six.
Source: Central Statistics Office.

8. Exports

	1965	1986
	%	%
Live animals	26	3
Food and drink	34	21
Manufactured goods	27	65
Other exports	13	11
Total	100	100
Agricultural	54	19
Industrial	38	80
Other exports	8	1
	100	100

Sources: 1965 *Statistical Abstract* 1968 (CSO). 1986 *Trade Statistics of Ireland,* December 1986 (CSO).

9. Persons receiving full-time education 1983–4

First Level	575,500
Second Level	
Secondary and secondary tops	209,300
Comprehensive	8,700
Community	26,100
Vocational	76,900
Other second level	3,400
Total Second Level	324,400
Third Level	
Universities	25,200
Vocational Technological	6,500
Regional Technical Colleges	9,100
Teacher Training	2,500
Other third level	6,500
Total Third Level	49,800
Total	949,700

Source: Department of Education Statistical Report 1983–4.

NOTES TO TABLES

Population. Taking 1966 as base year is in some respects arbitrary. Population rose continuously from 1961, hence the 1961 Census figure is also given. Over the whole period, the population rose by 26 per cent, an astonishing change in relation to the experience of the previous 120 years.

Employment. April 1985 is the latest year for which figures are available. The main features of the period were a dramatic fall in agriculture (numbers fell by 55 per cent), a modest increase in manufacturing (up 14 per cent), an increase in building (over one-quarter), a substantial increase in services sector (up 45 per cent), mainly in public services, and the overall increase in total employment was only 2 per cent.

Unemployment. Figures given are for persons on the Live Register. Another estimate of unemployment is based on Labour Force Survey statistics. These alternative statistics in respect of mid-April 1985 are as follows:

Unemployed of which:	225,000
having lost or given up previous job	189,000
looking for first regular job	36,000

Foreign Trade. Note that figures for 1965 are for the original *six* EEC countries.

The main features of the export table are the halving of the proportion of our exports going to Britain since 1965 (from 58 per cent to 28 per cent), and the near trebling of trade with the original *six* EEC countries (from 13 per cent to 35 per cent).

As regards the table on exports, note (a) drop in live animal exports since 1965 as a proportion of total exports (from 26 per cent to 3 per cent), (b) the reduction for food and drink exports (from 34 per cent to 21 per cent) and (c) the dramatic increase for manufactured goods (from 27 per cent to 65 per cent). Agricultural produce exported in 1986 represented less than one-fifth of exports as compared with more than one-half in 1965. On the other hand, the proportion of industrial exports in the total more than doubled, rising from under two-fifths of the total to four-fifths.

Education. Because of changes in the educational structure it is difficult to make comparisons between 1965–66 and 1983–84; the table attempts a comparison. A more detailed breakdown in respect of 1983–84 (latest year available) is also given.

Index